day trips® from
orlando

help us keep this guide up to date

We would love to hear from you concerning your experiences with this guide and how you feel it could be improved and kept up to date. Please send your comments and suggestions to:

editorial@GlobePequot.com

Thanks for your input, and happy travels!

day trips® series

day trips® from orlando

third edition

getaway ideas for the local traveler

john kumiski

travel

Guilford, Connecticut

All the information in this guidebook is subject to change. We recommend that you call ahead to obtain current information before traveling.

To buy books in quantity for corporate use or incentives, call **(800) 962-0973** or e-mail **premiums@GlobePequot.com**.

Text design: Linda R. Loiewski
Layout: Joanna Beyer
Maps: XNR Productions, Inc. © Morris Book Publishing, LLC.
Spot photography throughout © Natalia Bratslavsky/Shutterstock

ISSN 1541-0404
ISBN 978-0-7627-5337-6

Printed in the United States of America
10 9 8 7 6 5 4 3 2

to environmental scientists
jennifer dupree and jason liddle,
who were wed at washington oaks
state gardens on april 13, 2002

contents

preface. xi
travel tips xii
using this travel guide. xvii

north

day trip 01
celery and the st. johns river 2
oviedo 2
sanford. 4
debary 8

day trip 02
spiritualism and springs 9
cassadaga 9
orange city 13
deland 14
deleon springs 19

day trip 03
in the center of things. 22
barberville—crescent city 22
palatka 24

northeast

day trip 01
the birthplace of speed. 28
ormond beach 28
port orange 32
ponce inlet 33
new smyrna beach. 34

day trip 02
**the world's most
   famous beach** 38

daytona beach 38
palm coast—flagler beach 44

day trip 03
america's oldest city 47
st. augustine. 47
ponte vedra beach 61

east

day trip 01
the place for space 64
christmas 64
cape canaveral 67

southeast

day trip 01
the space coast's south side . . .76
sebastian inlet 76
vero beach 79

day trip 02
florida's cattle country 82
st. cloud. 82
melbourne 84

south

day trip 01
florida's "hill" country 88
poinciana 88
lake wales 88

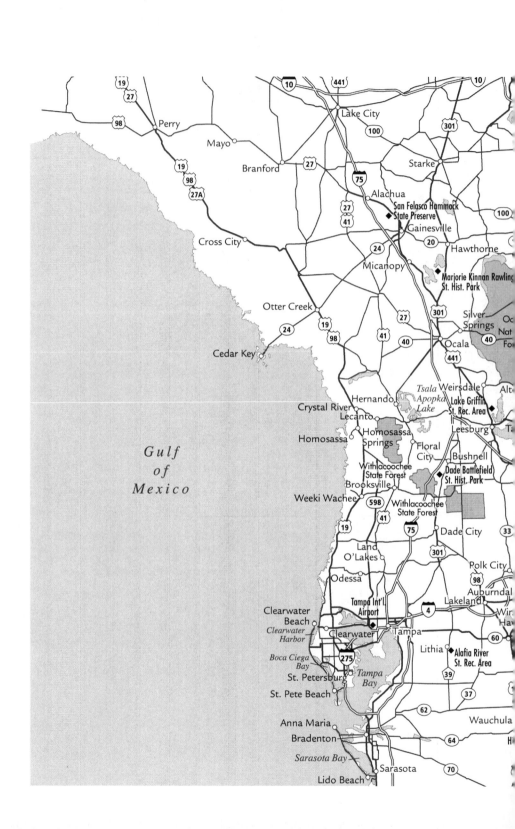

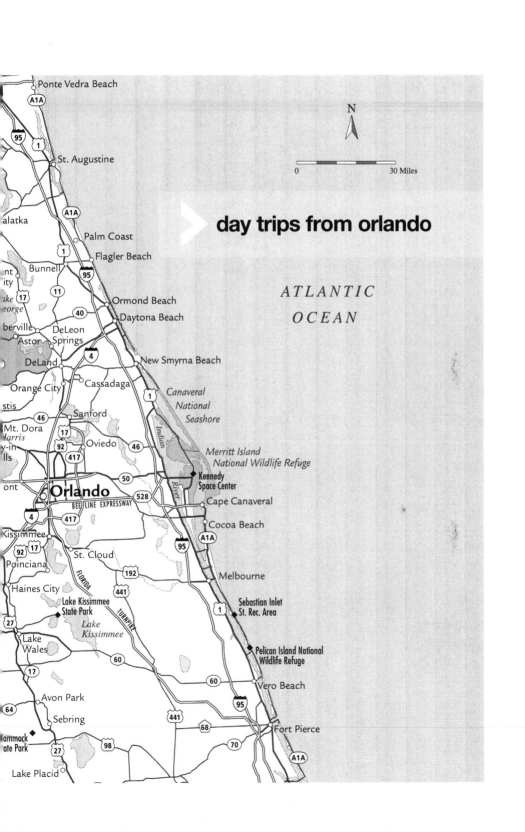

day trips from orlando

Ponte Vedra Beach
A1A

95 1

St. Augustine

A1A

alatka

Palm Coast

1

Flagler Beach

nt Bunnell
ity 95

ake 17 11

eorge 40 Ormond Beach

berville DeLeon
Astor Springs Daytona Beach

DeLand 4

Orange City Cassadaga New Smyrna Beach

stis 1

46 Sanford *Canaveral
National
Seashore*

Mt. Dora
arris 17
y-in 92 Oviedo 46
lls 417

50 *Merritt Island
National Wildlife Refuge*

ont Kennedy
Orlando Space Center
BEE LINE EXPRESSWAY 528

4 Cape Canaveral
417

Kissimmee Cocoa Beach

92 17 St. Cloud A1A

Poinciana 192 95

Haines City 441 Melbourne

Lake Kissimmee
State Park Sebastian Inlet
St. Rec. Area

27 *Lake
Kissimmee* 1

Lake
Wales Pelican Island National
Wildlife Refuge

17 60

60 Vero Beach

Avon Park 95

64 Sebring 441

ammock 68 Fort Pierce
ate Park 27 98 70

Lake Placid A1A

ATLANTIC

OCEAN

N

0   30 Miles

day trip 02
cattle, oranges,
and a speedway 93
avon park 93
sebring 96
lake placid 99

southwest
day trip 01
a land of lakes 102
polk city 102
lakeland 104

day trip 02
florida's first theme park 108
winter haven 108

day trip 03
the city on the bay 112
tampa 112

day trip 04
a tropical delight 121
st. petersburg–clearwater 121

day trip 05
culture on the beach 129
sarasota 129
bradenton 135

west
day trip 01
sleepy little towns 142
clermont 142
bushnell 145
dade city 146

day trip 02
a place for mermaids 148
brooksville 148
weeki wachee 150

day trip 03
quiet lakes and baseball 152
inverness 152

northwest
day trip 01
climb mount dora 158
mount dora 158
tavares 163
leesburg 163

day trip 02
the home of tarzan 165
ocala 165
silver springs 169

day trip 03
outdoorsman's paradise 171
ocala national forest 171

day trip 04
gator country 175
micanopy 175
gainesville 177
hawthorne 183

day trip 05
the nature coast 185
homosassa 185
crystal river 189
cedar key 191

regional information 193
festivals and celebrations 198
index 205
about the author 214

preface

The most-visited tourist attraction in the entire world is Walt Disney World, just south of Orlando in Lake Buena Vista. Whether the theme parks are the focus of your trip to Central Florida or you are a resident in search of side trips from the City Beautiful, we have exciting news for you. In drives of about two hours from Orlando, you can visit America's oldest city, Florida's finest beaches, the birthplace of speed, scuba destinations on offshore wrecks, springs fed by water so clear you can see fish 30 feet down, and miles of country roads that will remind you of sweet yesteryears.

Do we have a favorite day trip? No, because each trip we suggest here has an everyday personality as well as a special event or season that makes it the best place to be: DeLand or Palatka when azaleas bloom, Clermont during the harvest of wine grapes, Clearwater Beach under blue skies, St. Augustine for the reverent Blessing of the Fleet, a spring "run" in a canoe, Ocala National Forest on a brisk winter day, or Alexander Springs on a sweltering summer day for a cooling swim. Come join us in finding a Florida that is not themes and screams but placid, historic, and real.

So many of Florida's treasures are found within two hours of Orlando. In these pages you'll find villages such as Cassadaga and Lake Helen, where you can lose yourself in a time warp. Check into a posh resort at Ponte Vedra Beach or a 200-year-old inn in St. Augustine. Picnic in Micanopy under an oak tree that was a sapling when this was an Indian village. Walk sacred ground at Crystal River, where unknown tribes buried their dead in enormous mounds.

You'll want to take some of these trips with the children, some alone, some with your lover, and others with parents or grandparents who can tell you about the way things used to be. Whomever you decide to share your day with, take this book in hand, leave Orlando behind—and start day tripping.

travel tips

When is a beach not a beach? Where do Florida residents get special treatment? Here, in alphabetical order, are answers to these questions and others frequently asked about Florida travel. Whether you're an old Florida hand or are visiting for the first time, scan these listings for wrinkles, warnings, shortcuts, and discoveries.

Amtrak: Amtrak serves much of the region covered in this book. For information and schedules visit www.amtrak.com or dial (800) USA-RAIL.

Area codes: Area codes are being added throughout Florida at a head-spinning clip. In the 407 area of Greater Orlando, where a new area code—321—is being phased in for new subscribers, ten-digit dialing is required for every call, even if you are dialing next door.

Baseball: Central Florida hosts the following major league teams in March for spring training:

Atlanta Braves—Kissimmee

Detroit Tigers—Lakeland

Houston Astros—Kissimmee

Beaches: When reading hotel listings, take the word "beach" with a grain of salt. Some municipalities, such as Daytona Beach, have just one mailing address for the entire city; other communities, such as St. Augustine and St. Augustine Beach, have separate names. A Daytona Beach address could be as much as half an hour from anything even resembling a beach. Lodgings that brochures describe as "waterfront" may overlook an oily bay, dirty river, alligator-infested lake, or buggy swamp. "Beachfront" may mean rocks and shell rubble, or waters that you wouldn't let your dog swim in.

When in doubt, look up the address on a good map or in the *Florida Gazetteer,* or simply ask hosts exactly what body of water they're talking about. Florida has some of the best beaches in the world. You don't have to settle for less.

Bicycling: Paved bike paths within two hours of Orlando include the 18-mile West Orange Trail, the 46-mile Withlacochee Trail, the 34-mile Pinellas Trail, the 19.5-mile Flagler County Trail, and the 16-mile Gainesville-Hawthorne State Trail. One of the best guides to Florida bicycling is Jeff Kunerth's *Florida's Paved Bike Trails: An Eco-Tour Guide,* published by University Press of Florida. Also contact the Office of Greenways and Trails (877-822-5208;

www.dep.state.fl.us/gwt) or the Florida Trail Association (www.floridatrail.org). Bicycle tours of the state, some lasting a week or more, are organized by Bike Florida, P.O. Box 5295, Gainesville, FL 32627; www.bikeflorida.org.

Bird-watching: Florida is one of the major birding states in the nation, offering a huge variety of native, migratory, seasonal, and accidental sightings. Entry fees to Gateway sites on the Great Florida Birding Trail are often free—never more than a few dollars—and loaner optics are often available. Start by visiting www.floridabirdingtrail.com or calling (850) 488-8755 to learn where to find Gateway sites. Some trails require reservations or an appointment. Get a map ahead of time and arrive during the right time of year for the species the trail is best known for. Many of the sites are drive-in, making them suitable for those who have physical challenges.

Camping: Reservations for campsites and cabins in Florida state parks are available by calling (850) 245-2157 or by visiting www.dep.state.fl.us/parks.

Chain motels: Lodging chains offer familiar layouts and facilities. Properties must meet their chains' standards, are usually well located along the highway, and are often an excellent value. Chains located within two hours of Orlando include:

Best Western (800) 528-1234; www.bestwestern.com

Days Inn (800) 329-7466; www.daysinn.com

Holiday Inn (800) 465-4329; www.holiday-inn.com

Howard Johnson (800) 446-4656; www.hojo.com

La Quinta (800) 531-5900; www.laquinta.com

Motel 6 (800) 466-8356; www.motel6.com

Hospitality International Hotels (800) 251-1962; www.reservahost.com

Cruising: Central Florida is not just the theme park capital of the world and a place to stay within a short drive of both Atlantic Ocean and Gulf of Mexico beaches. It's also handy to two major and a couple of minor cruise terminals. In-the-know Orlando travelers book a cruise add-on with their Orlando stay.

- From **Port Canaveral,** cruise to the Caribbean or transatlantic with Carnival, Disney Cruise Line, or Royal Caribbean.

- From **Tampa,** sail to the Mexican Riviera with Carnival Cruise Lines or Holland-America.

- *Regal Empress* cruises seasonally out of **Port Manatee** in Sarasota.

A travel agent who specializes in cruises is your key to finding the right ship, cabin, rate, and itinerary.

Fishing and hunting: Florida residents pay $17 for an annual saltwater fishing license. For non-Floridians saltwater licenses are $17 for three days, $30 for seven days, and $47 per year. A freshwater fishing license costs $17 per year for Floridians or $47 for nonresidents, who can also buy a seven-day permit for $30. Divers, spearfishers, and people who set traps for marine life need the same licenses as other anglers. Licenses are not required for children under age sixteen or Floridians over age sixty-five with a valid driver's license or registration card. Visit http://myfwc.com/License/LicPermit_RecreationalHF.htm for more information.

Fishing licenses can be ordered by phone at (888) 347-4356. A credit card is required and a service fee is charged. Hunting licenses are $17.00 per year for Floridians and $151.50 per year or $46.50 for ten days for out-of-staters.

Excellent fishing information is included in the free vacation guide available from the Central Florida Visitors & Convention Bureau (800-828-7655), www.visitcentralflorida.org. Listed are fishing guides, fish camps, public landings, boat rentals, license centers, fishing piers, and tips on catching largemouth bass, bluegill, shellcracker, crappie, and catfish.

An hour's drive east of Orlando lies the Indian River Lagoon system, consisting of the Indian River Lagoon, the Banana River Lagoon, and the Mosquito Lagoon. All offer world-class sight fishing for spotted sea trout, redfish, and black drum. Tarpon, snook, and crevalle are available in season. A few minutes of extra driving lets you access the Atlantic Ocean through Port Canaveral. Florida is justly famous for its saltwater fishing, and this area offers some of the best in the state.

Florida National Scenic Trail: It isn't yet continuous throughout all of Florida, but eventually hikers will be able to hike Florida from stem to stern, connecting with other national trails. For now, major segments of the trail can be hiked in state and national forests, in Big Cypress National Preserve, and around the entire circumference of Lake Okeechobee. It's a project of Florida groups and government and the United States Department of Agriculture. Contact the USDA Forest Service, 325 John Knox Rd., Suite F-100, Tallahassee, FL 32303. For information on the Florida Division of Forestry's Trailwalker program, call (850) 414-0871 or visit www.fl-dof.com.

Florida residents: When making hotel reservations or buying theme park tickets, always ask if a Florida resident discount applies. Often you can get a price break, albeit sometimes with blackout dates. Some theme park annual passes cost little more than two or three days' admission yet can be used year-round, including special festivals and events.

Getting around: Coastal communities on both the east and west shores of Florida have their own cluster of barrier islands, each with its own beach. Some can be reached by coastal roads that hop from island to island. Others require starting at the mainland and taking the only bridge that serves that particular island. It's fun to drive these coastal roads, but traffic can be stop-and-start and there's always the chance of a long delay for a bridge opening. Consult a good map.

Golf: With its gentle hills and benign weather, Central Florida is a natural for golf courses. It's possible to build entire day trips around golf courses in every corner covered in this book. Write to the resources listed in the back of the book, and ask for special brochures on their golf facilities.

Greyhound bus: Second only to a rental car for convenience is traveling Florida's outback by Greyhound. The line serves almost every community listed in this book. Ask about the Florida Pass, which allows unlimited travel for a given time period at a given price. For information visit www.greyhound.com or call (800) 229-9424; tickets (800) 231-2222.

Hurricane season: The chances of a hurricane affecting your day trip are very small. Still, hurricanes happen and should be respected. The three stages of alert are hurricane advisory, watch, and warning. If you travel Florida's coastal areas during hurricane season—roughly June 1 through the end of October—note highway signs indicating evacuation routes. If a storm is forecast, follow instructions and evacuate early; it can take many hours to evacuate barrier islands over narrow roads and even narrower bridges or causeways. At the first indication of a hurricane watch, fill the car with gas. Traffic jams can occur on evacuation routes; you could be stuck for hours. Stock up on food and water for the trip home. If a hurricane warning is issued, follow authorities' instructions as quickly as possible. If you have pets, children, or medical problems, prepare even earlier. Pets aren't allowed in most shelters.

Mapping your route: If you want to get to, say, Indian Rocks Beach west of Tampa, you could take the slow, scenic, coastal route—SR 699—through every hamlet, or take a quicker route via I-4, I-275, and SR 688 directly to the island. Maps in this book are provided for planning and orientation, but you'll need a good state map or, better still, the *Florida Gazetteer* (DeLorme Publishing) to fine-tune your route. In coastal areas almost every route will be determined by bridges and causeways rather than by a straight-arrow route from here to there.

Pets: It's against Florida law to leave an animal in a closed vehicle, even if a window is cracked to provide ventilation. Temperatures soar quickly in the sunshine, even on a cool day. Animals suffer and die needlessly; you risk a fine or even prosecution.

Sales tax: Some attractions list their prices including tax, others without. Be prepared to pay 6 to 7 percent state sales tax on top of published prices. Hotels rarely include tax or gratuities in their published rates. Hotel rates are plus state sales tax, any county option sales tax, and bed tax—adding 12 to 13 percent to the total tab, not counting tips, service charges, and the occasional surcharge for a special event.

Self-catering: Central Florida is awash in time-shares, suites, condos, apartments, duplexes, and even entire neighborhoods of single-family homes that rent by the night, week, or month. When booking accommodations, understand what services are provided.

Resorts usually provide daily maid service, including kitchen cleanup. At other lodgings you may have to make your own bed, do all your own housekeeping, and pay a cleaning-fee deposit in case you don't leave the place clean enough for the next tenant.

Smoking: If you're a smoker, or a nonsmoker who wants to avoid breathing others' smoke, it's wise to call ahead to inquire about a restaurant's smoking policy. Laws and policies are changing, but most restaurants in Central Florida do not permit smoking. Cigars are verboten almost everywhere except in cigar bars.

State parks: Admission to most state parks, gardens, historic sites, and recreation areas is by the carload, usually $4 to $5 for up to eight persons or $1 per walk-in or biker. Passes good for all state sites are $40 per year for an individual and $80 per family. See www.florida stateparks.org for more information.

Swimming safety: It's always best to swim within sight of a lifeguard station. Observe warning flags and signs that may indicate such pests as stinging jellyfish, hazards such as run-outs, or weather problems. In addition to water hazards, Florida is the lightning capital of the United States. When lightning is in the area, get off the beach or golf course or away from other open areas.

Wheelchair access: Thanks to the Americans with Disabilities Act, you no longer have to wonder whether most places have access. Still, it's wise to check ahead to see whether particular facilities suit your needs, because "handicap accessible" may mean only that a wheelchair can get through the door and not that a hotel room has a wheel-in shower, lowered light switches and closet bars, TDD telephone access, information in braille, acceptable facilities for a guide dog, and so on. Check ahead, too, to see what park facilities are available if you need a paved nature trail or a wheelchair-accessible bathroom.

Wineries: For a list of Florida wineries that are open to the public, contact the Florida Grape Growers Association, 111 Yelvington Rd., Suite 1, East Palatka, FL 32131 (386) 329-0318; www.fgga.org.

 # using this travel guide

Highway designations: Federal highways are designated US. State routes and are indicated by SR (State Road).

Restaurants: This book uses dollar signs to indicate whether a hotel or restaurant is inexpensive, moderate, or expensive. Assume roughly that you'll pay $10 or less per person for a typical meal at a $ restaurant, $25 or less at $$, or more than $25 at $$$. If $$$$ is indicated, it's likely you'll spend $50 and up per person. Call ahead to see if reservations are accepted or required and to ask about special concerns such as parking, handicap facilities, or the availability of vegetarian meals.

Accommodations: Lodgings priced $50 or less are indicated as $. You'll pay $50 to $100 at $$ rates and $100 and up at $$$ listings. Hotels priced at $$$$ are truly luxury properties where you'll pay $200 or more.

north

day trip 01

celery and the st. johns river:
oviedo, sanford, debary

oviedo

Barely over the county line north of Orange County, enter Seminole County near Oviedo. You're still in Greater Orlando with its ever-devouring growth, but this is also lake and river country, with some remaining greenspace for the angler, canoeist, and wildlife observer. To reach Oviedo from Orlando, drive east on SR 50, then north on SR 434, also known as Alafaya Trail.

where to go

Black Hammock. 2316 Black Hammock Fish Camp Rd.; (407) 365-2201 restaurant; (407) 365-1244 marina; www.theblackhammock.com. Black Hammock is a center for boat rentals, nature tours aboard pontoon boats, alligator viewing in a nature exhibit, airboat rides, bait and tackle—and some of the best catfish meals in the South.

Gator Ventures. 2536 Black Hammock Fish Camp Rd.; (407) 977-8235. Come during the day for sightseeing, fishing, duck hunting, and wildlife watching, or take a night ride for frogging or gator watching. A free alligator exhibit is on the grounds. Ride the wetlands around Lake Jesup, a 10,000-acre wilderness alive with bird life, wild boar, bobcats, and alligators. Adventures are by appointment and are priced by the hour.

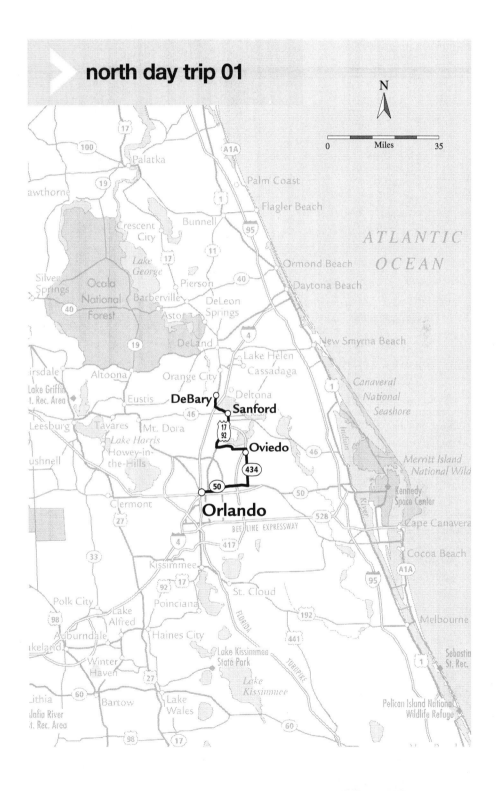

north day trip 01

N

0   Miles   35

Pappy's Patch U-Pick Strawberries. Florida Avenue (just off SR 434, 1 mile north of Oviedo center); (407) 366-8512. They are open seasonally and close once the weather gets too hot. That means Pappy's Patch typically opens around the end of Dec and closes around the end of April. We pick fresh strawberries there at least once a week. The berries are great and the people that run the place are wonderful.

where to eat

Black Hammock. 2316 Black Hammock Fish Camp Rd.; (407) 365-2201 restaurant, (407) 365-1244 marina. Of the many activities that can be enjoyed here, one of the best is eating. Try farm-raised gator as well as fried or blackened catfish, barbecue, mahimahi done your way, burgers, chicken, or steak. The Shrimp Feast features three kinds of shrimp with all the trimmings, or have the Surf 'n' Turf or the Swamp 'n' Turf (steak and gator bites). Prime rib, steak, and chicken are charbroiled. For dessert have the Kentucky Derby pie. Beer is sold by the can, bottle, or pitcher; wine is served by the glass or carafe. On the first and third Sundays of the month, live music starts at 2 p.m. in the Tiki Bar. Open Tues and Wed from 4 p.m., Thurs through Sun from 11:30 a.m. Closed Monday. $–$$.

El Potro Mexican Restaurant. 15 Alafaya Woods Blvd., Suite 101; (407) 977-3075. A family-owned and -operated establishment serving authentic Mexican cuisine. Enjoy live music at selected times. Voted Orlando's best Mexican restaurant. My favorite item is the mushroom quesadilla. $–$$.

Giovanni's Italian Restaurant & Pizzeria. 4250 Alafaya Trail, Suite 132; (407) 359-5900. Although this restaurant is located in a nondescript shopping area, it may remind visitors of upscale pizza houses in Boston or New York. Tile floors, comfortable booth seating, and a display case all help to set the mood. This spot offers a broad pasta selection. The spaghetti, linguini, angel hair, etc., can be topped with any of six sauces. The menu also boasts lasagna, manicotti, and other baked favorites. The cost of most pasta dishes is very reasonable. The pizzas are also popular, as are calzones. Very family friendly! Lunch and dinner daily. $–$$.

Peppino's Ristorante. 100 Carrigan Ave.; (407) 365-4774. If you're looking for a dressy-casual place to feast on authentically prepared Italian specialties, especially veal and chicken, this is it. There's always a seafood specialty, too, and good steaks. Have a drink from the full bar. Open for lunch and dinner weekdays; dinner only Saturday and Sunday. $$.

sanford

Sanford is slipping out of its small-town role and is increasingly perceived as part of Greater Orlando because so many Orlando-bound travelers arrive here at the international airport or at Amtrak's Auto Train terminus. Many plunge on south to the theme parks, missing out on the treasures that Sanford itself has to offer. Boats with a draft of up to 8 feet can still sail from the Atlantic Ocean all the way to Sanford on the St. Johns River. The city remains an important port, just as it was in the steamboat days when the river was central Florida's chief "highway." Its historic downtown deserves a day or two, and its Lake Monroe is a boating and fishing paradise. To reach Sanford from Oviedo, pop back onto SR 434, exit at US 17/92/Sanford, and continue into Sanford.

where to go

Central Florida Zoo. 4755 Northwest US 17/92; (407) 323-4450; www.centralfloridazoo .org. This small zoo has been a local favorite since 1933. See rare and endangered species from all over the world, as well as an impressive collection of rare Florida native plants. Trained volunteers educate visitors about animals, birds, elephants, big cats, snakes, and much more. Shop for gifts; cold drinks and light meals are sold at the canteen, which can also stage a children's birthday party if you make arrangements in advance. Adults $8.95, children ages three to twelve $4.95, and seniors age sixty or over $6.95. Open every day 9 a.m. to 5 p.m.

Lower Wekiva River State Preserve. Mailing address: c/o Wekiwa Springs State Park, 1800 Wekiwa Circle, Apopka, FL 32712; (407) 884-2008; www.floridastateparks.org/lower wekivariver/default.htm. Located 9 miles west of Sanford on SR 46, this preserve covers more than 17,000 acres along the St. Johns River. Access to these fragile wetlands is limited, so be sure to call ahead to inquire about any hiking, primitive camping, horseback camping, or canoeing you want to do. Lucky visitors see black bear, river otters, alligators, wood storks, and sandhill cranes. Except for trails and primitive campsites, there are no facilities.

Museum of Seminole County. 300 Bush Blvd.; (407) 665-2489; www.seminolecountyfl .gov/leisure/museum. Because Sanford was a major steamboat stop in the decades before people arrived in Florida by rail or motorcar, the town is drenched in history, and this museum is the place to learn about it. Displays depict agriculture, the steamboat era, a typical country store, hospital memorabilia, and artifacts from the first police and fire stations, and the days when Sanford was the Celery Capital. As you enter the building, note the camphor tree, said to be the third largest in the nation. The building itself began as a home for the indigent and elderly, who became largely self-sufficient through operation of their own orange grove, vegetable garden, chicken farm, and dairy barn. Open Tues through Fri 1 to 5 p.m., Sat 9 a.m. to 1 p.m. Admission is $3.21 for adults (tax included), $1.07 for children ages four to eighteen and students (tax included). Children under four are admitted free.

Rivership *Romance*. 433 North Palmetto Ave.; (800) 423-7401 or (407) 321-5091; www .rivershipromance.com. Your cruise can be a relaxing glide on the St. Johns River or a fun-filled evening of feasting and dancing. On day cruises, bring binoculars for the wildlife show that goes on along the banks of the river. View egrets, herons, and ospreys, sunning alligators and turtles, and perhaps a rare manatee. Dine at your reserved table in the air-conditioned dining room, gazing through a picture window at the passing scene. Menus offer a choice of six entrees, including one seafood and one vegetarian. Luncheon cruises sail Wed, Sat, and Sun 11 a.m. to 2 p.m. and Mon, Tues, Thurs, and Fri 11 a.m. to 3 p.m. Moonlight Dinner cruises with live music and dancing sail Fri and Sat at 7:30 p.m., docking at 11 p.m. Cruises are priced $37 to $53, including the meal. Bar beverages and tips are additional. Reservations are required.

Sanford Museum. 520 East First St.; (407) 688-5198. This small effort captures the rich history of "Celery City" with well-displayed mementoes. It's housed in a Mediterranean Revival building on the colorful waterfront. The archives and research library are also open to the public. Admission is free Tues through Fri 11 a.m. to 4 p.m. and Sat 1 to 4 p.m.

Self-guided walking tour. Write ahead (see Regional Information) for a brochure and map describing the Sanford Historic Downtown District. Picture the city as it was at the turn of the twentieth century, bustling with steamboat traffic and farm wagons laden with produce. Pass the movie palace, the opera house, and buildings that were once the livery stable, saloon, post office, banks, and dime stores. At 1000 East First St., the old Hotel Forrest Lake is now the home of the New Tribes Mission. The exterior is original.

Wekiwa Springs State Park. 1800 Wekiwa Circle, Apopka; (407) 884-2008. Off SR 434 or 436, the park takes its name from an Indian word meaning "spring of water." Bring your own horse and ride the 8-mile equestrian trail, or hike 13.5 miles of verdant pathways. Camp, swim in the springs, picnic, bicycle, or bird-watch for Carolina chickadees, bald eagles, limpkin, hawks, and wood storks. With luck, you may spot a black bear, gray fox, or bobcat. Deer, gopher tortoises, and other critters are more common. Open 8 a.m. to sunset every day. State park fees apply.

where to shop

Fleaworld. 4311 Orlando Ave.; (407) 330-1792. Fleaworld bills itself as America's Largest Flea Market, with over 1,700 dealer booths spread out over 104 acres. It is located on US 17/92 in Sanford. There is free admission and parking. Also home to Funworld family amusement park.

Gallery on First. 211 East First St.; (407) 323-2774; www.galleryonfirst.com. A unique gallery and working space for professional and emerging artists that invites the public inside the artistic process through shows, events, education, and conversations with artists. Voted one of the top twenty galleries in America by *GO Magazine*.

a thing for fleas?

Located on US 17/92 in Sanford, Fleaworld is a sprawling monument to the small entrepreneur. Advertised as America's largest flea market, the place has roughly 1,700 different vendors and the widest variety of merchandise imaginable—everything from antiques to tires, arts and crafts to windows. I even bought a tarantula and cage here once! My son Alex put it thusly during a recent visit: "The stuff they have here is so random." Even people who don't normally enjoy shopping like coming to Fleaworld.

Take some time to wander the aisles. While, of course, much of the merchandise here is junky, there really are some good bargains to be had. It's like being on a treasure hunt.

Fleaworld is also a superb place to people-watch. We've all heard the phrase, "it takes all kinds," and with the possible exception of wealthy folks, they all come through here. You can buy some snacks and sit down to watch the show that constantly parades by. The conversations you'll hear are another remarkably entertaining way to pass some time.

Speaking of shows, there's even an entertainment pavilion that offers free shows daily. Recent shows have included circus performers, magicians, and animal acts.

So take a break from Disney World and browse through Fleaworld, a place that is truly worlds apart. Who knows, maybe you'll develop a thing for fleas.

The Sanford Historic District Shopping Area, Downtown Sanford. Hidden treasures await visitors in the many antiques shops and specialty boutiques in historic downtown Sanford.

Seminole Towne Center. 200 Towne Center Circle; (407) 323-1843. The 1.5-million-square-foot, bi-level Seminole Towne Center features five anchor tenants—Dillard's, JCPenney, Parisian, Burdines, and Sears—along with about 120 specialty stores, and an innovative array of dining and entertainment options featuring a state-of-the-industry design. Located at exit 101C and I-4 in Sanford.

where to eat

Don Pablo's Mexican Kitchen. 100 Towne Center Blvd.; (407) 328-1885. Don Pablo's is a popular chain that features made-from-scratch salsa, tortillas, and sauces as well as an entire range of authentic Mexican specialties. From the hearty Conquistador combo to burritos, fajitas, and real margaritas, Don Pablo's serves up an authentic experience. $–$$.

Hollerbach's Willow Tree Cafe. 205 East First St.; (407) 321-2204. This is a special place that has it all—great food, fabulous German wines and beer, camaraderie, and an efficient and caring staff. The best time to come is on the entertainment nights, Thursday through Sunday. Reservations are a must as they are always busy. Even if you do not like German food, do not miss this place. They have other choices on the menu and everything is fresh and homemade. The desserts are European in style and are to die for. Their apple strudel is scrumptious! $$.

Sergio's. 2895 Orlando Dr.; (407) 323-4040. Italian classics are served with gusto in this locally popular Italian place, found just behind the ABC liquor store north of Lake Mary Boulevard. There are pastas galore, saucy chicken or a steak with a side of spaghetti, juicy veal scaloppine, shrimp Diavolo, and desserts such as tiramisu. Start with antipasto or a green salad with vinegar and oil and slabs of the crusty bread. $$–$$$.

debary

In the days when steamships brought Northerners to inland Florida for the winter, DeBary caught the eye of Samuel Frederick deBary, who owned his own side-wheelers and made his fortune carrying cargo, including Mumm's champagne. His winter home, once a lonely but elegant outpost on the St. Johns River, is now surrounded by a fast-growing community that bears his name. Continue north on US 17/92 north to DeBary.

where to go

DeBary Hall Mansion. 210 East Sunrise Blvd.; (386) 736-5953; www.debaryhall.com. This is the fully restored winter home of wealthy wine importer and steamship line owner Frederick deBary. Count deBary is recognized as bringing the first "tourists" to the area on his riverboats that steamed the waters of the St. Johns River between Jacksonville and Lake Monroe. DeBary Hall now features historic photographs and interactive exhibits that tell the region's story. Volusia County grants and other sources have funded the restoration of DeBary Hall, which features a visitors' center with a state-of-the-art Imagidome Theater presentation. DeBary Hall is listed on the National Register of Historic Places. Open Tues to Sat 10 a.m. to 4 p.m. and Sun noon to 4 p.m. The last guided tour begins at 3:30 p.m. Admission: adults $5; seniors $4; children three to twelve $2; under three free.

Gemini Springs Park. 37 Dirksen Dr.; (386) 668-3810; http://volusia.org/parks/gemini .htm. This 210-acre park surrounds one of the springs that Florida is so famous for. There's a boardwalk and nature trails, a picnic area with restrooms, and swimming in the clear, deep spring waters. A wading pool for children is 2 feet deep. There's a 2-mile equestrian trail, campsites, a bike trail, canoe rental, and fishing from the fishing dock only. Open sunrise to sunset. Admission is free.

day trip 02

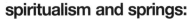

spiritualism and springs:
cassadaga, orange city, deland,
deleon springs

This jaunt covers 10,000 years of history in a nutshell, and you'll want to come back for more. The oldest canoe found in the Western Hemisphere was fished out of DeLeon Springs and sent to a museum in Tallahassee. Today the springs still pour thousands of gallons of water a day into a swimming pool that is the same temperature winter and summer. Ponce de Leon thought he would find the Fountain of Youth in these waters. Some locals swim here daily year-round. Your visit to Cassadaga takes you into the realm of spiritualism. DeLand is a college town abuzz with bustling students; Orange City is the home of Blue Spring. Like DeLeon Springs, the waters here gush up into a crystal pool that spills eventually into the St. Johns River. It's a favorite wintering spot for manatees, who know they'll find shelter and warm water here.

cassadaga

Go north from Orlando on I-4 (signs say east) toward Daytona Beach. Pass the Deltona exits, then take the DeLand–Orange City exit, turn left on Route 472, then turn right on Martin Luther King Boulevard. Turn right at the sign to Cassadaga, which is on County Road 4139.

The historic hamlet of Cassadaga in Central Florida was settled in 1894 by George P. Colby—a trance medium from New York—and his followers. They established Florida's first spiritualist camp, now known as the Southern Cassadaga Spiritualist Camp Meeting. Half

9

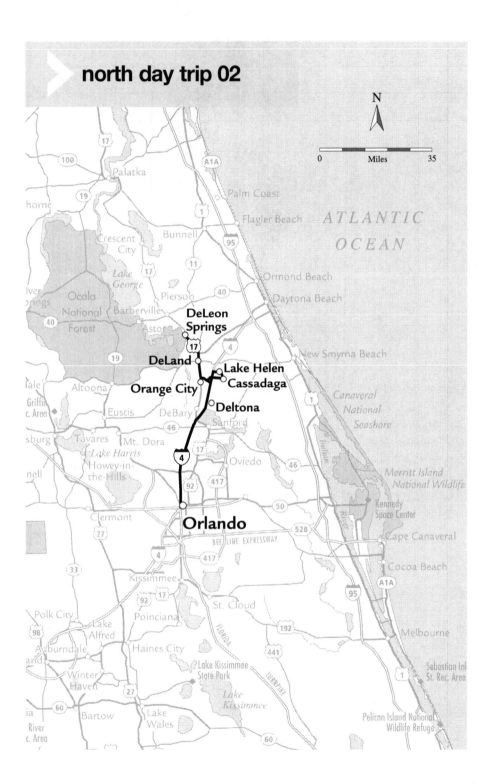

N

0   Miles   35

Palatka

Palm Coast

Flagler Beach

Bunnell

Ormond Beach

Daytona Beach

Pierson

DeLeon
Springs

New Smyrna Beach

DeLand

Lake Helen
Cassadaga

Orange City

Deltona

Canaveral
National
Seashore

Sanford

Altoona

Griffin
c. Area

Eustis   DeBary

Tavares   Mt. Dora

Lake Harris

Howey-in-
the-Hills

Oviedo

Merritt Island
National Wildlife

Clermont

Kennedy
Space Center

Orlando

Cape Canaveral

BEE LINE EXPRESSWAY

Cocoa Beach

Kissimmee

St. Cloud

Polk City

Poinciana

Lake
Alfred

Melbourne

Auburndale

Haines City

Winter
Haven

Lake Kissimmee
State Park

Sebastian Inl
St. Rec. Area

Bartow

Lake
Wales

Lake
Kissimmee

Pelican Island National
Wildlife Refuge

ATLANTIC
OCEAN

Ocala
National
Forest

Astor

Crescent
City

Lake
George

Barberville

Palatka

a day does nicely for strolling the streets, having a reading or two if you're into the psychic scene, shopping the bookstores for New Age music, and dining at the hotel.

Even if you're immune to superstition and fortune-telling, you'll feel the eerie presence here. The homes look like summer camps, unlike any other neighborhood in Florida, and they're packed tightly into one-lane streets. Outside many of them are signs announcing that a reader, healer, medium, or reverend lives inside. Most will give you a reading for about $50 a half-hour. A longer reading or a visit with a departed loved one might run $75. Or you can attend one of the free services, including healing services on Sunday and Wednesday. Minireadings by students cost only a few dollars, and mediums sometimes offer minireadings for half the going rate. There's such a crowd on some nights, you have to take a number.

where to go

Cassadaga Hotel. 355 Cassadaga Rd.; (386) 228-2323; www.cassadagahotel.net. The hotel lies in the heart of this tiny crossroads, and front desk personnel can arrange a reading with one of their resident psychics. The gift shop has a superb selection of New Age paraphernalia and souvenirs. Set a spell on the wide wraparound veranda or in the homey lobby. Start your tour by buying the annual Cassadaga Spiritualist Camp program here or in the other shops. The hotel has a map showing the community's buildings and parks and a schedule of services and events.

Colby Memorial Temple. On Stevens Street, a short walk from the hotel; (386) 228-3171; www.cassadaga.org/church_services.htm. The temple is the setting for spiritualist services. On Sunday the healing service is at 10 a.m., followed by a church service at 10:30. A demonstration message service is held Sun 12:30 to 1:30 p.m. On Wednesday healing is at 7 p.m. There's an admission charge to the message service that follows. On the second Friday of each month, spiritual healing is practiced by candlelight at 7:30 p.m. Oct through May the camp also offers adult lyceum every morning, in which teachers instruct in spiritualism and related topics. On the church grounds, note the plaque honoring the founding of Cassadaga. The small six-sided building is the Caesar Forman Healing Center, where healing is held on Sun 10 to 10:30 a.m. and Wed 7 a.m. to 3:30 p.m. by some of the community's dozen or so certified healers. Rites are free, although donations are appreciated.

Parks dot the little settlement. They all have names and meaning to locals, but for visitors they are just pleasant greenspaces with paths, carefully tended plantings, and sometimes a picnic table. Follow the map in the program mentioned above. Seneca Park, overlooking Spirit Pond, has a gazebo large enough to seat eight to twelve for a picnic.

Self-guided walking tour. Just walk up one street and down the other to soak up the strange atmosphere of a camp community. Occasionally you'll see a patch of the original brick paving peeking through. Roads are still mostly single-lane, lined with homes packed close together, and they're remarkably hilly for flat Central Florida. You'll pass Harmony Hall, Brigham Hall, the temple, several meditation gardens, and Spirit Lake.

where to shop

Cassadaga Hotel. Its gift shop is well stocked with New Age books and paraphernalia, incense, unique jewelry, and gifts for followers of the spirit world.

Cassadaga Spiritualist Camp Bookstore. 1112 Stevens St.; (386) 228-2880; www .cassadaga.org/bookstore.htm. A broad range of New Age philosophies is represented with books, music, trinkets, and icons. You'll also find soaps, scents, writing paper, and other souvenirs. Open daily.

Purple Rose. 1079 Stevens St.; (386) 228-3315; http://cassadaga-purplerose.com. The shop carries crystals, gems, jewelry, Native American and metaphysical paraphernalia, and butter-soft Minnetonka moccasins. Open every day.

where to eat

Lost in Time Cafe. 355 Cassadaga Rd.; (386) 228-2323; http://cassadagahotel.net/cafe3 .html. Located in the Cassadaga Hotel, the cafe is surprisingly conventional in this unusual, spiritualist setting. Choose from a nice variety of sandwiches and hot and cold dishes. You can even get a glass of wine with your meal. Open daily for lunch. $–$$.

where to stay

Ann Steven's House. 201 East Kicklighter Rd., Lake Helen; (386) 228-0310 or (800) 220-0310; www.annstevenshouse.com. This AAA three-diamond inn is housed in an 1890s Victorian mansion and carriage house. All rooms are different, so let the hosts know whether you want a soaking tub, in-room Jacuzzi, private veranda, or other feature. A full country breakfast is included. The inn also has an intimate pub, where it's fun to have a quiet drink after dinner. $$.

Cassadaga Hotel. 355 Cassadaga Rd.; (386) 228-2323. Built in 1927 to replace an even earlier structure that burned, the hotel is beyond quaint. Rooms are small, furnishings defiantly tatty, and bathrooms so minuscule that the tiny pedestal sink may be in the bedroom. Still, baths have all the essential plumbing and are en suite. Window units provide air-conditioning. Some rooms have a tub, balcony, or other special features, but all cost the same. Rates, which are higher on weekends, include continental breakfast. Rooms have no television, phone, radio, or other conveniences, but guests can watch TV in the lobby. The hotel also has a hair salon, a massage therapist—and mediums on call. $$.

orange city

A century ago, steamboats stopped at the docks at Blue Spring to load oranges picked in nearby groves. The main drag, US 17/92, has been the main highway from south Florida to the Midwest for almost a century, yet the heart of little Orange City hasn't budged out of the 1950s. Continue west on CR 4139 from Cassadaga. Turn south onto the Martin Luther King Beltway, then take CR 4145 west and US 17/92 south to Orange City.

where to go

Blue Spring State Park. 2100 West French Ave.; (386) 775-3663; www.floridastateparks .org/bluespring. The park has a view of the St. Johns River, a clear spring for swimming and snorkeling, a historic home, live oak trees for shade, and a boardwalk that takes you along the spring run to an overlook where, with luck, you'll see manatees. February is usually the top time for these "sea cows" to come in from the cold and live in spring waters that stay the same temperature year-round. The old homestead was built at a time when steamboats brought passengers upriver and left here filled with oranges. Bring a picnic lunch. Canoes are rented by the hour or day, and there is a boat launch, showers, and primitive campsites. Admission is $5 per vehicle and $1 per person for those who arrive on foot or bicycle. Hours are 8 a.m. to sunset.

St. Johns River Cruises & Tours. 2100 West French Ave.; (386) 917-0724; www.sjriver cruises.com. This cruise provides visitors with an award-winning two-hour narrated tour of the St. Johns River. They also have guided kayak tours and rentals. Tours depart daily at 10 a.m. and 1 p.m. Adults, $22; seniors sixty and older, $20; children ages three through twelve, $16.

U.S. Postal Museum. 300 South Volusia Ave.; (386) 774-8849; www.1876heritageinn .com/museum.htm. The U.S. Postal Museum, one of only three in the United States, was established for the preservation and appreciation of postal history and postal artifacts. In 1876 the first post office for the area that became Orange City was housed in the very same building as the current museum, which offers visitors a glimpse of rare postal artifacts in a re-created 1940s post office setting. Paperwork, books, forms, and clothing used more than fifty years ago are also displayed. Open Mon to Fri, 10 a.m. to 4 p.m.; Sat, 10 a.m. to noon. Admission is free.

where to eat

Jax Place. 481 Deltona Blvd., Deltona; (386) 860-3000. Located in the Best Western Del-tona Inn on the way to Orange City, Jax Place is a gem of a restaurant that's well worth a special stop for its elegant dinners. The lounge is famous for its large selection of martinis;

there's live music on special nights. Reservations are strongly advised. The restaurant is open daily for dinner; breakfast is provided for inn guests. $$–$$$.

Stavros Pizza. 413 South Volusia Ave.; (386) 775-2066. This is a family favorite for hot grinders, gyros, Greek salad, and all the pasta favorites, from spaghetti and meatballs to lasagna and fettuccine Alfredo. Veal, chicken, and eggplant are served parmigiana, with beer or wine if you wish. Open daily, except Mon, 11 a.m. to 10 p.m. $–$$.

where to stay

Best Western Deltona Inn. 481 Deltona Blvd., Deltona; (386) 860-3000 or (800) 528-1234; www.bestwestern.com. Located at Deltona exit 53 off I-4, with easy interstate exit and access, this is a twenty-three-acre oasis of calm just off the highway. Rooms have data ports, voice mail, and more than forty TV channels, including free HBO. The inn is also home to Jax Place restaurant, where breakfast is provided for guests. $$–$$$.

deland

Originally founded closer to the St. Johns River, the entire community was moved after a long-ago flood. Today a grid of streets shaded with picturesque live oaks, the city is home to Stetson University and an old downtown lined with trendy restaurants and shops. To see the campus, which includes the oldest continuously operating school building in Florida, start 3 blocks from downtown and walk north to the Holiday House restaurant. You'll pass the grand mansion occupied by Stetson's president, historic buildings in a variety of architectural styles, pleasant lawns, and the city's cultural-arts center. Peek in to shop the gift shop and to see what's showing in the small museum. Take US 17 north to DeLand.

where to go

African American Museum of the Arts. 325 South Clara Ave.; (386) 736-4004; www .africanmuseumdeland.org. The only museum in the region devoted primarily to African-American and Caribbean-American cultures and art. The museum presents six major exhibitions each year, featuring works by established and emerging artists. It is also home to a permanent collection of more than 150 artifacts, including sculptures and ceremonial masks from the countries of Africa. Open Thurs to Sat, 10 a.m. to 4 p.m. Admission is free.

Athens Theatre. 124 North Florida Ave.; (386) 738-7156; www.athenstheatre.org. The Athens Theatre opened in 1922. This local landmark was the center of DeLand entertainment and socializing for almost seventy years. Opening as a vaudeville house, one of its visiting performers, Sally Rand (the famous fan dancer), entertained there in the 1930s. It operated for many years as a movie theater—just a block from the historic DeLand High School, many recall first dates and first kisses there. Today, the Athens is a multipurpose venue for films, musical events, and community programs. Visit the Web site for a list of events.

DeLand Historic Mural Walk. Woodland Boulevard, (386) 738-0649; www.mainstreet deland.com. The DeLand Historic Mural Walk presents a chronological history of the community. Each of the twelve murals tells a story on its own, vividly portraying the arrival of Henry DeLand, the great St. Johns River, steamboats, statesmen, wildlife, first hotels, the Spanish sugar mill, the DeLand Naval Air Station, the citrus industry, the traditional African-American settlement (Red City), and more events, places, and characters from the community's past. Featuring the work of six artists, the murals act as illustrated pages of a history book with cleverly placed hidden elements to discover. A self-guided walking tour brochure is available.

DeLand House Museum. 137 West Michigan Ave., (386) 740-6813; www.delandhouse .com. A living history museum, complete with period furnishings of the nineteenth century, the Henry A. DeLand House is a popular destination for those interested in learning about the people, culture, and history of Volusia County. The West Volusia Historical Society operates the museum and offers year-round educational programs and special events designed to expand awareness of the area's rich and diverse heritage. An adjoining research center houses an extensive library of early maps, videos, rare photographs, books, and historical artifacts. Open Tues to Sat, noon to 4 p.m. Admission is free.

The DeLand Museum of Art. 600 North Woodland Blvd.; (386) 734.4371; www.deland museum.com. The DeLand Museum of Art has served as a cultural cornerstone of the city, dedicated to presenting and educating in the visual arts. The museum has grown from a small house into a shared cultural arts center providing high-quality exhibitions and programming for all ages. The museum has had national-caliber exhibitions such as Ansel Adams; Icons of the Twentieth Century: Portraits by Yousuf Karsh; The Spirit of Africa; Audubon in Florida, and Audubon Treasures; and It's a Dog's Life: Photographs by William Wegman from the Polaroid Corporation. The museum also showcases work of established and emerging Florida artists. Open Tues through Sat, 10 a.m. to 4 p.m., and Sun, 1 to 4 p.m.; closed Monday. Modest admission is charged.

DeLand Naval Air Station Museum. 910 Biscayne Ave. (in the airport complex); (386) 738-4149; www.delandnavalairstation.org. Although it's a small, modest effort, this museum looms large in the hearts of aviators, military buffs, and those who learned to fly here during World War II. This airport actually was a naval air station between 1942 and 1946, a training center for dive-bomber pilots. Displays of uniforms, guns, photographs, and aircraft models recall the story. Open Mon through Sat 1 to 4 p.m. Free, but donations are accepted. Also on the field and open the same hours is the **DeLand Naval Air Station Historic Hangar** (386-738-4149), showing historic war birds and World War II memorabilia.

Gillespie Museum of Minerals. 234 East Michigan Ave.; (386) 822-7330; www.gillespie museum.stetson.edu. This museum houses one of the largest private gem and mineral collections in the nation, attracting rock hounds from all over the world. See rare, unique, priceless, and gee-whiz rocks and fossils. Open Mon through Fri 9 a.m. to 4 p.m. Free admission.

Hontoon Island State Park. 2309 River Ridge Rd.; (386) 736-5309, http://floridastate parks.org/hontoonisland. The park occupies an island in the St. Johns River. Take US 44 west to Hontoon Road, then follow the signs. Timucuan tribes lived here hundreds of years ago, leaving behind an owl totem that wasn't found until 1955. A replica of the original— a rarity because totems were uncommon to Native American tribes in this area—stands on the island today. Take the free ferry to the island to picnic, fish, and camp in a rustic cabin or your own tent, observe wildlife, or climb the watchtower for a view of the river for miles around. Allow ninety minutes for the self-guided hiking trail. Free parking is on the mainland; ferries run from 9 a.m. to an hour before sundown daily. Bring everything with you; there are no supplies on the island. Dock your boat for the same fee paid by overnight campers.

Reptile Discovery Center. 2710 Big John Dr.; (386) 740-9143; www.reptilediscovery center.com. This education and conservation-based research development center is home to hundreds of reptiles and amphibians. It also houses the Medtoxin Venom Laboratories, where visitors can witness live venom extractions at 11:30 a.m. and 3 p.m. Open Thurs to Sun, 10 a.m. to 5 p.m., Oct 15 to Aug 23. Admission: adults $8.50; seniors $5.50; children four to seventeen, $5.50; children three and under, free.

Skydive DeLand. 1600 Flightline Blvd.; (386) 738-3539; www.skydivedeland.com. Skydive DeLand, one of the busiest drop zones in the world, offers the thrill of a lifetime in a tandem parachute ride with certified instructors. Tandem skydiving was developed in DeLand and is now done worldwide. Teams from all over the world come to Skydive DeLand to practice group formations. Skydive DeLand also features a restaurant and bar, as well as an observation platform. Open 8 a.m. to sunset. Call or visit the Web site for prices.

where to shop

Angevine's. 2999 South Woodland Blvd. (US 17/92); (386) 734-8553; www.angevinesfine silver.com. This establishment is the city's oldest antiques dealer, known for its fine silver, estate jewelry, and specialty pieces. Cliff Angevine Jr. is a sterling-matching specialist, and Sue Angevine Guess is a graduate gemologist. Open Mon through Sat 10 a.m., closing weekdays at 5 p.m. and Sat at 1 p.m.

BackHome Antiques. 110 South Woodland Blvd.; (386) 738-9967; www.backhome antiques.net. This store is owned by Graham and Petula Bartlett, who have been buying and selling antiques for ten years. Browse through their vast and varied array of nostalgic and sentimental items. Some of the items you will find in their store include antique furniture, mirrors, lamps, and rugs. Generally open Mon through Sat 11 a.m. to 5 p.m.

Doll & Hobby Shop. 138 South Woodland Blvd.; (386) 734-3200; www.doll-hobby.com. This is another of the very special shops that bring tourists to historic downtown DeLand from miles around. Shop for collectible and specialty dolls, everything you need for your Hot Wheels collection, Polar Lights, Barbie, and much more. Open Mon through Fri 10 a.m. to 4 p.m.

The Muse Book Shop. 112 South Woodland Blvd.; (386) 734-0278, http://themusebook shop.com/. The Muse is an old-fashioned bookstore crammed with books from the latest novels to rare, historical books. Stop in for Florida maps and books as well as to shop for gifts and your own library. Lose yourself among the high stacks, a book lover's paradise. Generally open Mon through Sat 10 a.m. to 6 p.m.

Uppity Woman. 135 West Plymouth Ave.; (386) 736-1117. This big old house is jam-packed with country collectibles, candles, copper, primitives, bath and body products, and a big teacup-and-teapot collection. It's off the beaten path but worth a special trip several blocks north of downtown center. Take US 17 north, then turn right onto Plymouth Avenue at the Eckerd Drug. Open Mon through Sat 9 a.m. to 5 p.m.

Wolfe Contemporary Gallery. 119 North Woodland Blvd.; (386) 740-1492; www.wolfe gallery.com. This is one of a growing number of high-quality art galleries in downtown DeLand. Many works are by area artists who are in the national spotlight. The gallery also specializes in fine crafts from all over the United States—blown glass, wooden boxes, hand-made jewelry, wind chimes, and more. Open Mon through Thurs 10 a.m. to 6 p.m., Fri and Sat until 9 p.m., and Sun from 1 to 5 p.m.

where to eat

Belly Busters. 930 North Woodland Blvd.; (386) 734-1611. This joint is a delightfully dumpy owner-operated place that loyal locals have been keeping to themselves for more than twenty years. Sandwiches are stuffed with at least a quarter pound of meat. For a cholesterol fix, order the double steak sub with cheese. Buddy and Jerry offer a large menu of subs, soups, and pita sandwiches. The interior is small and has no nonsmoking section, but you can eat on the picnic tables out back or grab a bag of belly busters to take with you for boating or picnicking. $.

DeLand Artisan. 215 North Woodland Blvd.; (386) 736-3484; www.delandartisaninn.com. This is the "in" place for lunch (ask for a table overlooking "The Boulevard") or a leisurely dinner in a softly lit dining room backed with the original brick walls. The chef does classic continental, fusion, Southwest, and Caribbean dishes with flair and finesse. Every day there's a new soup, quiche, sandwich, and specialty of the day featuring fresh seafood or a special cut of meat. There's a full bar, a lounge with live entertainment some evenings, and a comprehensive wine list. Open every day for lunch and dinner. Reservations are highly recommended. $$–$$$.

Holiday House. 704 North Woodland Blvd.; (386) 734-6319; http://holidayhouserestaurant .com. This is the original of a small Florida chain of buffet restaurants. It's an interesting concept, with unlimited self-serve for some foods but enough rules and limits that you have to mind your p's and q's. You can opt for the full meal (only one serving of meat), hot and cold buffet with no meat, or cold buffet only. The menu is limited but is a good choice for those who don't like buffets. This is basic, home-style southern family fare. Open 11:30 a.m. to 8:30 p.m. Tues through Sat and 11 a.m. to 8:30 p.m. Sun and holidays. They don't take reservations, but call ahead anyway and they'll do their best. On Sunday after church the wait can be long. $–$$.

Oudoms Thai Restaurant. 217 North Woodland Blvd.; (386) 740-0123. One-half of a dual-personality restaurant (the other half specializes in sushi), this is a superb place for Thai food. Order a Japanese beer, sushi, or a Thai specialty cooked to order—from unspicy to hot-hot. Open for lunch Monday through Friday and for dinner daily except Sunday. $$.

The Old House Cafe. 412 South Woodland Blvd.; (386) 734-7592; www.oldhousecafe .com. The Old House Cafe is a delightful blend of southern Victorian charm, old Florida recipes, soups, sandwiches, and salads. Try the gourmet food selections, or prepared foods to go for busy lifestyles. Open for lunch Monday through Friday, and for dinner Thurs and Fri 5:30 to 9 p.m. $$.

The Perfect Spot Restaurant and Bar. 1600 Flightline Blvd.; (386) 734-0088; www .skydivedeland.com. Located at Skydive DeLand, this restaurant offers a "birds-eye" view of skydivers at one of the most active drop zones in the world. It's the only place you will find in the area where world travelers, a wide variety of beers and liquor, and a large group of thrill seekers falling from the sky come together. Breakfast, a vegetarian menu, wings, burgers, and salads are served in a relaxing, friendly atmosphere. Open weekdays 8 a.m. to 8 p.m., weekends until 9 p.m. $$.

Sunrise Fish Camp. 1905 Hontoon Rd.; (386) 736-2970. Savor the flavor of authentic Florida on the St. Johns River at Lake Beresford in a laid-back, casual atmosphere where newspapers cover the wood tables. Known for its blue crabs, Sunrise also features steaks, shrimp, chowder, and some of the best hush puppies ever made! They also have soft-shell crabs in season. Always call ahead when you want a bucket full of blue crabs. $–$$.

where to stay

Comfort Inn. 400 East International Speedway Blvd.; (386) 736-3100 or (800) 424-6423; www.choicehotels.com. The motel is on the east side of DeLand on the highway to Daytona Beach. If you like a familiar, economical chain motel, headquarter here to sightsee both east and west Volusia County. Your day starts with a free continental breakfast; restaurants for lunch and dinner are nearby. Amenities include free cable television, swimming pool, whirl-pool, laundry for guest use, and Jacuzzi suites.

DeLand Artisan. 215 North Woodland Blvd.; (386) 736-3484; www.delandartisaninn.com. The Artisan was built in the 1920s, but you wouldn't guess it from the smart new face. One of the city's most chic places to dine as well as a plush suites hotel, it's within walking distance of the library and downtown's antiques shops, bookstore, and boutiques. $$–$$$.

DeLand Country Inn. 228 West Howry Ave.; (386) 736-4244; http://delandcountryinn. sitesvp.com. The inn lies in the heart of the city, within walking distance of downtown res-taurants and antiques shops. There's a screened swimming pool, basketball court, and a Florida room where guests can use the television and VCR. Take a single, double, or king room or the two-bedroom cottage that sleeps five. Children are welcome; pets are not. Rates include a full cooked English-style breakfast. $–$$.

Victorian Lace Bed and Breakfast. 5444 US 17 North; (386) 985-5223 or (877) 985-5223; www.victorianlacebedandbreakfast.com. Come and stay awhile among the antiques of your grandparents' time: quilts, crocks, hand-stitched verses, chamber pots, and porch rockers. Swing on the front porch while enjoying afternoon tea. Savor breakfast on the back porch while listening to the morning call of the birds. Reservations are required as is a deposit on accommodations of two or more nights. A two-night minimum stay is required during special events.

deleon springs

Today it's a hamlet with little more than a hardware store, convenience store, secondhand shops, a Mexican grocery, and a bank, but DeLeon Springs has been a part of Florida his-tory since the earliest explorers. Some historians believe these springs to be the Fountain of Youth that Ponce de Leon sought. Drive north from DeLand on US 17, once the major high-way between Florida and Chicago via Chattanooga. You'll still see mom-and-pop motels along the way, some of them derelict and others proudly maintained and still operating. Trains still run on old tracks parallel to the highway, where you'll see the remains of what was once a mighty orange-packing facility.

where to go

Deep Creek Stables. CR 3, DeLeon Springs; (386) 985-0520; www.deepcreekstables .net. Deep Creek Stables offers trail rides through Lake George Forest, where abundant wildlife is visible. They also offer skeet shooting, riding lessons, buggy rides, cabin rentals, RV hookups, parties, and hayrides. Hours: 9 a.m. to 4 p.m. Call or visit the Web site for rates.

DeLeon Springs State Park. 601 Ponce de Leon Blvd.; (386) 985-4212; www.florida stateparks.org/deleonsprings. This beautiful park, with centuries-old live oaks surrounded by azaleas that are a spectacle in February, is best known as the home of the Old Mill Res-taurant. Once a real mill, the building has a water wheel, cane grinder, old boiling kettles, and modern machinery for milling flour for the whole-grain breads and pancakes offered here. The tables are centered with grills where you can make your own breakfast or lunch. Rent a canoe, paddleboat, or kayak; swim in the clear, sweet spring; and tour the small but excellent museum. Admission is $5 per vehicle with up to eight people or $1 for a walk-in or biker.

Lake Woodruff National Wildlife Refuge. 2045 Mud Lake Rd.; (386) 985-4673, www .fws.gov/lakewoodruff. A whopping 21,500-acre wetlands out on County Road 4053, this is one of the best bird-watching spots in the state. Found here are about 200 species of birds and 42 species of mammals, plus countless reptiles, amphibians, and fishes. The refuge is remote and there are no facilities, so bring water, food, sun protection, and bug repellent—and tell someone where you're going and when you expect to return. If you run into trouble, you might not be found for weeks in this labyrinth of waterways. The area, once known as Spring Garden, has long been considered an Eden. John James Audubon came here to sketch birds almost 200 years ago. The refuge is open during daylight hours. Fishing and primitive hunting are permitted. Look for signs off US 17.

where to eat

Karling's Inn. 4640 North US 17; (386) 985-5535; www.karlings-inn.com. The inn is an Alpine chalet transplanted along a lonely highway twenty-five years ago by a German chef and his wife. The superb food and charming service couldn't be kept a local secret for long, and today it's essential to call ahead for reservations. Meals begin with a wonderful soup from one of the chef's age-old recipes. Try the cucumber salad, then one of the chef's daily specials. At least one game dish and a fresh fish are offered, plus sauerbraten, steaks, chicken, or veal, followed by a roly-poly German dessert. Hours vary seasonally, but the inn is generally open for lunch Tues through Fri and Sun, and for dinner Tues through Sat from 5 to 9 p.m. $$–$$$.

Old Spanish Sugar Mill Restaurant. DeLeon Springs State Park, 601 Ponce de Leon Blvd.; (386) 985-5644; www.planetdeland.com/sugarmill. Park admission is required. Explore the grounds of this old mill, which once milled grain thanks to power supplied by the spring run. Then feast on pancakes or sandwiches made from whole grains, or buy some of the breads to take home. Open Mon through Fri 9 a.m. to 4 p.m. and weekends 8 a.m. to 4 p.m. Reservations are taken only for groups of ten or more, so waits can be long. $–$$.

day trip 03

north

in the center of things:
barberville—crescent city, palatka

Once upon a time, each of these communities was a waypoint for streams of north-south traffic on the highway, railroad, and river; but the interstates stole their thunder, and there are still long stretches of solitude between them. Barberville is still a mere crossroads. Pierson is the fernery capital of the state and the home of the oldest Swedish Lutheran Church in Florida. It's found on the town's main street, which runs parallel to and 1 block west of US 17. The town itself is tiny, but members come from miles around to attend services at this beloved old landmark. Palatka is an old river town now known for its ravishing azalea gardens, established during the Depression of the 1930s as a public works project.

barberville—crescent city

Begin your day trip on I-4 east, exit at SR 44 (DeLand) and follow US 17 north to Barberville and Crescent City.

where to go

Crescent City. On US 17 between Barberville and Palatka. Write ahead (see "Putnam County" under Regional Information) for a free self-guided walking tour of the little village, which was settled in the mid-1800s high on a bluff overlooking lakes that are part of the St. Johns River system. The settlement flourished thanks to the steamboat trade, abundant orange crops, and the patronage of wealthy northerners who wintered here. Old homes,

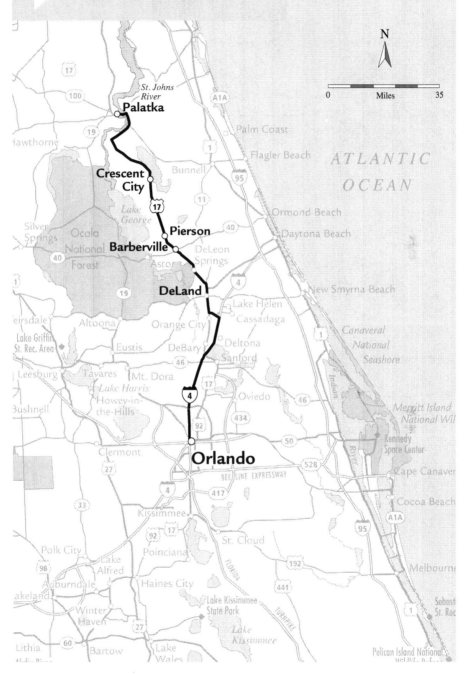

N

0 Miles 35

St. Johns River

Palatka

Crescent City

Lake George

Pierson

Barberville

DeLand

Orlando

ATLANTIC OCEAN

Palm Coast

Flagler Beach

Ormond Beach

Daytona Beach

New Smyrna Beach

Canaveral National Seashore

Merritt Island National Wil...

Kennedy Space Center

Cape Canaveral

Cocoa Beach

Melbourne

Sebast... St. Rec...

Pelican Island National

churches, and commercial buildings are privately owned, but you can walk the streets to ponder the history of American architecture. The brochure explains who built each structure and when.

Pioneer Center for the Creative Arts. Mail address: P.O. Box 6, Barberville, FL 32105; (386) 749-2959; www.pioneersettlement.org. Located just west of US 17 on SR 40, the center began with an old wooden schoolhouse, built in 1919 and in session here until 1969. Many of the hardworking volunteers here attended this school, and their love for the land shows in everything from the biscuits they bake to the crops they tend. More than a dozen other buildings have been moved here, creating a community that includes a railroad depot, a church, cabins, a turpentine still, homes, a firehouse, workshops, and stores. Don't miss the special events and reenactments held here. Open Mon through Fri 9 a.m. to 4 p.m. and Sat 9 a.m. to 2 p.m.; usually closed Sun and holidays. Admission is $6 for adults and $4 for children age twelve or under. Admission may be higher during special events.

Take a ferry ride on an ancient ferry that has transported people, wagons, horses, and vehicles across this part of the St. Johns River since 1856, saving travelers the 45-mile trip to the Palatka Bridge. From Crescent City, go west on County Road 308 to County Road 309, then north to Mount Royal Avenue; follow the signs to the Fort Gates Ferry. The ferry runs from 7 a.m. to 5:30 p.m. daily except Tuesday. One-way fare is $9 per vehicle. (386) 467-2417.

where to eat and stay

Sprague House Inn & Restaurant. 125 Central Ave., Crescent City; (386) 698-2622; www.spraguehouse.com. The Sprague House is a rambling wooden hotel just a block from the lake, on a quiet street that hasn't changed much since the turn of the twentieth century except for the addition of highlights of city history that someone carved in the sidewalk. Rent a boat, fish from the dock, or take a walking or bicycling tour of streets that time forgot. The standard room has twin beds, cable TV, and private bath. Children should be age twelve or older. Suites are sweetly old-fashioned; the honeymoon suite has a tiled bathroom with stained-glass windows, bidet, and a shower big enough for two. $$–$$$, including breakfast. Open for brunch on the second Sunday of every month. Open for dinner on most holidays by reservation only. $$–$$$. Don't miss the old-fashioned bar and the antiques shop. Sailors and street ladies are reminded to use the back entrance.

palatka

Continue north on US 17 through layers of history laid down by the river, then the railroad, and finally by the motorcar. Palatka was founded on the banks of the St. Johns in 1821 and named for an Indian word meaning "crossing." The settlement was burned in the Seminole

War of 1836 and rebuilt as Fort Shannon. Among notables who served here were Winfield Scott, Zachary Taylor, and William T. Sherman. The city was occupied by the North during the Civil War. After the war, Yankees returned here in winter to soak up the southern sun. The old downtown has seen better days, but empty storefronts are slowly finding new owners with drive, brains, and a love for these old buildings.

where to go

Bronson-Mulholland House. 100 Madison St.; (386) 329-0140; www.rootsweb.ancestry .com/~flpchs/virtual_tour.htm. Hours for this Greek Revival home filled with period furnishings and relics from the city's past are Thurs through Mon from noon to 5 p.m. Admission is free but donations are encouraged.

Ravine State Gardens. 1600 Twigg St.; (386) 329-3721; www.floridastateparks.org/ ravinegardens. This geological wonder was formed by nature's forces, as swirling waters sculpted deep ravines like no other in the state. In time, grasses and shrubs took root, slowing the erosion. In 1933 the federal Works Projects Administration set up a work camp to make the ravine a botanical showplace. Hundreds of azaleas were planted, some of them now house-high. Camellias bloom through the winter, to be replaced in early spring by a symphony of azaleas that inspire the annual Azalea Festival. Drive the 1.8-mile loop road, or stroll trails along a spring-fed creek. The gardens are at their busiest and most beautiful in Feb and March, but they're worth walking through any time to see the wildlife and enjoy the cool green of the magnolia, live oak, hickory, and sweet gum trees. Open daylight hours. Admission is $4 per vehicle.

where to shop

Classic Impressions. In the Palatka Mall on SR 19; (386) 325-0507. This quaint gift shop carries a wide range of name-brand collectibles such as Yankee Candle, Boyds Bears, Cherished Teddies, Fenton Glass, Willow Tree Angels, and Ty Plush. Open from 10 a.m. to 6 p.m. Mon through Sat.

Elsie Bell's Antique and Art Mall. 111 North Fourth St.; (386) 329-9669; www.elsiebells antiquemall.com. The mall is filled with individual stalls operated by dealers, each with his or her own interests and specialties. Hours vary seasonally, but the mall is generally open Mon through Sat from 10 a.m. to 5 p.m. and on Sun from noon to 5 p.m.

where to eat

Angel's Diner. 209 Reid St.; (386) 325-3927. The oldest diner in Florida, this intimate, traditional diner is filled with 1950s decor and serves delicious burgers, onion rings, fried okra, and many more traditional diner foods. The diner is located in a converted railway train car and they are open twenty-four hours a day. $.

Corky Bell's Seafood of Palatka. 211 Comfort Rd.; (386) 325-1094. This restaurant is one of a small chain known for its big menu of fresh seafood served up with coleslaw, onion rings, hush puppies, and french fries. There isn't much here for vegetarians, but some offerings can be ordered broiled to cut down on the calories. This place is enormously popular and doesn't accept reservations, so expect long waits at peak hours. Call for hours, which vary seasonally. $–$$.

where to stay

Azalea House. 220 Madison St.; (386) 325-4547; www.theazaleahouse.com. This establishment is for those who prefer a historic setting and the personal service of a bed-and-breakfast inn. The 1878 Queen Anne house has a pool and spa in its secluded garden. Breakfast can be served on the pool deck if you like. Rates also include cookies at bedtime and a picnic lunch. The house has four guest rooms, three of them with private bath. Children under age twelve and pets aren't accommodated; smoking is permitted outdoors only. Ask about packages that include dinner at a nearby restaurant or a romance package that includes dinner, chocolate, roses, and champagne. $$–$$$.

Best Western Inn of Palatka. 119 US 17 South; (386) 325-7800 or (888) 325-7801; www.bestwesternflorida.com/east-palatka-attractions-lodging. This is one of a respected, reliable chain known for clean, spacious rooms and a generous continental breakfast at no added charge. Enjoy the swimming pool and whirlpool, use the guest laundry, and walk only half a block to the river. Suites have a wet bar with minirefrigerator, coffeemaker, and microwave. Golf packages are available, and a public boat launch is nearby. $$.

Quality Inn Riverfront. 201 North First St.; (386) 328-3481; www.qualityinn.com. Book a room with a view of the St. Johns River, and dine in the waterfront restaurant. There's also a full-service lounge, with live music on some nights. Arrive by car or boat. Docks and fishing guides are available. $$.

northeast

day trip 01

northeast

>>>

the birthplace of speed:
ormond beach, port orange, ponce
inlet, new smyrna beach

Drive up I-4 from Orlando to I-95, then north to SR 40, which goes east to Ormond Beach. If you start here, you can work your way south past Daytona—saving it for another day trip—to Port Orange, Ponce Inlet, and New Smyrna Beach via I-95, US 1, or Highway A1A.

This string of communities has attracted beachgoers to their shores for more than a century—some to speed across the flat sands in their race cars, others to find new lives in the New World, and most to vacation in sun-warmed communities that haven't yet succumbed to the tourism stampede. Although Daytona's special events spill over and you may not be able to book a room during those times, these Atlantic-front communities should be explored one by one by beach-starved Orlandoans.

ormond beach

The city calls itself the Birthplace of Speed because of early motorcar speed records that were set on the beach by the likes of Barney Oldfield and R. E. Olds. Ormond Beach started as a retirement community in the 1880s, when an enormous wooden hotel was built over-looking the Halifax River. An early resident was John D. Rockefeller, who loved the area so much that he built his own home across the street. (The hotel fell to the wrecker's ball, but his mansion remains.)

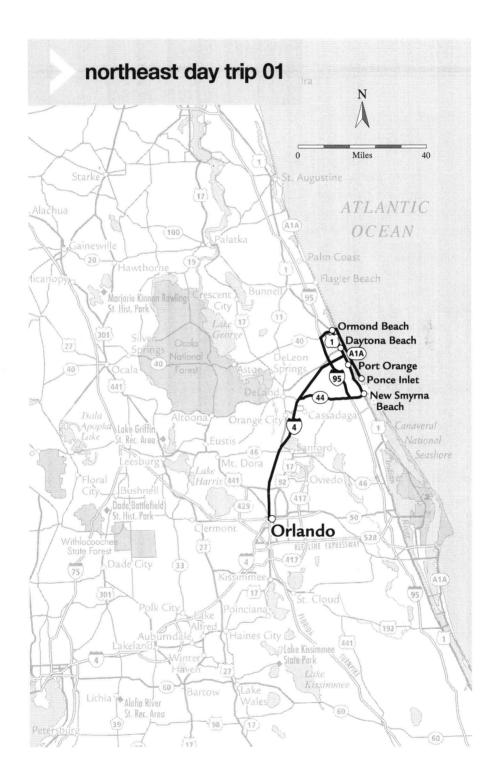

N

0   Miles   40

ira

St. Augustine

ATLANTIC
OCEAN

Starke

Alachua

Gainesville

Hawthorne

icanopy

Marjorie Kinnan Rawlings
St. Hist. Park

Crescent
City

Bunnell

Palm Coast

Flagler Beach

Palatka

Silver
Springs

Ocala
National
Forest

Lake
George

DeLeon
Springs

Astor

DeLand

Ormond Beach
Daytona Beach

Port Orange
Ponce Inlet

New Smyrna
Beach

Ocala

Tsala
Apopka
Lake

Lake Griffin
St. Rec. Area

Altoona

Orange City

Cassadaga

Canaveral
National
Seashore

Eustis

Leesburg

Floral
City

Bushnell

Dade Battlefield
St. Hist. Park

Lake
Harris

Mt. Dora

Sanford

Oviedo

Clermont

Orlando

BEE LINE EXPRESSWAY

Withlacoochee
State Forest

Dade City

Kissimmee

Polk City

Poinciana

St. Cloud

Lake
Alfred

Auburndale

Haines City

Lake Kissimmee
State Park

Lakeland

Winter
Haven

Lake
Kissimmee

Lithia

Alafia River
St. Rec. Area

Bartow

Lake
Wales

Petersburg

If you're an RV traveler, skip Ormond Beach. Strict laws apply to where and how long you can park (including your own driveway), and many shopping centers have NO RV PARKING signs.

where to go

The Casements. 25 Riverside Dr.; (386) 676-3216; http://echotourism.com/cultural/casements.htm. This mansion was once the winter home of John D. Rockefeller. Indoors, see vestiges of the opulent life lived by the powerful tycoon, as well as a Boy Scout Museum and a museum of Hungarian folk art. Special events often take place on the grassy riverfront grounds. Stroll them to view lush greenery and giant live oaks. Open Monday through Friday and Saturday morning. Donations are appreciated.

Ormond Memorial Art Museum and Garden. 78 East Granada Blvd.; (386) 676-3347; www.ormondartmuseum.org. This small but important museum is surrounded by lush gardens, waterfalls, and a koi pond. The building itself is of historical interest, and it's filled with the works of Florida artists. Donations are appreciated; $2 is the suggested minimum. Open Mon through Fri 10 a.m. to 4 p.m. and weekends noon to 4 p.m.

Tomoka State Park. 2099 North Beach St.; (386) 676-4050; www.floridastateparks.org/tomoka. This greenspace at the confluence of the Halifax and Tomoka Rivers is a place where Native Americans once powwowed under the enormous live oak trees. Spanish explorers visited the settlement in 1605, a story told in the visitor center's museum and art gallery. Rent a canoe, fish, picnic, boat, camp, or walk the nature trail. The park is open 8 a.m. to sunset daily. State park fees apply.

where to eat

Barnacle's Restaurant & Lounge. 869 South Atlantic Ave.; (386) 673-1070. This place has a whopping big seafood menu and plenty of steaks, baby back ribs, prime rib, and pasta specialties. Create your own combination platter. The salad bar is one of the city's biggest and best, and the children's menu offers treats for kids. Early-bird specials and happy hour are offered every day. $–$$.

Frappes North. 123 West Granada Blvd.; (386) 615-4888; www.frappesnorth.com. A consistent award-winner, from soup to the sinful desserts, Frappes is offbeat and innovative. Go conventional with the Black Angus burger and bistro fries, or go gourmet with the walnut-crusted chicken breast with goat cheese and spinach or the veal chop Milanese with sage butter, rosemary potatoes, and balsamic organic greens. Open for lunch and dinner. Call for hours and reservations, which are highly recommended. $–$$ ($$$ with an expensive wine).

Jerusalem Kosher Restaurant. 366 West Granada Blvd.; (386) 671-0033. If you've never been to Israel but wondered what the food was like there, this is the place to visit. It's a nice place to eat and sample a wide variety of Jewish and Israeli cookery. Try the matzo ball soup, a latke, some mango drink, a shwarma in pita, and some baklava. $–$$.

La Crepe en Haut. 142 East Granada Blvd.; (386) 673-1999; www.lacrepeenhaut.net. Yes, they serve crepes, but the gourmet menu offers much more—all prepared in French classic style and served in an elegant setting. Start with French onion soup or ravioli with porcini mushrooms, then the *salade maison* and an entree of veal medallions with Maine lobster, filet *au poivre,* salmon in almond crust, or duck a l'orange. Have a strawberry or praline crepe for dessert, or splurge on the bananas Foster, prepared tableside for two. Choose from the selection of French vintages. Open for lunch Tuesday through Friday and for dinner daily except Monday. $$$.

Stonewood Tavern & Grill. 140 South Atlantic Ave.; (386) 671-1200; www.stonewoodgrill .com. This is a familiar name because the founders have restaurants in other Florida locales. The setting is warm mahogany, with good smells coming from the oak-burning grill. Aged steaks are hand cut; seafood comes fresh from local fleets or is flown in from Chesapeake Bay or the Pacific. Try herb-crusted rack of lamb, pork Adirondack, or big, herb-basted black tiger shrimp. Chicken potpie and pot roast are comfort-food classics; quesadillas are made with handmade flour tortillas, and the chef does a fantastic pasta with fire-roasted vegetables. Add chicken or shrimp if you like. There's a modest, well-selected wine list. Open for dinner only; call for reservations. $$.

where to stay

Coral Beach Motel. 711 South Atlantic Ave.; (800) 553-4712; www.coralbeachmotel.com. The world-famous automobile racing at the Daytona International Speedway actually began at the turn of the twentieth century on the firm beaches just outside this motel. This resort motel features an indoor heated pool, a large outdoor pool and deck from which you can observe the breaking surf of the Atlantic Ocean, a game room, and a shuffleboard court. If you enjoy miniature golf, you only need to cross the street to play. The Coral Beach is located near shopping, restaurants, theaters, the Daytona International Speedway, and dog racing. $$.

Driftwood Beach Motel. 657 South Atlantic Ave.; (386) 677-1331; www.daytonahotels .com/Driftwood/index.php. Relax by the large heated pool located right on the beach or swim in the Atlantic. Efficiencies and suites with kitchens are available. Located within walking distance of Daytona Beach restaurants and shops. $$.

port orange

Rich, black soil attracted early settlers to these lands north of Spruce Creek. They planted acres of sugarcane and thrived until the Seminole Wars, when every plantation south of St. Augustine was put to the torch. Today their ruins are one of the community's most compelling attractions.

where to go

Cracker Creek Canoeing. 1595 Taylor Rd.; (386) 304-0778; www.oldfloridapioneer .com. Rent a canoe or take a tour on a pontoon boat down Spruce Creek, a scenic Florida waterway. Hardwood forests, cypress swamps, and saltwater marshes line this meandering stream, providing habitat for a number of threatened and endangered animal species. Reservations are recommended for the boat tours.

Gamble Place. 1819 Taylor Rd.; (386) 255-0285; http://volusia.org/echotourism/heritage/ gamble.htm. This was once a hunting and fishing retreat owned by Proctor & Gamble magnate James Gamble. This 150-acre property features beautiful cypress trees, alligators, pileated woodpeckers, and ospreys, and includes a hunting lodge, Cracker-style home, and old citrus-packing house. The Snow White cottage, modeled after the one in the Walt Disney movie, is of special interest to children. Admission is free. The property is open from Wednesday through Sunday, but this changes seasonally. Guided one-hour tours ($5) are given Fri at 10 and 11 a.m. and 1 and 2 p.m. but this also changes seasonally. For up-to-the-minute information, call Cracker Creek Canoeing at (386) 304-0778.

Sugar Mill Gardens. 950 Old Sugar Mill Rd.; (386) 767-1735; www.dunlawtonsugarmill-gardens.org. Towering trees and flowering shrubs surround the ruins of a sugar plantation with botanical glory. Bring your camera; it's a favorite of fashion photographers. The sugar mill was burned out during the Seminole Wars, but troops stayed on this land during the Civil War. A century later an attempt was made to turn it into a dinosaur theme park. Huge old statues of prehistoric creatures still sit incongruously amid the rusted boilers, live oaks, and tangled shrubs. Picnics and bicycles are prohibited. Admission is free; open sunrise to sunset every day.

where to eat

Aunt Catfish's on the River. 4009 Halifax Dr.; (386) 767-4768; www.auntcatfish.com. Aunt Catfish's serves great seafood with a wonderful water view and excellent service. This is many locals' favorite restaurant and is kid-friendly. They offer a salad bar, their famous cinnamon rolls, chicken shortcake, birthday celebrations, a playground, music, and Granny sitting at the door. Try the Banana Banshee! $–$$.

Marko's Chick-fil-A Heritage Inn. 5420 South Ridgewood Rd. (US 1); (386) 756-1004. Birthplace of the popular fast-food chain, this one's located in an old farmhouse—with a museum thrown in. See race cars, antiques, and Remington statues. Dining rooms are themed for race fans, motorcycle fans, beach vacationers, and families. Serve yourself from the soup-and-salad bar, or order one of the tasty Chick-fil-A specialties or a hand-cut steak, fresh seafood, chicken and dumplings, a smoothie, or one of the scrumptious desserts. Open for lunch and dinner daily except Sunday. $–$$.

ponce inlet

Ponce Inlet lies east of Port Orange, a residential community. The easiest way to reach it is to hop back on I-95 and cruise south to the Taylor Road–Dunlawton exit, then south on Nova Road to US 1. Both US 1 and Highway 1A are clogged with local traffic and should be avoided on this day trip as a way of getting through Daytona Beach.

where to go

Ponce de Leon Inlet Lighthouse. 4931 South Peninsula Dr.; (386) 761-1821; www.ponce inlet.org. This is one of the East's most scenic lighthouses. Climb 203 steps to the top for a bird's-eye view. Tour buildings and the grounds for a glimpse of the life of a lighthouse keeper at the turn of the twentieth century. (The beacon was first lit in 1887.) See the 600-pound bronze bell that was recovered from a sunken sea buoy, the oil storage house built in 1887 with a unique double ventilation system, the old radio shack dating to just before World War II, keeper's quarters, and much more. Shop the gift shop for souvenirs and lighthouse memorabilia. Open 10 a.m. daily until 8 p.m. in summer and 4 p.m. in winter. Admission is $5 for adults and $2 for children age eleven or younger.

where to eat

Down the Hatch. 4894 Front St.; (386) 761-4831. This long-running, family-operated local favorite overlooks the inlet. Dine indoors or out in a laid-back, calypso setting where a clean T-shirt does for dress-up. Anglers gather here for breakfast, and the salty scene goes on through spectacular sunsets and into a starlit night. The catch of the day is always a good bet, right off the boat. There are also daily specials, burgers, chicken, and steaks. Vegetarians will have to get by with salad and potatoes. Open every day 7 a.m. to 10 p.m. $–$$.

Inlet Harbor Marina & Restaurant. 133 Inlet Harbor Rd.; (386) 767-5590; www.inlet harbor.com. This is a local favorite, not just for great seafood fresh from the restaurant's own fleet but also for a 1,000-foot river walk with nonstop nature watching and a view of the romantic Ponce de Leon Inlet Lighthouse. Arrive in time for the spectacular sunset and dine indoors in air-conditioned comfort or outside on the breezy RiverDance Deck. Start with the smoked fish dip and crisp crackers, then have peel-and-eat shrimp, snow crab, or fresh fish cooked your way and served with all the trimmings. Chicken, wings, steak, and ribs they call Bimini Bones also highlight the menu. For dessert enjoy Chocolate Suicide, key lime pie, mud pie, or the cheesecake of the week. This popular hangout also offers shopping for arts and crafts, so plan to arrive early and linger late, dancing to live music on the deck. Charter fishing by the day and half day can be arranged through the restaurant by calling (386) 767-5705. Open daily, except Monday, at 11 a.m.; closes at 10 p.m., later on Friday and Saturday. $$.

new smyrna beach

The first Greek settlement in the Americas, this area has a fascinating history filled with intrigue. People from Minorca were brought here as indentured servants by Scottish entrepreneur and medical doctor Andrew Turnbull in 1768. Florida was a British colony and events in faraway Boston and Philadelphia, where a revolution was brewing, were remote and irrelevant. The more than 1,200 immigrants who were brought in to work Turnbull's land grant fled to St. Augustine after years of disease, crop failures, and Indian attacks. Archaeologists are still cataloging and uncovering the marvelous works the immigrants created out of wilderness. Resettlement didn't begin in earnest here until after the Civil War.

New Smyrna Beach calls itself the redfish capital of the world, so wet a line on your own or book a guided outing. Surf fishing, backwater and river fishing, and deep-sea fishing are all on the menu here. From New Smyrna Beach, drive west on SR 44 to I-4 and south to Orlando to complete the loop.

where to go

Canaveral National Seashore. 7611 South Atlantic Ave.; (386) 428-3384, ext. 10; www .nps.gov/cana. Canaveral National Seashore features the longest undeveloped beach in this part of Florida, a spectacular strip of sand and dunes. Surfers and bathers can have a blast here. During the summer park rangers arrange night walks on the beach to watch sea turtles lay their eggs. Behind the beach is the Mosquito Lagoon, an angler's and bird-watcher's heaven. Kayakers and canoeists can also find happiness here. A boardwalk climbs to the top of Turtle Mound, an Indian shell midden that's the highest point around. In addition to the sea turtles, manatees, alligators, bald eagles, and other threatened and endangered species find refuge here. Daily admission is $5 per car.

Chamber of Commerce. 115 Canal St.; (877) 460-8410; www.nsbfla.com. Stop in for information, including a brochure describing a self-guided walking tour of the historic area. Two dozen buildings are highlighted and described. You'll see the history of small-town American architecture in old movie palaces, stores, a library that houses a museum of local memorabilia, and the park where Dr. Turnbull's home once stood. (Also useful is a self-guided-tour brochure published by the Southeast Volusia Historical Society, P.O. Box 968, New Smyrna Beach, FL 32170.) Chamber personnel can also provide a current list of outfitters and guides who will take you to Turtle Mound or along the backwaters of Canaveral National Seashore, the Intracoastal Waterway (Halifax River), or the St. Johns River.

Historic Conner Library Museum. 201 Sams Ave. (in Old Fort Park); (386) 424-2196, www.nsbhistory,org. See a permanent display depicting the Turnbull Colony, early settlers from Minorca. One or two temporary displays are always worth seeing, too, based on Florida arts, history, or nature. Free admission. Open 10 a.m. to 2 p.m. Tues through Sat.

Smyrna Dunes Park. At the north strip of Highway A1A; (386) 424-2935; www.volusia .org/parks/smyrnadunes.htm. Take SR 44 east, then left at the park. This windswept stretch of dunes and creamy surf is on the south end of Ponce Inlet. A boardwalk lets you walk over the impressive dunes without damaging the delicate sea oats. Bring a picnic lunch and spend the day nature watching, walking the seaside and trails, fishing from the jetty or in the surf, and enjoying the view from the observation tower. Rangers guide nature walks every Sat at 11 a.m. No lifeguards are on duty, so swim with caution. Admission is $3.50 per vehicle, $1.00 per person for more than eight passengers, or $30.00/$50.00 for an annual resident/nonresident pass.

where to shop

Arts on Douglas. 123 Douglas St.; (386) 428-1133; www.artsondouglas.net. This superb gallery in a community known as an art colony is home to many artists, sculptors, photographers, and potters. Open Tues through Fri 10 a.m. to 5 p.m., Sat 11 a.m. to 3 p.m., and by appointment. Other galleries include the Clay Gallery, 302 South Riverside Dr. (386-427-2903; http://clay-gallery.com), and Artist Workshop Gallery, 114 Canal St. (386-424-9254; www.artistsworkshopinc.com).

Flagler Avenue is the historic heart of New Smyrna, and many of its boutiques and specialty shops are open every day. Come here to browse for unusual gifts, swimwear, accessories, and souvenirs. You'll find funky places to dine, nosh, or have a coffee. Sometimes the street fills with street parties and entertainers.

where to eat

Heavenly Sandwiches & Smoothies. 115 Flagler Ave.; (386) 427-7475. This establishment is part of the historic downtown scene. Breakfast begins at 8 a.m., and the goodness goes on through early dinner. Drive through if you like. Dine on healthy alternatives to burgers and fries. Have a fruit smoothie, a refreshing salad, a wrap, or the soup of the day. $.

J.B.'s Fish Camp and Restaurant. 859 Pompano Ave.; (386) 427-5747; http://jbsfish camp.com. Drive 7 miles south on Highway A1A to find this funky fish camp, a longtime local hangout. At the table behind you will be a group of bikers, at the table next to you astronauts and rocket scientists, over there a group of fishing guides finishing up their day. The clientele is that eclectic. Much of the seafood is fresh from the Mosquito Lagoon, right underneath you if you dine on the patio. Try the alligator sampler for an appetizer, and follow it with an oyster sandwich. You might want to try some blue crabs, fresh from the lagoon, while you're at it. Relax, there's no hurry! $$.

Norwood's Restaurant & Wine Shop. South Causeway; (386) 428-4621; www.nor woods.com. Norwood's is known for its fine wine cellar as well as continental cuisine with a Florida spin. Have the catch of the day, steak, chicken, or the chef's most recent whim. Dine indoors or out. Kids can order from their own menu. Open 11:30 a.m. to 10 p.m. daily. Reservations strongly suggested. $$–$$$.

Riverview Restaurant. 101 Flagler Ave.; (386) 428-1865; www.restaurant.com/river view. Start with sundowners at happy hour prices on the deck of this rambling waterfront place along the Intracoastal Waterway. The menu is extensive and includes such house specialties as Riverview Wellington en croute, bourbon molasses New York strip, sesame-encrusted chicken breast, and stuffed pork loin. The filet mignon is always a good bet, as are the fresh-seafood dishes, especially Kelsey's Grouper Gourmet, crusty with almonds and topped with artichoke pesto. For dessert, have bananas Foster and flaming citrus coffee followed by dancing and nightcaps serenaded by live music. Owner-hosts Jim and Christa Kelsey, formerly of the landmark Faro Blanco Resort in the Keys, took over the old Riverview Charlie's, and this popular spot shines brighter than ever. Reservations are suggested. Open for lunch and dinner daily until 9 p.m., later on Friday and Saturday. Call about happy hour specials and Sunday brunch, one of the area's best. After dessert, visit the quaint gift shop. $$.

where to stay

Atlantic Plaza Condo Hotel. 425 South Atlantic Ave.; (386) 427-4636; www.atlanticplaza .net. This property puts you in a two-bedroom, two-bath, all-electric home away from home that accommodates four to six people. Full kitchens have full-size appliances and everything you'll need for cooking breakfast, snacks, or complete meals to eat on your balcony over-looking the Atlantic. The swimming pool is heated. Rentals are by the night or week; higher rates and a three-night minimum apply during race and bike weeks. $$–$$$.

Buena Vista Inn. 500 North Causeway; (386) 428-5565; www.buenavistainn.com. The inn is so close to the Indian River that you can walk out the back porch and straight out on the fishing pier. They'll also provide bikes to get to the beach, 5 blocks away. One-room units have refrigerators; one-bedroom units have complete kitchens. Pets are welcome for a modest extra fee. Children under age twelve stay free. The office and reservations desk are open only from 9 a.m. to 8 p.m. $$.

Coquina Wharf Bed and Breakfast. 704 South Riverside Dr.; (386) 428-9458, (866) 428-9458; www.coquinawharf.com. A historic bed-and-breakfast inn located on the Intracoastal Waterway. In the living room a cozy 17-foot living room sofa rests on heart-of-pine floors surrounded by family antiques. Lush flowered grounds hide inviting seating nooks. Breakfast is served in the sunroom. Wireless Internet and docking are both available. In walking distance of the beach, shopping, restaurants, and more. $$$.

Coronado del Mar. 701 South Atlantic Ave.; (386) 428-2970 or (800) 700-9445. This is an excellent value if you don't mind doing your own housekeeping. Every unit at this oceanfront condo offers an Atlantic view from the balcony. Kitchens are fully equipped, or you can walk to local restaurants as well as to the beach, tennis courts, and shops. Units have two bedrooms and two or two-and-a-half baths and rent by the week. It's an ideal meeting point for families who want to get together on the beach. $-$$$.

Night Swan Intracoastal Bed & Breakfast. 512 South Riverside Dr. at Anderson Street; (386) 423-4940; www.nightswan.com. Chuck and Martha Nightswonger host this stately mansion along the Intracoastal Waterway. Rooms are all different, but all have private bath, telephone, and cable television. There's also a private cottage with a Florida room. Breakfast is included in all rates, and the proprietors can also arrange a catered dinner for one to four couples, a sweetheart package with surprises for your loved one, in-room massages, bicycle rental, and a good choice of fishing and sightseeing outings. $$-$$$.

Riverview Hotel. 103 Flagler Ave.; (386) 428-5858 or (800) 945-7416; www.riverviewhotel.com. The Riverview is an elegantly restored relic of the flamboyant Flagler era, when tourists came to Florida on the new railroad to winter in big hotels with spacious quarters for themselves and their servants. Built as a hunting and fishing lodge in 1885, it became the Riverview Hotel in 1924. Rates include a generous continental breakfast—served in your room or on your private patio—use of bathrobes, bicycles, and evening turndown. Beach towels are provided at the heated swimming pool. The hotel is a few blocks from the ocean on the Intracoastal Waterway and has a popular restaurant overlooking the water. Stay in a standard hotel room, suite, or a two-bedroom cottage that sleeps four. If you arrive by boat, you can dock overnight for 75 cents per foot. $$.

day trip 02

northeast

the world's most famous beach:
daytona beach, palm coast—
flagler beach

Take I-4 north (the signs say east) from Orlando to the Daytona Beach exit, where I-4 ends. From here, I-95, US 1, or Highway A1A takes you north to Flagler Beach and Palm Coast.

daytona beach

Most visitors look at this area as one, long beach playground from Ormond Beach south to Ponce Inlet. Other little communities are found along the way, with such names as Wilbur-by-the-Sea, Holly Hill, and Daytona Beach Shores, but it's all strung together like beads on a chain. US 1, Highway A1A, and I-95 provide easy access to beachside hotels and restaurants. Inland are attractions galore and some of the best golf courses in the state, including the home of the Ladies Professional Golf Association.

Daytona calls itself the World's Most Famous Beach because, in addition to its boardwalk, it's one of the few beaches in the world with sands firm enough to drive on. It's a right zealously guarded by some beachgoers and bitterly contested by others. If you like the idea of driving to the water's edge to offload your cooler and beach umbrella, that's good. If you don't want to sunbathe on a beach where cars are permitted, well, that's bad.

If you aren't quite sure what to make of Daytona Beach, you're not alone. To some tourists it's a place for a cheap drunk during spring break. To others it's nothing but auto racing. Still others associate it with motorcycle mania. Critics call it "binge" tourism. Unless

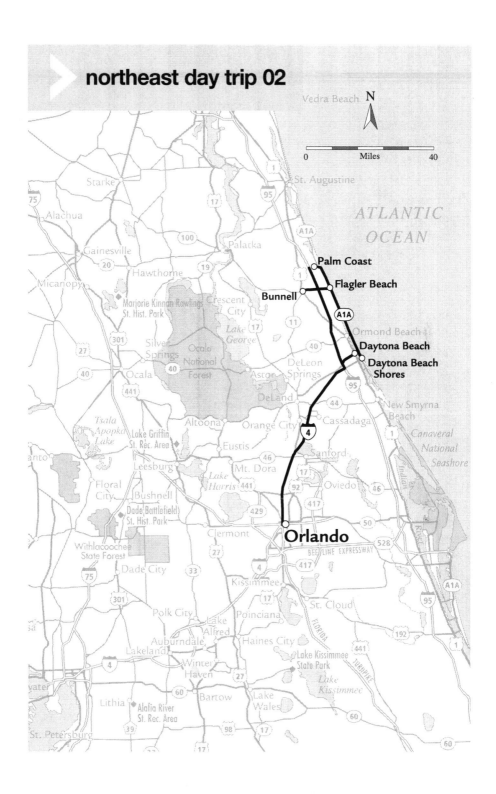

Vedra Beach **N**

0   Miles   40

St. Augustine

Starke

Alachua

Gainesville

Micanopy

Hawthorne

Marjorie Kinnan Rawlings St. Hist. Park

Silver Springs

Ocala National Forest

Ocala

Tsala Apopka Lake

Lake Griffin St. Rec. Area

Floral City

Bushnell

Dade Battlefield St. Hist. Park

Withlacoochee State Forest

Dade City

Palatka

Crescent City

Lake George

DeLeon Springs

Astor

DeLand

Altoona

Orange City

Eustis

Leesburg

Lake Harris

Mt. Dora

Clermont

Palm Coast

Flagler Beach

Bunnell

A1A

Ormond Beach

Daytona Beach

Daytona Beach Shores

New Smyrna Beach

Cassadaga

Sanford

Oviedo

Orlando

ATLANTIC OCEAN

Canaveral National Seashore

Indian

BEELINE EXPRESSWAY

Polk City

Lake Alfred

Auburndale

Lakeland

Winter Haven

Lithia

Alafia River St. Rec. Area

St. Petersburg

Kissimmee

St. Cloud

Poinciana

Haines City

Lake Kissimmee State Park

Lake Kissimmee

Bartow

Lake Wales

FLORIDA TURNPIKE

you're here to participate, give Daytona Beach a wide berth when these events are held. Traffic congeals, hotel rates rise out of all proportion, and many locals flee town to get away from the melee.

In short, Daytona Beach is a different city depending on when you are here, so choose your dates carefully. However, the city has enormous variety to offer and is not to be missed. Take I-4 northeast from Orlando to the Daytona Beach exit, which brings you into town on US 92.

where to go

Daytona Beach Drive-in Christian Church. 3140 South Atlantic Ave., Daytona Beach Shores; (386) 767-8761; www.driveinchurch.net. Drive-in movies have all but disappeared, but Florida still has a few drive-in churches like this one. Services are held Sun at 8:30 and 10 a.m. Drive in and tune your radio to 680 AM or 88.5 FM. Nursery and toddler care are available in the church building for both services.

Daytona USA. 1801 West International Speedway Blvd.; (386) 947-6800; www.daytona usa.com. From I-95 or I-4, take the US 92 exit and go east. Expect a sizzling half day of fast-paced fun, even if you're not a race fan. Start with the larger-than-life movie, then join a pit crew to change a tire. View displays of historic cars and drivers, make a recording of your report on a race, and try the "virtual" race machines. Tickets—$24 for adults, $19 for seniors, and $19 for children—pay for the indoor attractions and a tour of the speedway and track when weather and conditions allow. The Richard Petty Driving Experience ($135) lets you take three laps at 150 mph or more. Shop the gift store for NASCAR collectibles. Open daily, except Thanksgiving and Christmas, 10 a.m. to 6 p.m., sometimes later.

Halifax Historical Museum. 252 South Beach St.; (386) 255-6976; www.halifaxhistorical .org. The museum is worth visiting once to see the displays and often thereafter to participate in special events such as moonlight river walks or candlelight museum nights. It's housed in one of Daytona's earliest buildings in a row of shops, an architectural delight, now filled with specialty items. Admission is $5 for adults and $1 for children under age twelve. Open Tues through Sat 10 a.m. to 4 p.m.

LPGA International. 1000 Champions Dr.; (386) 274-5742; www.lpgainternational.com. This is the headquarters of the Ladies Professional Golf Association, but men can also play this eighteen-hole, par 72 championship course. Collared shirts are required. Greens fees and other fees apply. The course's restaurant is a fun little place for lunch.

Main Street Pier. (386) 238-1212. At the end of Main Street at the ocean is a fishing pier and an old-fashioned honky-tonk waterfront loaded with fun. Ride the Sky Lift, climb the Space Needle for an eagle's view of the sea, or rent tackle and go fishing. $–$$.

Museum of Arts and Sciences. 1040 Museum Blvd.; (386) 255-0285; www.moas.org. This is one of the state's finest small museums and home to three blockbuster attractions. One is the largest and most complete giant sloth skeleton ever found. This 150,000-year-old leviathan was found in a clay pit near here. Second is the largest collection of Cuban art in the free world. Third is the Root collection of railroad cars and memorabilia, Coca-Cola memorabilia, and quilts. The museum also has a sculpture garden, Florida wing, and galleries filled with permanent exhibits and a changing panorama of special shows. The children's wing, filled with hands-on exhibits, is worth a special trip with the kids. Admission is $12.95 for adults, $10.95 for seniors and students, and $6.95 for children; planetarium shows are included in the admission. Open Tues through Sat 9 a.m. to 5 p.m., Sun 11 a.m. to 5 p.m.; closed Monday.

Arrange through the museum to tour the Gamble Place on the 175-acre Spruce Creek Nature Preserve. Built in 1907 by James N. Gamble of Proctor & Gamble fame, the estate has a typical old Florida house with antiques and exhibits, gardens, a citrus-packing house, acres of primeval wetlands, and a whimsical playhouse built in 1938 following 1937's popular *Snow White and the Seven Dwarfs*.

Ocean Waters Spa. 600 North Atlantic Ave.; (386) 267-1660; www.oceanwatersspa.com. Located in the Plaza Resort & Spa, this is a place to get away from it all for a day or half day. Construct your own day from a menu of eight massages, nine facials, salon treatments for men and women, nails, waxing, body wraps, tanning, or therapies. They're all priced a la carte; for example, $90 for a fifty-minute Swedish massage or $155 for an anti-aging myoxy-caviar facial. By appointment only.

Seaside Music Theater. 1200 West International Speedway Blvd.; (386) 252-6200 or (800) 854-5592; www.seasidemusictheater.org. The Seaside is in the Daytona Beach Community College Theater Center. Some performances are also held in the theater downtown at 176 North Beach St. See Broadway favorites, enthusiastically performed. Ask your concierge what's playing.

A Tiny Cruise Line. 425 South Beach St., Halifax Harbor Marina; (386) 226-2343; www.visitdaytona.com/tinycruise. This company's cruises are always different, always a delight, thanks to a nonstop nature show that can't be predicted. The little boat itself is a replica of a fantail launch once used to ferry early hotel guests. Take a midday waterway cruise, a look at estates that front the water, a combination nature and sightseeing cruise, or the sunset cruise. Prices range from $13.61 to $20.42 for adults and $8.21 to $12.20 for children. Call ahead for reservations, or walk in and take your chances for any but the sunset cruise, which includes a snack and soda, or you can BYOB. Cruises sail every day but Monday.

World's Most Famous Beach. The beach hot line is (386) 239-SURF; http://volusia.org/beach. Accessed at multiple spots along Highway A1A, the beach allows cars in some areas, so you can drive to a good spot and off-load the beach umbrella and playpen without having to haul everything from the parking lot. Swim near a lifeguard station (run-outs, stinging jellyfish, and sharks have been a problem), and observe the 10-mph speed limit. No alcohol, pets, or loud music allowed. Hours vary through the year. Beach access is $5 except for those with handicap ID. Nonresident annual passes are $40.

where to shop

Angell & Phelps. 154 South Beach St.; (386) 257-2677 or (800) 969-2634. This has been a downtown icon since 1925. Let your nose guide you to a domain drenched in luscious chocolate sights and smells. Take a free guided tour Mon through Fri between 10 a.m. and 3 p.m. (call ahead), or shop Mon through Sat 9:30 a.m. to 5:30 p.m. for fine chocolates, ice cream, and gifts for the chocoholic in your life.

Daytona Flea and Farmers' Market. US 92 at I-95; (386) 253-3330. This is one of the world's biggest and best flea markets, as well as a place to shop for fresh produce and plants. Antiques are sold in an air-conditioned building. The two restaurants are also air-conditioned, and nine snack bars dot the massive complex. Admission is free. Open Friday through Sunday.

Riverfront Marketplace. 300 North Beach St.; 386-872-3272; www.hometownshopping .com/bd/riverfrontmarketplace. In the heart of Old Daytona Beach with over 110 shops, 30 eateries, and entertainment including professional baseball, marinas, theater and concerts, museum exhibits, and nightlife and dancing.

where to eat

Angell & Phelps. 154 South Beach St.; (386) 257-2677. See Where to Shop, above.

Boondocks at Adventure Yacht Harbor. 3948 South Peninsula Dr.; (386) 760-9001; www.boondocksdining.com. Boondocks, located in a marina, has a wonderful view of the Halifax River and the finest sunsets in this part of Florida. Dress is casual, as might be expected in a restaurant this close to the beach. Although the menu has a variety of items, seafood is a specialty, and is unloaded from the fishing boats daily. For those who like oldies music, the satellite system plays tunes all day long. $–$$.

Jackie's Mango's on the Beach. 2043 South Peninsula Dr.; (386) 258-8204; www.cfar .net/jackie.htm. If you're looking for a quiet, romantic dinner spot, you'll want to avoid this place. It's where Daytona goes to party! If you're looking for a fun night out, this ought to be one of your stops. This is a fun and friendly place with very good edibles, especially the cheesesteak and potato salad. There's nothing glitzy or fancy here. It's just the kind of place you can go to and let your hair down and have a good time. $–$$.

Ocean Deck. 127 South Ocean Ave.; (386) 253-5224; www.oceandeck.com. This is a locally popular place for lunch, drinks at sundown, or after-dark noshing on seafood, sandwich platters, or pastas featuring sauces so popular that they're for sale by the jar. For snacks order a frigate of fries with chili and cheese, nachos, salsa and chips, or onion rings. Almost everything on the menu is under $10—but for a whimsical touch, you can add a bottle of Dom Perignon champagne for $125. Park behind the Reggae Republic. Open daily from 11 a.m. $.

Teauila's Hawaii Dinner Show. 2301 South Atlantic Ave., Daytona Beach Shores; (386) 255-5411 or (800) 922-3023; www.teauilashawaii.com. Located in the Hawaiian Inn, this is one of the area's longest-running hits, and it never fails to charm. You'll dine on American and Polynesian foods while a whirl of hula, fire dancing, and sweet music surrounds you. It's a treat for all ages. Call for reservations for dinner or matinee shows. $$.

where to stay

Hilton Daytona Beach Resort. 100 North Atlantic Ave.; (386) 254-8200 or (800) 444-2326; www.hiltonhotels.com. One of the finest hotels on the World's Most Famous Beach, this is the center of the massive oceanfront complex called the Ocean Walk Resort. The complex begins with the beach, fishing pier, and historic band shell and spreads over acres of hotel rooms, shopping space, dining venues, and entertainment. Rooms are smartly furnished and have in-room movies, hair dryer, iron and ironing board, minibar, data ports, and coffeemaker. The hotel has bars, lounges with entertainment, and casual and fine dining; or order from room service and dine on your balcony overlooking the sea. No cars are permitted on this part of the beach. $$–$$$.

Best Western Mayan Inn Beachfront. 103 South Ocean Ave.; (386) 252-BEST or (800) 443-5323; www.bestwestern.com. It's hard to beat the value offered by this chain hotel, especially when you can find one right on the beach with a bountiful breakfast thrown in. All 112 rooms have an ocean view, and most have a balcony. Kitchens and Jacuzzi suites are available. Every room has a coffeemaker, free stays for kids under age eighteen with parents or grandparents, cable TV with premium channels, in-room safe, and data port. The pool is heated, which is a plus during Daytona's occasional cold spells. $–$$.

Hilton Daytona Beach Oceanfront Resort. 2637 South Atlantic Ave.; (386) 254-8200 or (800) HILTONS; www.daytonahilton.com. This high-rise hotel is right on the beach, with a sparkling pool, a wide swath of pristine sand, and the Atlantic beyond. Amenities include a kids' pool, whirlpool, gift shop, and fine dining or quick deli bites. Have a drink in the Blue Water Lounge overlooking the ocean. Every guest room has a refrigerator, voice mail, data port, cable TV with pay-per-view movies, iron and ironing board, hair dryer, safe, and coffeemaker with free supplies. Balcony rooms are available, and the hotel also has six suites. $$–$$$.

Sun Viking Lodge. 2411 South Atlantic Ave., Daytona Beach Shores; (386) 252-6252 or (800) 815-2846; www.sunviking.com. This family resort offers free accommodations to children under age seventeen in their parents' room. You don't have to worry about rowdy spring breakers here. Singles under age twenty-five aren't accommodated. Cribs are free, roll-aways are $10 extra, and some of the units have sofa beds. Choose from a wide range of layouts ranging from a motel room with two queen beds to a three-bedroom cottage with full kitchen and beds for up to eight persons. The lodge lies on a sugar-sand beach where you can walk or ride a bicycle for miles. Planned activities include children's programs and a family ice-cream social on Tuesday. Swim indoors or out, soak in the hot tub, and use Nautilus equipment in the fitness room. Dining and shopping are close by. Ask about packages, including golf deals. $–$$$.

Tropical Manor Beach Motel. 2237 South Atlantic Ave.; (386) 252-4920 or (800) 253-4920; www.tropicalmanor.com. Located on Highway A1A, this is one of Daytona's many small, resident owner–managed resorts. Other than having a refrigerator, all rooms are different, ranging from motel rooms to efficiencies, suites, and a fully furnished cottage that sleeps up to eleven. Balcony suites overlooking the Atlantic are perfect for a romantic weekend. Walk a block to a supermarket, or drive to a nearby fishing pier, charter boats, golf courses, and the Speedway. Restaurants are as near as next door. Picnic tables, chaises, barbecues, a gazebo, chairs, and tables with umbrellas are on the grounds for guest use. Adult and kiddie pools on the oceanfront are heated. $–$$ (ask about weekly rates).

palm coast—flagler beach

Barely a dot on the map a decade ago, Palm Coast has mushroomed into a major community, with miles and miles of residential streets filled with moderately priced homes. Older neighborhoods are along the coast and waterway. Both Flagler Beach and Palm Coast are north of Daytona Beach via I-95. Nearby Bunnell is on US 1 just west of Flagler Beach.

where to go

Bulow Plantation Ruins State Historic Site. Mail address: P.O. Box 655, Bunnell, FL 32110; (386) 517-2084; www.floridastateparks.org/bulowplantation. Find this wilderness on Old Kings Road, 3 miles west of Flagler Beach off County Road 2001 between SR 100 and Old Dixie Highway. Major Charles Bulow was master of a 4,600-acre wetland along a tidal creek where sugarcane, cotton, and rice flourished. One of the rich planter's visitors was John James Audubon, who was charmed by the abundance of bird life here. By the outbreak of the Second Seminole War, the major was dead and his son in charge of the plantation. As the Seminoles became more hostile, Bulow and his slaves fled the property, which was subsequently burned by the Seminoles. Heartbroken, the twenty-six-year-old Bulow fled to Paris, where he died three months later. Hike among the ruins of the house, sugar mill, and slave quarters; have a picnic; or launch your boat in Bulow Creek, a state canoe trail. The park is open daily 9 a.m. to 5 p.m. Entry is $3 per vehicle.

Gamble Rogers Memorial State Recreation Area. 3100 South Hwy. A1A; (386) 517-2086; www.floridastateparks.org/gamblerogers. On this barrier island bordered by the Atlantic to the east and the Intracoastal Waterway to the west, you can walk a nature trail through coastal scrub. Swim in the ocean or fish in the creamy surf. Launch your boat on the ICW, picnic, or camp. Shelling can be good, especially at low tide. Watch shorebirds pick their way through the restless waterline, pecking at meaty morsels while pelicans soar in updrafts. May through September, sea turtles come ashore here to lay their eggs. Hiking trails, restrooms, and picnic shelters are provided. Open 8 a.m. until sundown. State park fees apply.

Princess Place Preserve. 2500 Princess Place Rd.; (386) 313-4020; www.flaglerparks.com/princess/preserve.htm. From US 1 take Old Kings Road (a dirt road) east, following the signs. While this reserve isn't the most polished or accessible in the state, it has a fascinating story and is the home of the oldest existing homesteads in the county. The king of Spain granted this land to Francisco Pellicer in 1791. Later a settler planted orange groves, and in 1886 a wealthy New England sportsman, Henry Cutting, bought the grove and surrounding property along Pellicer Creek. His hunting lodge is said to be the only Adirondack Camp–style structure in the state. It has stables, tennis courts, and the first in-ground swimming pool in the state. Cutting died and his widow married an exiled Russian prince, thus becoming a princess. They returned to the grove, known ever since as Princess Place. Because the preserve is at the confluence of Pellicer Creek and the Matanzas River, it's alive with birds, small mammals, and a profusion of plant life. Bring a picnic lunch; there are no facilities. Camping and kayak rentals are available. The preserve is open daily from 7 a.m. to 6 p.m. Taking shape here is the Florida Agricultural Museum, so facilities will gradually be added.

Washington Oaks State Gardens. 6400 North Oceanshore Blvd.; (386) 446-6780; www.floridastateparks.org/washingtonoaks. This 400-acre preserve on Highway A1A is built around flourishing gardens that were established for a private home in the 1930s. Picnic, walk along a bouldery shoreline pounded by surf, or stroll along the river under towering live oaks past azaleas and mirrored ponds. Stop at the interpretive center, housed in the original 1930s home, to learn about natural flora and fauna, then hike the nature trails. Open daily 8 a.m. to sunset. Admission is $4 per vehicle.

where to eat

Blue–Dining with a View. 1224 South Oceanshore Blvd.; (386) 439-4322. Occupying the site formerly known as the Topaz Cafe, Blue is still one of the most popular restaurants in the area. Blue offers a fine wine list to go with its excellent menu offerings. Reservations are needed for parties of five or more. $$–$$$.

Chicken Pantry. US 1 South, Bunnell; (386) 437-3316. This is a country place that reels in the city folk for mountains of southern fried chicken, black-eyed peas, green beans, squash, eggplant, and all the trimmings. Turkey with dressing is served on Thursday; fresh

St. Augustine shrimp or macaroni and cheese leads the fare on Friday. For lunch have a club sandwich and a platter of onion rings. Open for breakfast, lunch, and dinner 7 a.m. to 8 p.m. daily except Sunday. $–$$.

Cracker Barrel. 4 Kingswood Dr.; (386) 445-2127. This is an outlet of the popular roadside chain that everyone loves for the rustic decor and modest prices. Order your favorite comfort food: chicken and dumplings, eggs and grits, Salisbury steak with real mashed potatoes, or roast pork with applesauce, followed by a slab of pie. It's open most of the time and can be crowded at peak times, but it's big and well organized so waits are usually bearable—especially if you shop the country store until your name is called. $–$$.

High Jackers. 202 Airport Rd.; (386) 586-6078; www.highjackers.com. While eating here among the South Pacific decor you can watch the planes come and go from the Flagler airport. Main flight dinner entrees include coconut shrimp, chicken O'Gara, and southwest tuna and come with black beans and rice, fries, or garlic mashed potatoes and two fritters. $$.

where to stay

Country Hearth Inn. 2251 Old Dixie Hwy., Bunnell; (386) 437-3737; www.countryhearth .com/hotels/fl-bunnell.htm. This is a reliable, traveler-friendly roadside inn handy to exit 90 off I-95. Stop in for a swim, a meal in the restaurant, and a restful night at modest prices. Continental breakfast is included. Pets are permitted. $$.

Topaz Motel & Hotel. 1224 South Oceanshore Blvd.; (386) 439-2545 or (800) 555-4735; www.flaglercounty.com/topaz. This property has been here since the flapper era but in recent years has become very "in," a favorite weekend hideaway for job-weary fugitives from nearby cities. Rooms overlook the Atlantic; the restaurant, Blue, is one of the most popular in the area. The motel consists of standard rooms that are predictable, clean, and comfortable. The hotel, by contrast, is more of a B&B, furnished in antiques. Discuss your preferences when you make reservations, because so many different accommodations are available. Pets are welcome in the motel but not the hotel. $$–$$$.

White Orchid Bed & Breakfast. 1104 South Oceanshore Blvd.; (386) 439-4944 or (800) 423-1477; www.whiteorchidinn.com. Located on Highway A1A, this romantic spa getaway on the ocean has a heated swimming pool and an extensive menu of spa treatments and services, ranging from Hot Stone Therapy ($110) to a Hydralessence Radiance Facial ($85), plus packages that include half a dozen or more services. Included in the rates are a full breakfast and wine with afternoon snacks. Ask for a room with a two-person Jacuzzi, and let your hosts arrange everything else you'll need, from fine dining to suggested sightseeing. Bicycles are available for guest use. All spa packages include use of the mineral pool. $$$.

day trip 03

america's oldest city:
st. augustine, ponte vedra beach

st. augustine

From Orlando, zip northeast on I-4 to Daytona Beach, where you pick up I-95 and a quick route northward to America's oldest city and, just north of it, one of Florida's least known but most exclusive beach communities. The scenic route is Highway A1A, which you might pick up at Flagler Beach, Crescent Beach, or Palm Coast. It takes you past Marineland, no longer the tourist attraction it once was as Florida's first marine park but now a development and research station. Beaches, beach overlooks, parks, beach motels, and beach restaurants line the route and make the going slower but more interesting than the interstate. The beaches of St. Johns County alone (Marineland to Ponte Vedra) stretch for 42 miles.

Timucuan Indians lived well in this area, tending crops and harvesting shellfish, until the coming of the Spanish in 1513, more than seventy years before Sir Walter Raleigh founded his English settlement on what is now the Outer Banks of North Carolina. By 1565 French Huguenots had arrived. Massacre followed, with the Catholic Spaniards driving out the Protestant French. Sir Frances Drake burned St. Augustine in 1586, but the strongly fortified Spanish settlement held until 1763, when Florida was ceded to Great Britain by Spain under the terms of the Treaty of Paris, which ended the French and Indian War. Twenty years later, another treaty gave Florida back to Spain for almost forty years before it became a U.S. territory.

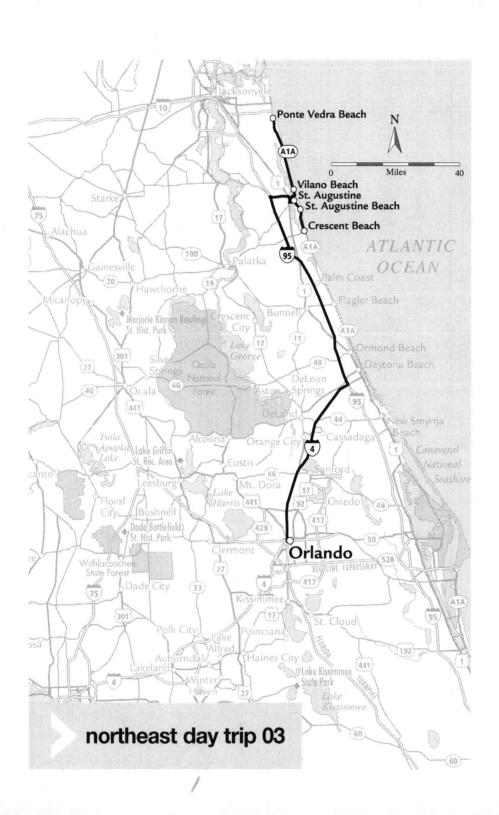

northeast day trip 03

History can be confusing—the following St. Augustine timeline will help:

Amerindian Period	Prehistory to mid-1500s
First Spanish Period	1513–1763
British Period	1763–1783
Second Spanish Period	1783–1821
U.S. Territory Period	1821–1845
U.S. Statehood Period	1845–1861
Confederate Period	1861–1865
Reconstruction Period	1865–1877

Visitors come back to St. Augustine time and again to try the great variety of accommodations, from lavish beach and golf resorts to bed-and-breakfast inns housed in 200-year-old buildings. You can spend years of weekends just trying the B&Bs. World Golf Village is new and trendsetting. Casa Monica, which dates to the flamboyant Flagler railroad era, is a luxury hotel steeped in rich history.

The Marriott at Sawgrass Resort alone has ninety-nine holes of world-class golf. World Golf Village is home to the Senior PGA Tour's Legends of Golf Tournament. The Ponte Vedra Inn & Club is the home of a 1974 Robert Trent Jones classic course, and the eighteen-hole course at the Radisson Ponce de Leon Golf and Conference Center was designed by Donald Ross himself. In fact, the whole area is such a golf destination that there's a separate booking number just for golf vacations: (866) 794-3324; www.florida-golf.org.

In the "living history" attractions, people go about their daily tasks as though it's still the seventeenth or eighteenth century, so visits here are always new, always absorbing. During reenactments, which occur often throughout the year, it's a time warp to be entered time and again. Wear period clothing and join in. Driving is difficult, parking impossible, so park at the visitor center and sightsee on foot, in a horse-drawn carriage, or on the trolley.

In addition to the hot spots listed in the next section, take time to visit the historic churches and cemeteries, where the thoughtful traveler will find the real history and passion of this centuries-old city. Christian Indians were buried in the Tolomato Cemetery across from the Castillo; the National Cemetery on Marine Street has been used as a burial ground since 1763 and is the resting place of soldiers killed during the Second Seminole War. The Huguenot Cemetery, a burying place for Protestants, who weren't permitted burial in the Catholic city, was probably named for the French Huguenots who arrived in 1564. All the churches have a story, a monument, a shrine, or a placard that will enrich your understanding of St. Augustine's history. The Cathedral of St. Augustine, Memorial Presbyterian Church, St. Photios Chapel, and Trinity Episcopal are usually open for sightseeing. Ancient

City Baptist, Grace United Methodist, and St. Ambrose Catholic Church are historically significant churches that are usually open only during worship services.

Note that Anastasia Island and St. Augustine Beach are the same community. The names are used interchangeably and have the same zip code. A car is required to get to the historic area from the island.

where to go

Castillo de San Marcos National Monument. 1 South Castillo Dr.; (904) 829-6505; www.nps.gov/casa. This is the heart of the city, a fortress with echoing dungeons and walls that never fell to enemy invasion. It's the oldest masonry fort in the nation, dating to 1672. Allow an hour or more for exploring the rambling ramparts, seeing exhibits, chatting with costumed characters, and photographing sea views from the highest towers. Admission is $6 for adults, free for children. Open from 8:45 a.m. to 5:15 p.m. every day of the year except Dec 25.

Dow Museum of Historic Houses. 250 St. George St.; (904) 823-9722; www.old-staug-village.com. The main entrance is on Bridge Street. A complex of nine ancient buildings, galleries, and gardens, this is a place to spend half a day. Costumed interpreters pose as French pirates, Spanish conquistadors, seventeenth-century cooks, storekeepers, and Cracker cow hunters in an era when Florida was a rawboned frontier. Check the *Village Almanac* to see what's doing today and where. One of the houses was once the home of Napoleon's nephew, Prince Murat, a place where Ralph Waldo Emerson wrote and movie star Greta Garbo dined. On the grounds are the ruins of a colonial fort, the oldest hospital, and one of the oldest bridges in the United States. Open daily from 10 a.m. to 4:30 p.m. and Sun from 11 a.m. to 4:30 p.m. Admission is $8.95 for adults, $7.95 for seniors, and $6.95 for students.

Faver-Dykes State Park. 1000 Faver-Dykes Rd.; (904) 794-0997; www.floridastateparks .org/faver-dykes. The park follows wildly beautiful Pellicer Creek through pine flatwoods and mesic hammock, 15 miles south of St. Augustine. The park offers family camping with electric hookups, picnic tables, rental canoes by reservation, fishing, and nature walks. State park fees apply. Open 8 a.m. to sundown daily.

Fort Mose. Two miles north of St. Augustine off US 1; watch for signs; (904) 823-2232; www.floridastateparks.org/fortmose. There isn't a lot to see here, but you'll feel the powerful history of a community of free blacks who escaped from their owners in the Carolinas and took refuge in Florida, where slavery was not practiced under Spanish rule. When the British attacked from Georgia, blacks fought on the Spanish side; when the British won Florida in a European treaty deal, most blacks fled to Cuba. The fort is open during daylight hours; admission is $2 per vehicle or $1 for walk-ins.

Fountain of Youth. 155 Magnolia Ave.; (904) 829-3168 or (800) 356-8222; www.fountain ofyouthflorida.com. Touristy but with a serious, archaeological side, this was the site of the Indian village of Seloy, noted by Ponce de Leon. See the old spring, the burial grounds for Indian Christians, and the site of the first settlement of St. Augustine. Take the tram or walk the park. Hours vary seasonally, so call ahead. Admission is charged.

A Ghostly Experience walking tour. The tour starts at the north end of St. George Street at 8 p.m. nightly; (904) 461-1009; www.aghostlyexperience.com. A 500-year-old city is sure to have a lot of ghosts, legends, and juicy stories, which are described by lantern light as you walk with a guide for ninety minutes of spooky, good fun. It's G-rated, so don't hesitate to bring Grandma and the kids. Everyone pays $12 except children under age six, who walk free.

Government House Museum. 48 King St.; (904) 825-5079; www.staugustinegovernment .com/visitors/gov-house.cfm. This museum takes you through the city's history from early Native American settlements through the Flagler era. See gold and silver from Spanish shipwrecks, archaeological treasures, and presentations that walk you through the city's culture, history, and economy in quick and digestible bites. Open Mon through Fri 9 a.m. to 4:30 p.m. and Sat and Sun 10 a.m. to 4:30 p.m.

Kayak in the rivers and wetlands that surround St. Augustine. For lessons and canoe or kayak rents, call Anastasia State Park Canoe and Kayak Concession (904-460-9111), www .floridastateparks.org/anastasia; or Outdoor Adventures (904-393-9030). For information about area water sports, hiking, and outdoor adventures, request the *Vacation Guide* from the St. Johns County Visitors & Convention Bureau. (See Regional Information at the back of this book.)

Lightner Museum. King St.; (904) 824-2874; www.lightnermuseum.org. Located in the City Hall Complex, this museum offers a gilt trip into an ornate Victorian era. Housed in what was built in 1888 as a luxury hotel, the museum shows antique musical instruments, costumes, furniture, and works of Louis Comfort Tiffany. See the hotel's old casino, grand ballroom, and what was once an indoor swimming pool. Admission is $10 for adults and $5 for children ages twelve to eighteen. Children under age twelve are admitted free with an adult. Open from 9 a.m. to 5 p.m. daily (closed Christmas Day).

Memorial Presbyterian Church. 36 Sevilla St.; (904) 829-6451; www.memorialpcusa .org. The church was built by a grief-stricken Henry Flagler after he received word that his daughter, Jennie, had died delivering his first grandchild. Workers toiled around the clock to finish this magnificent structure in one year, and it opened on the first anniversary of her death. Flagler and his family are buried here in the magnificent Venetian Renaissance structure. Open daily 9 a.m. to 4 p.m. Free.

St. Augustine Alligator Farm and Zoological Park. 999 Anastasia Blvd.; (904) 824-3337; www.alligatorfarm.us. Cross the Bridge of Lions, then turn right on Highway A1A. One of Florida's oldest attractions, this has evolved from a mere curiosity to an important refuge and breeding ground for gators, which were once overhunted to the point where they needed protection. Spend the day. Walk boardwalks through wetlands to see nature's harmony in birds, buzzing insects, small mammals, monkeys, and slithery alligators. Special shows and exhibits highlight a spectrum of Florida wildlife from parrots to snakes, plus imports from all over the world. Bring the children to learn about nature's beasts, including one of the world's greatest collections of crocodilians. Open every day from 9 a.m. to 5 p.m. Admission is $21.95 for adults and $10.95 for children; under age five free. Discounts for AAA and seniors.

St. Augustine Lighthouse & Museum. 81 Lighthouse Ave., St. Augustine Beach; (904) 829-0745; www.staugustinelighthouse.com. Climb to the top of this 165-foot tower off Highway A1A for a bird's-eye view of the area. See artifacts from shipwrecks including the British sloop *Industry,* which was lost on St. Augustine Bar on May 6, 1764. See the working Fresnel lens, hear the story of the "mission impossible" restoration of the damaged light, see the lighthouse keeper's quarters, and shop for lighthouse memorabilia in the gift store. Hours are daily 9 a.m. to 6 p.m., with longer hours in summer. Admission is $9. for adults, $8. for seniors age fifty-five or over, and $7 for children ages seven to eleven. Note that children must be at least seven years old and 48 inches tall to climb the 219 steps to the tower. Free museum admission and activities are offered to children under age seven with an accompanying adult.

St. Augustine Sightseeing Trains. 170 San Marco Ave.; (904) 824-1606 or (800) 226-6545; www.redtrains.com. These narrated tours are the best way to get your bearings and some background before you set out on your own. Park at the visitor center just north of the Castillo, one of the few places in the historic area with ample parking, and see the orientation films, then take a tour. Trains cover 7 miles, with twenty scheduled stops where you can get off, stay as long as you like, then reboard. Tickets are good for three days. Call for rates for seven different tour plans. Admissions to attractions are extra. A number of other tours are available, from flight-seeing to individually guided tours on foot or by carriage. Ask about them while you're at the visitor center, or call (800) OLD-CITY.

St. Augustine Trolley Tours are arranged through your hotel or at the Old Jail Complex, 167 San Marco Ave.; (904) 829-3800 or (800) 868-7482; www.trolleytours.com/st-augustine. The 7-mile narrated tour is the best way to get oriented in the city before striking out on your own. Tours run 8:30 a.m. to 5 p.m., and you can get off and on as you please. There's a wide range of prices and options, from $20.70 on up, depending on whether a package includes other admissions. All tickets are good for three days.

San Sebastian Winery. 157 King St.; (904) 826-1594 or (888) 352-9463; www.san sebastianwinery.com. This is a surprising find in a state that has so few wineries. Taste the wines, including a delightful cream sherry, then shop for wine by the case, wine gifts and accessories, and gourmet foods. There's plenty of parking for cars and even big RVs. Complimentary tours and wine tasting run about every 20 minutes, take approximately 45 minutes, and are offered seven days a week, except for major holidays. Open Mon through Sat, 10 a.m. to 6 p.m., and Sun, 11 a.m. to 6 p.m.

Spanish Quarter Museum. Mailing address: P.O. Box 210, St. Augustine, FL 32085; (904) 825-5033; www.historicaugustine.com. The complex spreads along St. George Street from Government House Museum to the Spanish Quarter Museum. Start at Government House to see exhibits explaining 500 years of city history, then go to the Spanish Quarter to see them come alive. "Townspeople" in authentic costumes go about their daily lives as merchants, carpenters, soldiers, homemakers, gardeners, and idlers. They'll be glad to talk to you about their concerns with hunger, homesickness, the fear of English invasion, or the next attack of malaria or yellow fever. Admission is $6.95 for adults, $4.25 for students ages six to seventeen, $16.95 for families (two parents and related children ages six to seventeen), $15.95 for seniors (age sixty-two and older), and free for military personnel. Open daily, except Christmas, 9 a.m. to 5:30 p.m.

Victory III sails out of the Municipal Marina south of the Bridge of Lions on a seventy-five-minute cruise of the waters just off the Old City. She's skippered by members of a family that has been here for 500 years, so the narration is informative and exciting. See the shore as seen by the earliest Spanish and English settlers. You'll also see a world of wildlife and, with luck, bottlenose dolphins. Adults are $16.75, seniors $13.75, children ages thirteen to eighteen $9.75, and those ages four to twelve $7.75. Sailings are daily except Christmas, but schedules vary seasonally. (904) 824-1806 or (800) 542-8316; www.scenic-cruise.com.

World Golf Village. 1 World Golf Place; (904) 940-4000 or (800) WGV-GOLF; www.wgv .com. An entire community devoted to golf, it's the home of the PGA Tour Golf Academy, a 300-seat IMAX theater, the World Golf Hall of Fame, two par-72 golf courses, plus restaurants and resorts. (See Where to Stay.) Play The King & The Bear golf course, designed by Arnold Palmer and Jack Nicklaus, or The Slammer and The Squire, designed by Gene Sarazen and Sam Snead. Walk the half-mile-long Walk of Champions around Kelly Lake on granite slabs signed by members of the World Golf Hall of Fame. Play the eighteen-hole putting course, and dare the 132-yard Island Challenge Hole. Dine in the **Murray Brothers' Caddy Shack, Sam Snead's Tavern,** or the many hotel restaurants; and shop for golf memorabilia, including autographed mementos, at the museum store. The village also has a toy shop, art studio, ice cream and fudge, a travel shop, and a fly-fishing center where you can buy supplies or take lessons in fly-tying or casting.

Sign on for lessons from top professionals at the PGA Tour Golf Academy, then try your skills in the Full Swing Golf Simulator in the Renaissance Resort. If you stay on the grounds, excursions can be booked for the historic area.

where to shop

Old City Farmers' Market in the St. Augustine Amphitheater, Highway A1A South, Anastasia Island; (904) 471-3733, www.staugamphitheatre.com/farmers.php. The market is open Saturday morning only, selling homegrown produce, homemade baked goods, and lovingly tended plants. Free programs on nature and wildlife are also offered. On Tuesday morning the same spot hosts a combination farmers' market and flea market. A farmers' market is held on Wednesday morning, rain or shine, at 370 Beach Blvd., St. Augustine Beach.

Prime Outlets St. Augustine. 500 Belz Outlet Blvd.; (904) 826-1311; www.primeoutlets .com/locations/st--augustine.aspx. From I-95, take the SR 16 exit. Seventy-five stores are spread under one roof here. Shop for bargains in such brands as Fossil, Zales, Samsonite, Nike, Timberland, Black & Decker, Le Creuset, Royal Doulton, Polo Ralph Lauren, Coleman camping equipment, Tommy Hilfiger, and many more. When you're hungry, choose among the snack shops and fast-food places. Open daily. Also at this exit, the **St. Augustine Premium Outlets** (904-825-1555) offers ninety-five more stores and a trolley to take you around. Shop for books, Harry & David, Levis, Jockey, Van Heusen, Seiko, L'Eggs/Hanes, and dozens of other famous names. Open daily except Thanksgiving and Christmas; limited hours on Easter.

Whetstone Chocolate Factory. They have three locations around St. Augustine: 248 SR 312; (904) 825-1710; 42 St. George St.; (904) 825-1720; 13 Anastasia Blvd.; (904) 825-1725; www.whetstonechocolates.com. This is a working chocolate factory where you can see a video, take a self-guided tour, and shop for delectable chocolates and souvenirs in the Factory Outlet Store. The different stores have differing hours, so call ahead.

World Golf Village. 1 World Golf Place; (904) 940-4000; www.wgv.com. This is one of the largest and most complete golf-related shops in the state. Shop for clothing, logo merchandise, gifts, souvenirs, golf-theme accessories and furnishings for the home, and the finest golf equipment. Hours vary, so call ahead.

where to eat

A1A Ale Works. 1 King St.; (904) 829-2977; www.a1aaleworks.com. Enjoy award-winning culinary creations while dining indoors or on the outdoor veranda overlooking Matanzas Bay and downtown. A1A Ale Works offers pasta, chicken, and steak, and specializes in seafood dishes. The A1A Beer Cheese Soup has become famous and is an absolute must for many diners. Entrees include seared tuna, key-lime shrimp and lobster over fettuccini, and seafood paella. A1A Ale Works features six ales and lagers, brewed on-site for the freshest beers in town. Call in advance for priority seating. $$–$$$.

Avilés Restaurant. 32 Avenida Menendez; (904) 829-9727; www.avilesrestaurant.com. It's worth the trip for the Hunan Whole Crispy Fish, a fresh red snapper caught that day. Sides could include the crab whipped potatoes, Swiss chard, and sweet and sour chili glaze. Top it off with a glass of fine white wine. You'll also find other entrees of delectable local seafood and meats. Dinner is served from 4 to 10 p.m. $$–$$$.

Barnacle Bill's. 14 Castillo Dr.; (904) 824-3663; www.barnaclebillsonline.com. The fresh catch of the day can be served fried or broiled at this popular seafood center located across from the Visitor Information Center. Order gator tail, mahimahi, red-hot wings, oysters, scallops, catfish, or one of a half-dozen shrimp concoctions. If you don't do seafood, there's steak, chicken, and ribs. The combination platters are fun and adventurous for big eaters. Open daily 11 a.m. to 9 p.m. $–$$.

Columbia Restaurant. 98 St. George St.; (904) 824-3341; www.columbiarestaurant.com. This is an outlet of the family-operated chain that was founded in Tampa in 1905. Don't miss the classic 1905 Salad. The paella takes some advance planning but is worth the wait. It can be ordered for a couple or a crowd. Try one of the fish dishes, meltingly tender beef and pork, or the chicken with yellow rice, all served traditionally with rice and beans and fried plantains. All the desserts are good, but the flan is irresistible. After you eat, don't miss the gift shop. Open daily for lunch and dinner and for Sunday brunch. Call for reservations, which are strongly recommended. $$–$$$.

Conch House. 57 Comares Ave.; (904) 829-8646 or (800) 940-6256; www.conch-house.com. Dine in a Caribbean island resort where you can enjoy your meal in a grass shack right on the water. Start with a honeydew daiquiri or the goombay smash. Breakfast choices range from conventional waffles and omelets to tangy huevos rancheros. At lunch have a veggie burger, Caribbean chicken sandwich, shrimp and chorizo, or a specialty burger. Fried seafood, including cracked conch, is on both the lunch and dinner menus. So are a tempting list of salads and appetizers. House specialties include a couple of chicken dishes, a vegetarian stir-fry, and shrimp Anastasia served over pasta. Certified Black Angus beef steaks are served at dinner with a long list of other choices, including the catch of the day with grilled pineapple, baby back ribs, or Jamaican chicken served with beans and rice. In season, steamed crab legs are served by the pound; steamed shrimp is sold by the half pound. Open Sun to Thurs 11 a.m. to 9 p.m., Fri and Sat 11 a.m. to 10 p.m. $–$$$.

Cortessés Bistro. 172 San Marco Ave.; (904) 825-6775; http://cortessesbistroandflamingoroom.com. The bistro is also home to the Flamingo Room and some of the city's most sizzling nightlife. Come for cocktails and dinner, then stay for the jazz. The menu offers a huge choice ranging from soups and "light plates" to salads, hot and cold sandwiches, pasta specials, and a bistro menu (herb-crusted lamb chops, Minorcan fish stew, veal Oscar, and Black Angus beef) served from 5 p.m. on. The international wine list is impressive. Open daily for lunch and dinner. $$–$$$.

Dairy Queen. 100 San Marco Ave.; (904) 824-1224. Deliciously out of place in the midst of all this oldness, DQ is a beacon of familiarity where you can pick up a take-out meal or eat in cool comfort. The menu is pretty simple: hotdogs and hamburgers with fries. Kids like the Pick-Nic meals that include a sweet and a toy. The Blizzards, Smoothies, and Mud Slides are indescribably delicious on a hot day. Open daily 7 a.m. to 10 p.m., until 11 p.m. Fri and Sat. Lunch served from 10 a.m. $.

Gypsy Cab Company. 828 Anastasia Blvd.; (904) 824-8244; www.gypsycab.com. In an ideal location between the historic district and the beach, this place serves what they call urban cuisine. It starts with a great soup from a choice that includes Bahamian clam chowder, cream of chicken tarragon, black bean, lentil, or gazpacho. Then come appetizers and salads. For lunch have the grouper, chicken with black beans and rice, Italian sausage sauté, or seafood Santa Fe. Dinner entrees include chicken stuffed with Gorgonzola, veal in bacon-horseradish cream, braised lamb shank, and much more. The Florida peach and hazelnut icebox cakes are favorite desserts. Open every day for dinner from 5:30 p.m.; weekend brunch is served 10:30 a.m. to 3 p.m. The Gypsy Bar & Grill next door serves tapas, appetizers, and drinks. Live entertainment is offered Wed, Fri, and Sat nights. $–$$

Harry's Seafood, Bar, and Grille. 46 Avenida Menendez; (904) 824-7765; www.hooked onharrys.com. New Orleans lives in the Old City in a laid-back restaurant that serves fried oyster po'boys, red beans and rice with smoked sausage, crawfish, gumbo, or catfish Pontchartrain. The menu is as wide as Bourbon Street, offering burgers, fish, fried platters, soups, and just plain steaks or chicken for those who don't do Cajun. Have the bananas Foster for dessert. There's a children's menu, and kids get Mardi Gras beads to keep. $$.

The Kings Head British Pub. 6460 US 1 North; (904) 823-9787. If you love all things English, come here for the pub ambience (darts, "draught" ales on tap), and pub grub such as fish-and-chips, steak and kidney pie, bangers and mash, pasties, and Scotch eggs. Vegetarian dishes are available, too. On Sunday make reservations for a traditional roast-beef-and-Yorkshire-pudding feast. On the first Sunday of the month, classic and antique cars gather here. Open daily except Monday. $$.

La Pentola. 58 Charlotte St.; (904) 824-3282; www.lapentolarestaurant.com. Located in the Sebastian Harbor Marina Mall, La Pentola's gifted chef creates pastas, fresh seafood, and meats in the Mediterranean tradition. Start with escargot or brie baked in crust, then choose one of the many pastas, including a vegetarian selection. Or order fresh fish, shrimp, lamb, steak, veal, pork, or chicken, served with rosemary-garlic potatoes and all the trim-mings. Wild game and other exotics are a house specialty, and there's an impressive list of wines and beers. Open for lunch and dinner daily except Sunday. Reservations are suggested. $$.

La Strada. 4075 South Hwy. A1A, St. Augustine Beach; (904) 471-0081. This pleasant Italian bistro offers indoor or patio dining on classics (lasagna, veal Marsala) or inventive specialties (penne with cauliflower, raisins, and pine nuts or roasted duckling in cranberry and port wine sauce). Open daily for dinner; early birds are served 4:30 to 6 p.m. Reservations are suggested.

Le Pavillon. 45 San Marco Ave.; (904) 824-6202; www.lepav.com. Le Pavillon is a continental restaurant in one of the city's fine old homes downtown. Luncheon main dishes include the quiche of the day, a choice of salads, an omelette, or an oyster platter, as well as any of the dinner entrees, which are available during lunch. Begin dinner with oysters, escargot, the soup of the day, or the pâté, then dine lightly on one of the half-dozen crepe choices (Florentine, beef and mushroom, chicken, seafood, or a combination) or more heartily on main dishes from all over the world. They include sauerbraten with spätzle, veal Francaise, curried chicken Bombay, Viennese schnitzel, and New York strip steak. The crème de menthe parfait is a refreshing dessert. There's a full bar. Open daily 11:30 a.m. to closing. $$.

95 Cordova. 95 Cordova St. (at King Street); (904) 810-6810; www.95cordova.com. Elegance has been reborn at this restaurant in the splendid Casa Monica Hotel, one of the great railroad hotels built at the turn of the twentieth century. Have a drink first in the Cobalt Lounge, then try the New World Eclectic cuisine in the dining room and return to the lounge for dancing to live music. Open breakfast through dinner; for lighter dining, pick up pastries and sandwiches in the Gourmet Deli ($) to take on a picnic or enjoy on the patio. $$$.

O. C. White's. 118 Avenida Menendez; (904) 824-0808; www.ocwhites.com. Dining is simple and basic in this old Spanish structure overlooking the marina, Bridge of Lions, and bay—good fish or meat with salad, vegetables, and freshly baked bread. Try the crab cakes, scallops, a steak or chicken specialty, or the shrimp. There's live entertainment for happy hour Monday through Friday. Open every day for dinner and for lunch in season. $$.

Raintree. 102 San Marco Ave.; (904) 824-7211; www.raintreerestaurant.com. This restaurant is operated by a couple who sailed from England to America on their 45-foot yacht, bought a Victorian building that took them ten months to restore and turn into a restaurant, and lived happily ever after. The food is superb, the wine list one of the finest in the state, and the dessert bar a world in itself. Many people come here just for dessert, coffee, and a nightcap, but do treat yourself to dinner here sometime. Menu highlights include mahimahi and blue crab baked in puff pastry, beef Wellington, cashew-crusted pork tenderloin, Black Angus beef, and much more. $$$.

South Beach Grill. 45 Cubbedge Rd., Crescent Beach; (904) 471-8700; www.south beachgrill.net. On the ocean a block south of SR 206 on Highway A1A, this casual spot where you dine outdoors almost at the water's edge is a favorite with beachgoers. The catch of the day is served grilled, blackened, or sautéed, or have the fragrant cioppino made with half a dozen different seafood treats. Chicken fajitas are served in a wrap, or you can get a Black Angus sirloin steak, chicken jambalaya with andouille sausage, or the char-grilled chicken breast house specialty. Platters, burgers, and wraps are popular at lunch. Open for lunch and dinner daily; early-bird specials and happy hour from 4:30 to 6 p.m. $–$$.

Verrazano Pizza & Sub. Publix Plaza, St. Augustine Beach; (904) 461-9797. Verrazano's is a New York–style pizza joint where you can't go wrong with the pizzas, poppers, hot and cold subs, or a spaghetti dinner. Delivery is free anywhere on the island. The menu is pretty standard, with anything you'd want in a pizza topping. There are also calzones and saucy meatball or chicken hot subs. Dinner choices are spaghetti with meatballs, eggplant Parmesan with spaghetti, or chicken Parmesan with spaghetti, all served with bread and salad. $.

Zaharia's Restaurant & Lounge. 3496 Hwy. A1A South, St. Augustine Beach; (904) 471-4799. Lamb, chicken, choice steaks, and fresh seafood are served with a Greek or Italian accent at this longtime, family-run favorite. Start with calamari, escargot, or oysters Rockefeller, then choose from the kebabs, prime rib, fresh fish, ribs, and much more. Children get their own menu. There's a full bar. Dinner dishes are available from 3 p.m., and early-bird specials run till 7 p.m. Open daily until 9:30 p.m. Reservations are accepted. $$.

where to stay

NOTE: St. Augustine has far more historic bed-and-breakfast inns than can be listed here. If you like the personal service and homey ambience of a B&B, book through www.getaway 4lovers.com, or request a list of Superior Small Lodgings (hotels under fifty rooms that meet the program's standards) from (800) OLD-CITY (653-2489). Decide if you want lodgings on the beach, handy to the interstate west of town, or in the old city, where almost everything is within walking distance. If your focus is on the restoration area, it's handiest to stay here, park the car at your lodgings, and walk everywhere.

Anastasia Inn. 218 Anastasia Blvd.; (904) 825-2879 or (888) 226-6181; www.anastasiainn .com. Just across the Bridge of Lions, this is an excellent location for getting to the beach, the old city, shopping, sightseeing, and restaurants. It's a modern two-story motor hotel with refrigerator, microwave, and coffeemaker in every room, satellite TV with HBO, heated swimming pool, and a whirlpool. City tours pick up free at the hotel. If you fly in, ask about the airport shuttle. Continental breakfast is included. $$–$$$.

Beacher's Lodge. 6970 Hwy. A1A South; (904) 471-8849; www.beacherslodge.com. This condo-style hotel offers oceanfront suites with furnished kitchenettes, a guest laundry, and cable television. Swim off the beach or in the oceanfront pool. There is no restaurant on-site. $$–$$$.

Casa Monica Hotel. 95 Cordova St.; (904) 827-1888 or (800) 648-1888; www.casa monica.com. The Casa Monica is a splendid restoration of a grand hotel built in 1888 to lure affluent travelers to Florida on Henry Flagler's railroad. Flagler didn't spare the horses when it came to extravagance in design, furnishings, and service. With the restoration of the hotel, the golden age is back. Walk to attractions and restaurants in the old city. Swim in the second-story pool. Work out in the fitness center, and don't miss the fine dining in the hotel restaurant. Take a guest room or one of the romantic tower suites. $$–$$$.

Centennial House. 26 Cordova St.; (904) 810-2218 or (800) 611-2880; www.centennial house.com. This property has been restored from rafters to roost to create romantic rooms with gas fireplaces, luxury baths with oversize whirlpool tubs, cable television, and VCRs (choose your program from the video library). The hotel's in the heart of the historic district, within walking distance of attractions and restaurants. Watch horse-drawn carriages pass on Cordova Street, or find privacy in the garden courtyard away from city sounds. Rates include full breakfast. $$$.

Comfort Inn. 901 Hwy. A1A South, St. Augustine Beach; (904) 471-1472 or (800) 221-2222; www.comfortinn.com. This property is a short walk from the beach. Suites have Jacuzzi tubs and kitchenettes. Ask if you want a microwave and refrigerator. Rooms have two doubles or a king and big TVs with cable channels including HBO. There's a big swimming pool and a heated whirlpool. Continental breakfast is included, but there is no on-site restaurant. $$–$$$.

Comfort Suites at World Golf Village. 475 Commerce Lake Dr.; (904) 940-9500 or (800) 228-5150; www.hotelchoice.com. If golf is your game, this place puts you in the center of a 6,300-acre resort that is devoted to world-class golf. Swim in the heated indoor or outdoor pool and work out in the fitness center. Each of the suites has a separate bedroom, living area with sofa sleeper and desk, a wet bar with microwave, refrigerator, and coffeemaker, and two phones with data ports. Rates include continental breakfast. $$$.

Day's Inn Historic Downtown. 1300 Ponce de Leon Blvd.; (904) 824-3383; www.days inn.com. This is a good choice for those who want to stay in the historic area and prefer the amenities of a motor inn. It's the home of a Denny's Restaurant and Riley's Pub and is handy to sightseeing, shopping, other restaurants, and the historic area. Rooms have coffeemaker, hair dryer, 25-inch television with free HBO, and iron and ironing board. The big swimming pool is long enough for swimming serious laps. Ask about AAA and AARP discounts. $$–$$$.

Grand Villas at World Golf Village. 100 Front Nine Dr.; (904) 940-2000 or (800) 456-0009; www.bluegreenrentals.com. Nightly rentals are available at this one- and two-bedroom time-share resort. Each villa has a private patio and full kitchen. Swim in the heated outdoor pool, play volleyball, or take to the lighted tennis courts; stroll out the door and you're on the golf course. Ask about golf packages and priority reservations at twenty-five area courses. $$$.

Hampton Inn. 430 Hwy. A1A Beach Blvd.; (904) 471-4000 or (800) HAMPTON; www .elitehospitality.com/hampton. (**NOTE:** The 800 number can also be used to book Hampton Inns in the historic district, west of town near the outlet mall, and north of here on Vilano Beach.) This hotel is right on the snowy sands edging the Atlantic surf. Play beach volleyball, use the fitness center, swim in the pool, soak in the whirlpool, and enjoy a free continental breakfast each morning. Family and Jacuzzi suites are available. Ask about a microwave and refrigerator, and be sure to specify an ocean view. $$–$$$.

Holiday Inn. 860 Hwy. A1A Beach Blvd., St. Augustine Beach; (904) 471-2555 or (800) 626-7263; www.holiday-inn.com. Step out the door to the pool and, just beyond it, the Atlantic beach. This is the home of Crabbies Bar & Grill, open seasonally, and the year-round Beach Garden Restaurant. Room service is available. Shopping and additional restaurants are nearby. Kids stay and eat free. $$–$$$.

Penny Farthing Inn. 83 Cedar St.; (904) 824-2100 or (800) 395-1890; www.pennyfarthing inn.net. In this six-room inn on three floors, you can sleep in an elegant bedchamber with a private bath, fireplace, and whirlpool tub. Relax on the porch swing, or take a personalized bicycle tour. There's parking on-site—a plus because you can walk to historic attractions without worrying about a parking place. Rates include a full breakfast. $$–$$$.

St. Francis Inn. 279 St. George St.; (904) 824-6068 or (800) 824-6062; www.stfrancisinn .com. One of the oldest structures in town, dating to 1791, the inn is as handy to everything today as it was centuries ago. There are sixteen guest rooms with plenty of choices in size, location, and decor. Some rooms have a private balcony, fireplace, and/or whirlpool. The inn has a Mediterranean-style garden courtyard, sometimes with live music, a swimming pool, in-room phones and cable television, bicycles for guest use, and private parking. Guests get free admission to the St. Augustine Lighthouse and Museum. Included in the rates are the evening social and a buffet breakfast. $$–$$$.

World Golf Village Renaissance Resort. 500 South Legacy Trail; (904) 940-8000 or (888) 740-7020; www.renaissancehotels.com. A destination in itself, this plush resort is surrounded by 6,300 manicured acres dotted with two eighteen-hole championship golf courses designed by Jack Nicklaus and Arnold Palmer. The resort is inland, so this isn't a beach vacation, but it has great swimming pools, grounds, and activities as well as the golf, so bring the family. Dine in a variety of restaurants, or order from room service. Enjoy the billiards room, cigar room, twenty-four-hour health club and sauna, and a big gift shop; enroll the children in the kids' club. All units have in-room coffee, wet bar, refrigerator, two TVs, two phones, and hair dryer. Suites have balconies and microwaves. $$$.

ponte vedra beach

Today this area just north of St. Augustine is one of the most affluent areas of northeast Florida, home to millionaires and tony resorts. It has a fascinating history. During World War I, when minerals were mined from local sands for the war effort, the place was called Mineral City. The first golf course was built here in 1922 for the use of miners. During World War II, four German soldiers came ashore here from a submarine, carrying explosives and intent on sabotage. (They were caught before they did any damage.) A marker on the beach shows their landing place. On the sands of Pablo Beach in 1922, Jimmy Doolittle took off for San Diego, breaking a transcontinental air-speed record and earning the Distinguished Flying Cross. Since earliest explorations, the beauty of these beaches has attracted adventurers, hoteliers, and travelers in search of the solace of waved-washed sands. From St. Augustine, cross the bridge to Vilano Beach and follow scenic Highway A1A north to Ponte Vedra Beach.

where to go

Bicycling is the ideal way to see Flagler and St. Johns Counties with their endless acres of conservation areas and parks, Washington Oaks State Gardens, beaches, and designated bicycle routes. For a map of the bicycle trails, contact the Northeast Florida Regional Planning Council, 9143 Phillips Hwy., Suite 350, Jacksonville, FL 32256, and request *Bike Ways of Northeast Florida*. (904) 279-0880; www.nefrpc.org.

Guana River State Park. 2690 South Ponte Vedra Blvd.; (904) 825-5071; www.florida stateparks.org/guanariver. The park comprises a vast expanse of golden marshes, pine flatwoods, coastal strand habitat, and miles of beaches as flat as a mirror. One account by a Spanish historian leads today's researchers to think that these lands may have been the site of Ponce de Leon's first explorations in the sixteenth century. Fish in freshwater or salt, boat on the Guana and Tolomoto Rivers, swim and surf in the Atlantic, and hike or bike 9 miles of unpaved service roads. Bring your binoculars for the nature watching and a picnic lunch to spread on a beach blanket. The park is open 8 a.m. to sundown every day. State park fees apply.

where to stay

Ponte Vedra Inn & Club. 200 Ponte Vedra Blvd.; (904) 285-1111 or (800) 234-7842; www.pvresorts.com. This property has been dispensing excellence in hospitality since 1928. Stay in an ocean-view room or suite that has an oversize bathroom, robes for him and her, designer toiletries, twenty-four-hour room service, and nightly turndown service. In the morning you'll find the newspaper outside your door. The inn does a lot of conference business, but it's also a favorite for families or romantic getaways. Children ages four to twelve have their own programs June through Aug. The resort is best known for its two eighteen-hole golf courses, but there's also a sophisticated spa, a racquet club with fifteen Har-Tru courts, a business center with everything you'll need to stay in touch with the office, fishing, boating, a gym with individual Cybex stations, and four big oceanfront swimming pools. On the beach, kayaks, beach umbrellas, and beach chairs are available for rent. Dine in the elegant Florida Room, the rustic Outpost, or informally in the Golf Club or Surf Club. Have a drink in the Audubon Lounge, dance in the Seahorse Lounge, or have a frozen specialty drink at sundown in High Tides. Ask about packages. $$$$.

Sawgrass Marriott Resort. 1000 PGA Tour Blvd.; (904) 285-7777 or (800) 457-4653; www.sawgrassmarriott.com. Famed for its golf courses, this is a luxury resort by any standard, even if you don't go near the links. Luxuriate in the spa or swimming pools, hike or bicycle the sprawling grounds, and dine in a choice of casual or formal restaurants. Hotel rooms or spacious apartments are available in a wide range of prices and packages. $$$–$$$$.

east

day trip 01

east

>>> **the place for space:**
christmas, cape canaveral

Head east from Orlando on SR 50 and you'll be out of the traffic maelstrom by Christmas. It's no joke. There really is a Christmas, Florida, once just a quaint post office where people had their cards postmarked. Today it's quickly becoming a part of the Orlando crush, a greenspace and historic attraction. We've combined the communities from Titusville south through Merritt Island as one day trip known as Cape Canaveral, which is the home of Merritt Island National Wildlife Refuge, Kennedy Space Center, Cocoa Beach, and other close-clustered spots just east of Orlando via SR 50.

NOTE: *Before you go, you should be aware that the best beaches in the area for launch watching are Klondike, Floridana Beach, Canaveral National Seashore, Playalinda, and Sebastian Inlet. The best for lively beach action are Cocoa Beach, Satellite Beach, Indian Harbor Beach, and Melbourne Beach.*

christmas

During the Christmas season in 1837, as the Second Seminole Indian War raged in Florida, a force of 2,000 U.S. Army troops and the Alabama Volunteers established a supply depot in the pinewoods near this spot, handy to the St. Johns River. Most of them marched away to fight the Battle of Okeechobee on Christmas Day, but about eighty soldiers remained encamped here. By March the fighting had moved southward and the fort was no longer needed.

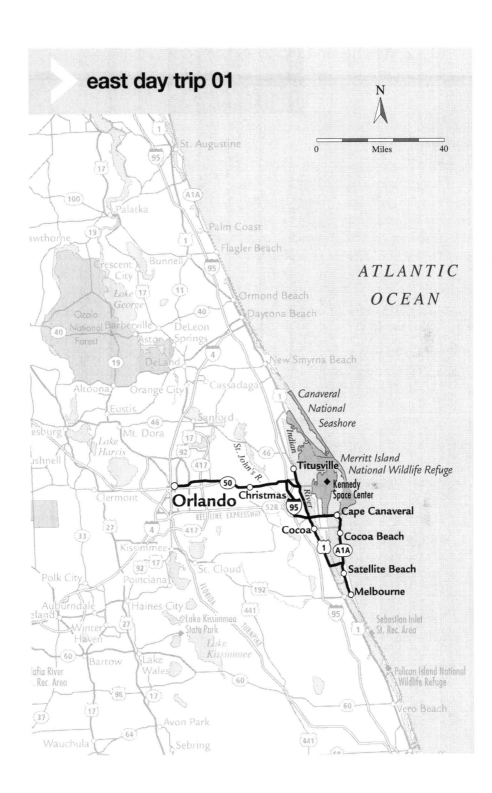

N

0   Miles   40

ATLANTIC

OCEAN

St. Augustine

Palatka

Palm Coast

awthorne

Flagler Beach

Crescent   Bunnell
City

Ormond Beach

Lake
George

Daytona Beach

Ocala
National Barberville   DeLeon
Forest   Aston Springs

New Smyrna Beach

DeLand

Altoona   Orange City   Cassadaga

Canaveral
National
Seashore

Eustis   Sanford

esburg   Mt. Dora   Merritt Island
National Wildlife Refuge

Lake
Harris

Titusville

St. John's R.

ushnell

Clermont

Orlando   Christmas   Kennedy
Space Center

Indian River

BEE LINE EXPRESSWAY   Cape Canaveral

Cocoa   Cocoa Beach

Kissimmee

Satellite Beach

Polk City   St. Cloud

Poinciana   Melbourne

Auburndale   Haines City

eland   Lake Kissimmee
State Park

Winter
Haven

Lake
Kissimmee

Sebastian Inlet
St. Rec. Area

afia River
. Rec. Area   Bartow   Lake
Wales

Pelican Island National
Wildlife Refuge

Vero Beach

Avon Park

Wauchula   Sebring

Although the fort was manned for less than four months, a small community grew up around it. Today centered on busy SR 50, Christmas has a Christmas tree that is lit all year, a manger scene, and a post office where you can mail letters and cards that are stamped with the Christmas postmark.

where to go

Fort Christmas Historical Park. Orange County Parks and Recreation Division, 4801 West Colonial Dr., Orlando; (407) 568-4149; www.orangecountyparks.net. Located 2 miles north of SR 50 on County Road 420, the park is free and fabulous—a real slice of history in a wooded setting where kids can run wild around the playground, and adults can picnic and relax or play tennis or basketball. Tour the fort, which houses an excellent museum. Stroll the grounds, where old Cracker homes, a school, and other historic buildings have been moved to save them from demolition. Covered picnic pavilions are available for rent by advance reservation. Admission is free. The park is open in the summer from 8 a.m. to 8 p.m. and in the winter from 8 a.m. to 6 p.m. The museum is open Tues through Sat 10 a.m. to 5 p.m. and Sun 1 to 5 p.m.

Jungle Adventures. 26205 East SR 50; (407) 568-2885 or (877) 424-2867; www.jungle adventures.com. Gators are raised for meat and hides on this working alligator farm. Take a jungle cruise for a look at gators in their natural environment, then stock up on frozen alligator meat in the gift shop. See exotic cats, walk the nature trail, see a replica of an early Spanish fort, take a guided tour of a sixteenth-century Seminole village, and see a wildlife show starring wolves, snakes, Florida panthers, and alligators. Adults $19.95, seniors $16.95, and $12.95 for children ages three to eleven. Open daily 9:30 a.m. to 5:30 p.m.

Orlando Wetlands Park. 25155 Wheeler Rd.; (407) 568-1706; www.cityoforlando.net/ public_works/wetlands. The Orlando Wetlands Park is an artificial wetlands built by the City of Orlando where you can relax and enjoy nature. The most popular activities include bird-watching, nature photography, jogging, and bicycling. Nature enthusiasts will be greeted by 1,650 acres of hardwood hammocks, marshes, and lakes. You'll find over 20 miles of roads and woodland trails crisscrossing the park. Open from Feb 1 to Nov 15 from sunrise to sunset. Admission is free.

Tosohatchee Wildlife Management Area. 3365 Taylor Creek Rd.; (407) 568-5893; http://myfwc.com/recreation/WMASites_Tosohatchee_index.htm. This wildlife manage-ment area covers 28,000 acres of wilderness that has been sculpted by fire and flood along the St. Johns River. Hike, bicycle the rugged trails, hunt or camp by permit, bring a horse to ride the trails, fish, or sit quietly to watch for wading and shorebirds, bobcats, gray foxes, gopher tortoises, owls, and other wildlife. Call ahead. Admission $3 per car.

cape canaveral

The communities of Cape Canaveral are lumped together because it's likely you'll stay in one community, shop and dine in many others, and sightsee in them all during the same trip(s). Melbourne is the chief city here, with a major airport. Cape Canaveral is the entire area, referring to the cape that juts out into the Atlantic Ocean. It is the home of Kennedy Space Center, Canaveral National Seashore, and Merritt Island National Wildlife Refuge. Port Canaveral has grown into the second-busiest cruise ship port in the nation.

To reach Cape Canaveral from Christmas, continue east on SR 50 (known as Colonial Drive in town and as Cheney Highway as it proceeds eastward), then go north or south on US 1 or I-95 to your destination. Canaveral National Seashore and Titusville are north; just about everything else in this Day Trip is south.

where to go

Ace of Hearts Ranch. 7400 Bridal Path Lane, Cocoa; (321) 638-0104; www.aceofhearts ranch.com. The ranch is an ecotourist's paradise. Call to see what's on the menu today: horseback rides on the beach, pony parties for little ones, a marshmallow roast, a rail ride along the river, or a wild airboat ride in the wetlands. In the petting zoo, make friends with Babe the pig, as well as chickens, ducks, and other critters. Prices are a la carte and vary according to the activity.

Airboat rides in the marshy uplands of the St. Johns River are available by reservation from Airboat Ecotours. (321) 631-2990 or (321) 638-9565.

Canaveral National Seashore. 212 South Washington Ave., Titusville; (321) 267-1110. This preserve is a 24-mile stretch of pristine beaches plus acres of wetlands, lagoons, dunes, and hammocks. To reach the visitor center, take exit 84A off I-95, then take SR 44 east to Highway A1A, then south for 10 miles. Playalinda, Klondike, and Apollo Beaches are part of this massive playland, which also has sites for hike-in or boat-in camping. Most people come here for a day at the beach, but there's much more for the angler, nature lover, bird-watcher, backpacker, kayaker, and hiker. Note that part of the Seashore is called Mosquito Lagoon for good reason. Bring plenty of bug dope. If a stiff wind is blowing, though, you may not need it, especially right on the beach. Some beaches are closed in turtle-nesting season, and prohibitions are strictly enforced. Don't trespass. Admission to the beaches is $5 per carload.

Cocoa Village. 430 Delannoy Ave., Cocoa; (321) 631-9075; www.cocoavillage.com. Located on SR 520 along the Indian River, the village is the historic heart of a coastal community that has grown west to the subdivisions and malls. Stroll brick sidewalks past old shops and former mercantiles that have been turned into smart boutiques and restaurants.

The streets of the old village often ring with festivals, but street entertainers might be here on ordinary days, too. Shop for jewelry, clothing, gifts, collectibles, beads, books, and arts galore. Dine in one of the restaurants, and visit the specialty shops for pastries and gourmet foods to take home. If you write ahead for maps and information, you'll receive discount coupons. Make an entire day of it by adding a lunch, brunch, or dinner cruise aboard the Cocoa Belle. Reservations: (321) 302-0544 or (321) 454-7414; www.islandboatlines.com.

A Day Away Kayak Tours. 3532 Royal Oak Dr., Titusville; (321) 268-2655; www.nbbd .com/kayaktours. A Day Away offers kayak trips on most central Florida waterways, including the Mosquito Lagoon, the Indian River Lagoon, and the Econlockhatchee and St. Johns Rivers. See all kinds of wildlife including dolphins, manatees, alligators, and dozens of bird species while paddling on tranquil waters through protected state and federal lands.

Kennedy Space Center Visitor Complex. Mail code DNPS, Kennedy Space Center, FL 32899; (321) 449-4444 or (866) 737-5235; www.kennedyspacecenter.com. From Orlando, take SR 528 east to SR 407 North and then SR 405 East. The route to the complex is well marked, so follow the signs. The moment you enter, look at the day's schedule so that you can make the best use of your time. There's more here than can be done in one day, especially if you're a serious space follower.

The Astronaut Encounter is usually held three times a day, depending on the season, and it's your chance to chat with a real astronaut. Take one of the bus tours to see where launches take place, view the IMAX and 3-D movies, photograph the Rocket Garden, walk through the full-size replica Space Shuttle, and watch assembly of the next batch of equipment slated for the International Space Station. If the children get restless, take them to the Play Dome for some high-voltage fun. Tickets are $38 for adults and $28 for children ages three to eleven.

Have lunch in one of the restaurants, or reserve well ahead to participate in the "Dine with an Astronaut" program. It's not offered every day, but for $22.99 for adults and $15.99 for children (in addition to the regular admission), you get a big meal, a special dessert called Chocolate Liftoff (complete with a chocolate space shuttle), an autographed souvenir, and the company of an astronaut, who will tell about his or her adventures in space.

Shop the gift store for one of the best selections of space souvenirs and educational space material on the planet. Real mission briefings are given hourly at the Launch Status Center. This is a living, working space center, always different and always in the news.

For $21 more per adult and $15 more per child, get the NASA Up-Close guided tour that includes stops at the A/B Camera Stop and the International Space Station Center, or choose the Cape Canaveral: Then and Now tour.

Merritt Island National Wildlife Refuge. The visitor center is 4 miles east of Titusville on SR 402; (321) 861-0667; http://merrittisland.fws.gov. In the shadows and smoke of giant rockets, a 140,000-acre wilderness is habitat to one of the largest and most diverse communities of common, rare, endangered, and threatened species in the United States, plus myriad plant communities of the forests, dunes, and wetlands. Start with orientation at the visitor center, where rangers and volunteers steer you right. Then take a self-guided drive along the one-way, 7-mile Black Point Wildlife Drive before striking off on foot on the 5-mile trail, complete with boardwalks and observation platforms. The visitor center is open Mon through Fri 8 a.m. to 4:30 p.m. and weekends 9 a.m. to 5 p.m. For safety reasons, the refuge is sometimes off-limits during space launches. Admission is free.

U.S. Astronaut Hall of Fame. 6225 Vectorspace Blvd., Titusville; (321) 269-6100; www .kennedyspacecenter.com/visitKSC/attractions/fame.asp. This is as much a must-see for space groupies as the Space Center itself. The heroes of the space frontier are honored here in displays and photographs, and you'll get a taste of space flight in a simulator. Drive the Shuttle Lander, ride a Mission to Mars, tour a full-size replica of the Space Shuttle, test your reflexes in a Mercury capsule, and see how many Gs you can take. Admission is included with general admission to the Space Center. The gift shop has serious space souvenirs, gifts, and books, and you can eat in the Cosmic Cafe. Hours are 9 a.m. to 5 p.m. daily, with no one admitted after 4 p.m. Hours may be extended in high season.

This is also the home of U.S. Space Camp Florida, where children and young adults can experience a five-day camp or children and their parents can plug into a parent-child weekend. For information on aviation programs, visit www.dogfite.com; for space camp details go to www.spacecamp.com.

Warbird Air Museum. 6600 Tico Rd., Titusville; (321) 268-1941; www.vacwarbirds.org. The museum showcases military aircraft from the two world wars, Korea, and Vietnam. You'll see the Valiant Air Command's fine collection of aviation memorabilia, including uniforms, gear, and arts. Many of the museum volunteers actually flew or worked on these birds, so don't be afraid to ask questions. The gift shop is well stocked with aviation gifts and collectibles. Hours are 9 a.m. to 5 p.m. except Thanksgiving, Christmas, and New Year's Day. Admission is $12 for adults and $5 for children age twelve or under. Military and seniors get in for $10.

where to shop

The Irish Shop. 818 East New Haven Ave., Melbourne; (321) 723-0122; www.the-irish-shop.com. The shop is located two doors down from Meg O'Malley's Irish Pub. Ask the Irish staff here about your favorite collectibles, Irish gifts and arts, and keepsake jewelry. They can even book you on a trip to the Emerald Isle. Hours vary seasonally, but it's generally open daily, except Sun, 10 a.m. to 5 p.m.

Ron Jon Surf Shop. 3850 South Banana River Blvd., Cocoa Beach; (321) 799-8888; www .ronjons.com. Ron's is a Florida icon, a must-see place to stop and shop along Highway A1A. Located 12 miles east of well-marked exits off I-95, the shop complex spreads over

a natural experience

One of my family's favorite day trips in Central Florida involves a visit to one of the few undeveloped beaches on Florida's east coast, Playalinda Beach in Canaveral National Seashore. The beach lies on the north side of the Kennedy Space Center, and the gantries of the Space Shuttle stand guard like two silent sentinels. They're the only works of man that are visible from this long strip of sand.

*After a morning spent sunning, swimming, and bodysurfing, a drive along a waterfront road in the **Merritt Island National Wildlife Refuge** follows. Their headquarters is 4 miles east of Titusville on SR 402, and their phone number is (321) 861-0667. Alligators, spoonbills, herons, the occasional otter or bald eagle, and all sorts of other spectacular wildlife are featured during one of these drives along the shore of the Mosquito Lagoon or the Indian River Lagoon. For manatee watching we drive to the viewing platform at the Haulover Canal. At times dozens of these homely but lovable creatures are visible from this boardwalk.*

*In spite of the snacks we've been ingesting, by now we're usually ready for some more serious feeding, and in the Titusville area we like one of two places. **Dixie Crossroads** (1475 Garden St., Titusville; 321-268-5000) features some of the best seafood going. The grilled rock shrimp are my personal favorite—they're to die for.*

*Dixie Crossroads always has long lines on weekends, although they now suggest reservations. If it's too crowded, we might head to **El Leoncito** (3800 South Washington Ave., Titusville; 321-267-1159). They feature Cuban and Mexican cuisine and seldom have a long wait, a feature that hungry humans appreciate. When I visit here I always have some black-bean soup and platanos. If you don't have to drive, you may want to sip on a margarita. Two will cross your eyes!*

two acres—a galaxy of goods for the beach or surf. Stock up on everything from floats to swim suits, clogs, sunblock, T-shirts, surfboards, and beach balls. While the original is in New Jersey and clones are popping up all over the world, including Orlando and Fort Lauderdale, this is still Florida's first. Like the beach, it's open twenty-four hours a day, seven days a week.

where to eat

Corky Bell's Seafood. 4885 North US 1, Cocoa; (321) 636-1392. Located between Cocoa and Titusville, Corky's is an old Florida landmark, delightfully ramshackle, where the deep fryer reigns and vegetarians find slim pickings. Seafood platters are bigger than

Neptune's chariot. The rib-eye steak dinner with baked potato, onion rings, hush puppies, and coleslaw is a belly buster. Waits can be long, especially on Friday and Saturday nights, and they don't take reservations. $$.

The Cove. 1462 Hwy. A1A, Satellite Beach; (321) 777-2683; www.thecoveonA1A.com. The Cove has been a local favorite for half a century. Bring the whole family for wholesome dining, dancing, and fun. The restaurant is best known for its ribs, crab legs, and prime rib, but there are also seafood dishes, steaks, chops, salads, chicken, and a kids' menu. Dine inside or outdoors on the patio. $$–$$$.

Dixie Crossroads. 1475 Garden St., Titusville; (321) 268-5000; www.dixiecrossroads .com. Enormously popular, Dixie Crossroads always has long lines on Friday nights and Saturday and Sunday afternoons. You can buy fish food and feed the tilapia while you wait. Once inside, try the house specialty, broiled rock shrimp. The owner invented the machine that cleans these succulent morsels. Prior to this invention, rock shrimp had no commercial value at all. All the shrimp, mullet, and crab are caught locally. Reservations are suggested for those busy times. Open daily, Sun through Thurs 11 a.m. to 9 p.m., Fri and Sat 11 a.m. to 10 p.m. $$.

The Dove. 1790 Hwy. A1A, Satellite Beach; (321) 777-5817; www.thedoverestaurant.com. This local icon is south of Patrick Air Force Base, and getting here on the seaside highway is part of the fun. The menu has an Italian accent with forays into the French Riviera. Your meal starts with a surprise appetizer of pasta e fagioli, so prepare yourself for a filling feast. Order a main course, and a salad will soon appear. Enjoy one of the veal dishes, chicken, fresh seafood, or a steak. A tangy lemon liqueur appears between courses. Open for lunch and dinner daily except Sunday. Reservations are recommended. $$–$$$.

Durango Oak Fire Steakhouse. 3455 Cheney Hwy., Titusville; (321) 264-2499. Located in the Space Shuttle Inn, the Durango does seafood as well as it does Colorado prime steaks. The oak fire is always burning, so you can order a grilled quesadilla, strip steak, porterhouse, top sirloin, bacon-wrapped shrimp, Campfire Chicken, and other fire-seared treats. There's also meatloaf, pasta, main-dish salads, and a list of side dishes for those who prefer to order a la carte. At lunch try one of the mammoth sandwiches with a mountain of seasoned fries. For dessert, tackle the Chocolate Avalanche or apple cobbler. Open daily for lunch and dinner. $–$$.

El Leoncito. 4280 South Washington Ave., Titusville; (321) 267-1159 http://elleoncito restaurant.com. This restaurant serves both Mexican and Cuban specialties and is a popular spot for locals. Cuban dishes are served with rice, black beans, and plaintains. A live mariachi band is featured the last Tuesday of the month from 6 to 9 p.m. Try a margarita if you don't have to drive! Open Sun through Thurs, 11 a.m. to 10 p.m., and Fri and Sat until 11 p.m. $$.

Gregory's Steak & Seafood Grille. 900 North Atlantic Ave., Cocoa Beach; (321) 799-2557; www.gregorysonthebeach.com. Certified Angus beef stars at this popular hangout, where Groucho's Comedy Club upstairs has 'em rolling in the aisles every Thurs at 9 p.m. Make an evening of it. Have a drink from the full bar, then dine on a big steak, cooked to order, or the best in fresh local and flown-in seafood. Select the right wine from a comprehensive list. Open daily 5 to 10:30 p.m. $$–$$$.

Pig & Whistle. 801 North Atlantic Ave., Cocoa Beach; (321) 799-0724. Located in the Galleria, this is a real English pub, complete with dartboard, beer on tap, fish-and-chips, and all your favorite pub grub, as well as hearty meat-and-potatoes fare. Play video games or pool. There's a full bar. Open daily 11 a.m. to 2 a.m. $–$$.

Punjab. 285 Cocoa Beach Causeway, White Rose Center, Cocoa Beach; (321) 799-4696. The Punjab serves Indian cuisine, including clay-oven specialties. Dishes are cooked to taste, with as much heat as you like or no heat at all. Open Mon through Sat 11 a.m. to 2:30 p.m. and for dinner nightly, except Sun, from 5 p.m. $–$$.

Roberto's Little Havana. 26 North Orlando Ave., Cocoa Beach; (321) 784-1868 or (866) 339-7042; http://robertoslittlehavana.com. This spot specializes in authentic Cuban sandwiches, main dishes, desserts, and coffees; they even serve Hatvey Cuban beer. Open daily for breakfast, lunch, and dinner. $–$$.

Rum Runners. 695 North Atlantic Ave. (Highway A1A), Cocoa Beach; (321) 868-2020. This is a must for visitors who like to party hearty in a good-times setting. Start with one of the fifteen rip-roaring specialty rum drinks. The clam chowder is a house specialty. Order from a long list of seafood, including the catch of the day, fresh crab cakes, frog legs, conch fritters, and shrimp. There's also chicken, pasta, and baby back ribs. Open every day 11 a.m. to 2 a.m. $–$$.

The Surf Restaurant. 2 South Atlantic Ave. (Highway A1A), Cocoa Beach; (321) 783-2401. The Surf gives you three eateries for the price of one. The big complex also contains **Fisher's Seafood Bar and Grill** and **Rusty's Seafood and Oyster Bar** (a clone is located in Port Canaveral in a picturesque setting in the shadow of the cruise ships). Show up early for happy hour and early-bird specials, or linger late over a lobster feast, fresh fish cooked to order, chicken, or a steak. Lunch on weekdays is a boffo buffet. Bring the kids, who will get their own menu. Hours vary seasonally, so call ahead. $–$$$.

where to stay

Best Western Space Shuttle Inn. 3455 Cheney Hwy., Titusville; (321) 269-9100 or (800) 523-7654; http://bwspaceshuttleinn.com. This property boasts a steakhouse and lounge, heated swimming pool, sauna, video game room, playground, free HBO, a fitness park with a fishing lake, picnic area with gazebo, guest laundry, and complimentary continental breakfast. Also offered are many creative packages that include nature tours, space attractions, or a casino cruise. Port Canaveral is only thirty minutes away, so it's also an affordable place to stay before or after a cruise. $$.

Casa Coquina Bed and Breakfast. 4010 Coquina Ave., Titusville; (321) 268-4653 or (877) 684-8341; http://casacoquina.com. A European boutique–style eclectic mansion built during the roaring '20s, furnished with treasures from around the world. Rooms include full breakfast and a complimentary happy hour with beer, wine, and popcorn. Stroll through the butterfly garden, watch the Space Shuttle launch from the second-floor deck overlooking the river, or sit under the 10-foot iron gazebo and stargaze. $$–$$$.

Clarion Hotel. 260 East Merritt Island Causeway (SR 520), Merritt Island; (800) -584-1482; www.clarionspacecoast.com. This hotel is everything a visitor could want in a home base for exploring the Space Coast or for a pre- or post-cruise stay near Port Canaveral. The courtyard is surrounded by tropical greenery and centered by a swimming pool. Rooms have a coffeemaker, and king rooms also have a microwave and refrigerator. The hotel has its own restaurant, lounge, tennis courts, and fitness center. $$–$$$.

Doubletree Oceanfront Hotel. 2080 North Atlantic Ave., Cocoa Beach; (321) 783-9222, (800) 222-TREE, or (800) 552-3224; www.cocoabeachdoubletree.com. The Doubletree is the perfect pied-à-terre for a stay along the Space Coast. Book an oceanfront room with a private balcony, or splurge on the concierge floor, where special perks include a lounge with free breakfast and snacks. A Doubletree trademark is the freshly baked chocolate-chip cookies that everyone receives on check-in. The hotel has an oceanfront lounge and restaurant serving Mediterranean cuisine, brick-oven pizza, and fresh seafood. Take the Beeline Expressway to where it turns south and becomes Highway A1A; the hotel is 5 miles south, on your left. $$$.

Radisson Hotel at the Port. 8701 Astronaut Blvd.; (321) 784-0000 or (888) 201-1718; www.radisson.com/capecanaveralfl. This is a good choice for space travelers, cruisers, a romantic weekend, or a business trip. It isn't on the ocean, but it's only a mile from the home port of the Disney ships and has a big outdoor heated swimming pool. Two-room whirlpool suites have one or two king-size beds with a queen-size sofa sleeper. Two-bedroom suites have microwave, refrigerator, wet bar, and 32-inch television. Eat in the restaurant or order from room service. $$–$$$.

Royal Oak Resort & Golf Club. 2150 Country Club Dr., Titusville; (321) 269-4500 or (800) 884-2150; http://royaloakgolfresort.com. Stay in a country club setting and play the championship eighteen-hole Dick Wilson golf course. The club is the winter home of many golf professionals, and the course provides a lovely stroll through rolling hills past sparkling lakes. Every room has a coffeemaker and refrigerator. Get a package that includes accommodations, eighteen holes of golf including greens fee and cart, a second round for the cart fee only, advance tee time reservations, and daily club storage and cleaning. Meals are served in the Terrace Room; a snack bar is halfway around the course. The resort also has an Olympic-size pool, driving range, and practice greens. $$–$$$.

southeast

day trip 01

southeast

sebastian inlet

Growth in Florida is spurting alarmingly, but developers and tourist hordes haven't yet over-run this stretch of the state. The community of Sebastian has parks, marinas, and yacht brokerages that lend a salty flavor and plenty of waterfront on the Intracoastal Waterway, the inlet, and the Atlantic. From Orlando, go east on SR 50 or the Beeline to I-95, then south to the Sebastian exit.

where to go

Mel Fisher's Treasure Museum. 1322 US 1, Sebastian; (772) 589-9875; www.melfisher .com. The museum houses many of the treasures that illustrate why this is known as the Treasure Coast. Unknown numbers of Spanish galleons sank on reefs just offshore, and their bounty continues to wash ashore. View a movie on treasure hunting, take a guided tour, and shop for real treasures from real wrecks. Open daily 10 a.m. to 5 p.m., Sun noon to 5 p.m. Admission is charged.

Pelican Island National Wildlife Refuge. On the Indian River Lagoon between Sebas-tian and Wabasso; (772) 562-3909; www.fws.gov/pelicanisland. Here, at the world's first national wildlife refuge, you may see loggerhead turtles, manatees, wood storks, green sea turtles, and bird life galore. This entire area is prime for birding, especially during spring and

southeast day trip 01

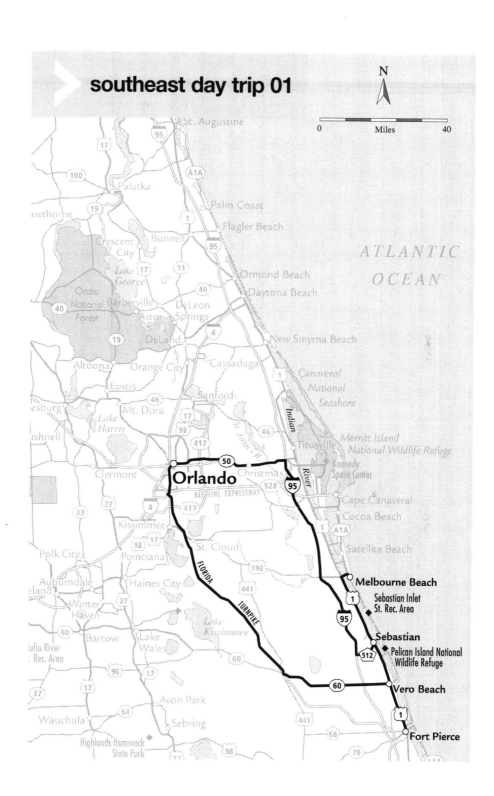

fall migrations. The Web site will tell all you need to know about visiting the refuge via boat tours.

River Queen **cruises.** 1660 Indian River Dr., Sebastian; (772) 589-6161 or (888) 755-6161; www.sebastianriverqueencruises.com. Enjoy narrated sightseeing and nature-watch trips on the Sebastian and Indian Rivers, usually at 10 a.m., noon, and 4:30 p.m. Bird-spotting is excellent, and you may also see alligators, manatees, and bottlenose dolphins. Drinks and snacks are available onboard. Dolphin-watch cruises last two and three hours; a sunset cruise that includes Pelican Island lasts about ninety minutes. Prices are $20 to $28 for adults, $12 for children ages three to ten; seniors get a $1 discount. Reservations are highly recommended.

Sebastian Inlet State Park. 9700 South Hwy. A1A, Melbourne Beach; (321) 984-4852 for park information; (800) 326-3521 for camping reservations; www.floridastateparks .org/sebastianinlet. This park is a favorite with surfers, offering some of the best combers in the East. It's also a great beach, park, and fishing area and the home to a museum housing real Spanish treasure. Arrive by car, or buzz over in your boat and dock at the marina. Bring a picnic lunch, everything you need for the beach, and your camera, and make a day of it.

fishing sebastian inlet

Sebastian Inlet is likely the best fishing hole covered in this book, and lots of anglers take advantage of it. Catwalks on top of both the north and south jetties provide access for anglers, and when a "run" is on, they are lined up in force.

Some of the fish commonly caught at the inlet include redfish, snapper, floun-der, crevalle jacks, bluefish, Spanish mackerel, and others, but the most popular is undoubtedly the snook, and the largest is the tarpon.

While you may want to stop by just to watch, local tackle shops dispense bait and advice and may even rent tackle so you can try your luck yourself. Imagine the fish story you'll have if you hook a one-hundred-pound tarpon!

During September and October huge numbers of mullet come through the lagoon system, and nearly every other creature that lives in or near the water preys on them. Pelicans, terns, and gulls will be diving, large numbers of big fish will be feeding, and the poor mullets will be trying to escape as best they can. This is the activity peak of the year, so if you're nearby, it's definitely a good time to visit.

Sebastian Inlet lies between Melbourne and Vero Beach on Highway A1A.

In 1715 a Spanish treasure fleet wrecked off these shores, and a treasure museum, sparkling with booty, now stands on the site where the shipwreck survivors camped. Little could be salvaged at the time, but bits of treasure continued to wash ashore for centuries afterward. Three glorious miles of sands and dunes are set aside for swimming, surfing, snorkeling, and scuba diving (no spearfishing). In June and July take a ranger-led moonlight walk to watch turtles lay their eggs. A concession near the beach picnic area sells basic items and serves breakfast and lunch daily. Fees apply for tours and services, and there's a small park entry fee. The park is open during daylight hours.

Skydive Sebastian. 400 West Airport Rd., Sebastian; (800) 399-JUMP; www.skydiveseb .com. Everyone is welcome, from the merely curious to the experienced parachutist. If you're a novice but want to try a jump, you can be strapped to a seasoned diver and float to earth without a care. Skydive University is on-site, training skydivers at all levels. Generally open during daylight hours; make an appointment for jumps.

where to eat and stay

The Key West Inn and Capt. Hiram's Resort. 1580 US 1, Sebastian; (772) 589-4345 or (800) 833-0555; www.hirams.com. Located on the Sebastian waterfront, Capt. Hiram's has indoor dining with weather control, or you can sit outdoors on the deck overlooking the river. There's live music after dark, so make an evening of cocktails, dinner, and dancing into the late hours. Seafood is cooked your way, including charcoal-grilled. Sumptuous sandwiches are popular at lunch. Peel-and-eat shrimp is available by the pound or half pound. Real Maryland crab soup shares the menu with crab cakes, shrimp, steaks, mussels, scallops, and chicken. The restaurant is open for lunch and dinner and has a delightful gift shop. The Bahamian Sandbar is right on the beach.

The inn offers rooms with balconies overlooking the water. Take a suite or efficiency apartment; rates include breakfast. From I-95, take exit 69; travel east on CR 512 for 7.5 miles to US 1, then left for another 0.5 mile. $$.

vero beach

According to one rating guide, little Vero Beach is one of the "Best Little Towns in America." From Sebastian, follow US 1 south to Vero Beach. (For a loop back to Orlando, take SR 60 west to the Florida Turnpike and follow the pike north to Orlando. Just off the turnpike is a rest stop with picnic tables and a hiking path to Blue Cypress Lake.) Along the shore are end-of-the-world resorts. In town, find upscale shops and smart dining.

where to go

Environmental Learning Center. 255 Live Oak Dr. off CR 510, near the Wabasso Bridge; (772) 589-5050 for the center; (772) 589-6711 for the Riding-Jackson house; www.elcweb

.org. Visit the butterfly garden. Walk the boardwalk through a mangrove forest and look for coon oysters. Ask at the visitor center about canoe trips and workshops. The home of poet Laura Riding-Jackson is on the grounds. It's a fine example of practical, homespun Florida "Cracker" design. The center is open daily during daylight hours except Monday. The home is open Tues through Fri 10 a.m. to 4 p.m., Sat 10 a.m. to 4 p.m., Sun 1 to 4 p.m. Admission is free.

Harbor Branch Oceanographic Institute's Ocean Discovery Center. 5600 US 1 North, Fort Pierce; (772) 465-2400, ext. 688; www.fau.edu/hboi. This is a serious research facility, not a tourist attraction, which makes for exciting discovery and participation. The center is the public gateway to Harbor Branch Oceanographic Institute. It houses interactive exhibits, small aquaria, a video theater, and other displays exploring the marine environment and depicting the research efforts of the institute. The exhibit continually evolves to give visitors a close-up look at the emerging technologies used by the marine research community. Open Mon to Fri 10 a.m. to 5 p.m., Sat 10 a.m. to 2 p.m. Admission is free but donations are welcomed.

Indian River Citrus Museum. 2140 Fourteenth Ave.; (772) 770-2263; www.veroheritage .org/CitrusMuseum.html. This museum remembers the pioneers who made a living by planting the citrus groves that are still the backbone of this area's agriculture. The words "Indian River Fruit" will be more meaningful after you've seen early tools and memorabilia from a bygone era. Open Tues through Fri 10 a.m. to 4 p.m. Donations are appreciated.

McKee Botanical Garden. 350 South US 1; (772) 794-0601; www.mckeegarden.org. Located just south of Indian River Boulevard, the garden has been here since 1932, when a family established a "jungle garden" in a true tropical hammock. They planted exotics from all over the world, but interest faded when flashier attractions came to the Sunshine State. The garden was closed for almost twenty years before it was resurrected in 2001. Hurray for its comeback! Start with the fifteen-minute video, which includes some charming 1930s footage. Walk quiet trails to see vestiges of the Florida that used to be, on your own or with a guide, then stop in the cafe for lunch or a snack. Shop the gift shop for souvenirs, pottery, and unique gardening goodies. Hours are 10 a.m. to 5 p.m. Tues through Sat and noon to 5 p.m. Sun. Admission is $7 for adults, $6 for seniors, and $4 for children ages five to twelve.

Riverside Theatre. 3250 Riverside Park Dr.; (772) 231-6990 or (800) 445-6745; www.river sidetheatre.com. This is the only professional theater on the Treasure Coast. Two stages present more than 250 performances each year, so check ahead to see what will be playing during your visit. Musicals, drama, comedy, and children's theater are on the menu.

where to shop

Artists Guild Gallery. 44 Royal Palm Pointe; (772) 299-1234; http://artistsguildgalleryvero beach.com. The Artists Guild Gallery is a cooperative gallery, with a membership of many diverse artists. Receptions are held the first Friday of every month. Classes in several mediums are offered in the gallery by guild member artists. Artists' work is refreshed at least monthly, so there are always new works of art to be seen. Receptions and viewings are free and open to the public. Hours are Wed through Fri 10 a.m. to 3 p.m., Sat 10 a.m. to 2 p.m.

The Outlets at Vero Beach. SR 60 at I-95; (772) 770-6097; www.verobeachoutlets.com. This is one of a chain of outlet malls known for big bargains on brand-name goods. Featured are Oneida, Springmaid, Wamsutta, BOSE, Book Warehouse, Remington, Dooney & Bourke, Zales, Hush Puppies, Dexter, Bass, Polo Ralph Lauren, Versace, Liz Claiborne, and many more, plus a sumptuous food court. Hours are 9 a.m. to 8 p.m. Mon through Sat and 11 a.m. to 6 p.m. Sun. Closed Easter, Thanksgiving, and Christmas.

where to stay

Disney's Vero Beach Resort. CR 510 at Highway A1A; (800) 500-3990; www.dvc.disney. go.com. This is pure Disney magic, set on a brown sugar–sand beach. Have breakfast with Goofy any Saturday morning. Swim in the big pool. Take part in planned activities. Dine in the Green Cabin Room, where you can order from the regular or appetizer menu 3 to 10 p.m. Live entertainment is offered seven nights a week, so linger over drinks and coffee. Elegant dinners are also served at Sonya's Restaurant; the casual Shutters serves breakfast, lunch, and dinner. Suites are actually time-shares, available for rent by the night. $$$.

Driftwood Resort. 3150 Ocean Dr.; (772) 231-0550; www.thedriftwood.com. Built entirely from ocean-washed timbers and planks, this hotel houses some beautiful art objects, antiques, and artifacts in a fascinating setting. The resort is located directly on the Atlantic Ocean amidst tropical landscaping. Choose a villa decorated in authentic period furnishings. Enjoy swimming pools, private Jacuzzis, and barbecue grills. Casual dining available either inside or poolside at Waldo's Open Air Deck. $$–$$$.

Holiday Inn. 3384 Ocean Dr.; (772) 231-2300 or (888) 897-0084. Take an oceanfront suite with wet bar, microwave, toaster, and refrigerator or a king room facing the ocean or pool. Dine in the prestigious Treasure Coast Grill or informally on the pool deck. Enjoy live music in the Treasure Coast Pub. All rooms have refrigerators, coffeemakers, and a free copy of *USA Today* every weekday. $$–$$$.

Vero Beach Inn Resort on the Beach. 4700 North Hwy. A1A; (772) 231-1600 or (800) 227-8615; www.verobeachinn.com. This is a good choice for "doing" Vero because it's on the pristine sand beach as well as handy to golf courses, tennis, water sports, and scuba diving. Book a double or king room, junior suite, or two-bedroom suite. Boogie boards, ironing boards, microwaves, and refrigerators are available to rent. There's no charge for the coffeemaker, hair dryer, pool towels, and iron. Swim in the spacious free-form pool, bubble in the hot tub, or run barefoot into the surf. The inn's restaurant serves breakfast, lunch, and dinner overlooking the ocean. $–$$$.

day trip 02

southeast

st. cloud

Beginning in the 1870s, soldiers who had served in the Civil War drifted into Central Florida to settle down on ranches or to cluster in small towns. St. Cloud retains some of the "cow town" flavor of those early years. Kissimmee and St. Cloud share one convention and visitor bureau, but it's rare to find St. Cloud mentioned in travel guides. That's because Walt Disney bought 50 square miles of land just west of Kissimmee, and most growth sprawled in that direction. St. Cloud, well to the east, plays a distant second fiddle, but that is just fine with most folks there.

At St. Cloud you can still find the Florida your grandparents saw when they came south in a pre-Disney era. Stroll the old downtown area to peek into boutiques, antiques shops, and cozy eateries. From Orlando take the St. Cloud exit off the Florida Turnpike South and head east on US 192. Stroll or drive the area from Tenth to Twelfth Streets on New York and Pennsylvania Avenues to find the best antiques shopping and offbeat dining.

where to go and eat

Forever Florida and the Crescent J Ranch. 4755 North Kenansville Rd.; (407) 957-9794, (866) 85-4EVER; www.foreverflorida.com. This massive 4,700-acre working cattle ranch and nature preserve honors the memory of the founder's son, who died of Hodgkin's disease when he was a teenager. While in the hospital, he shared his dream of preserving

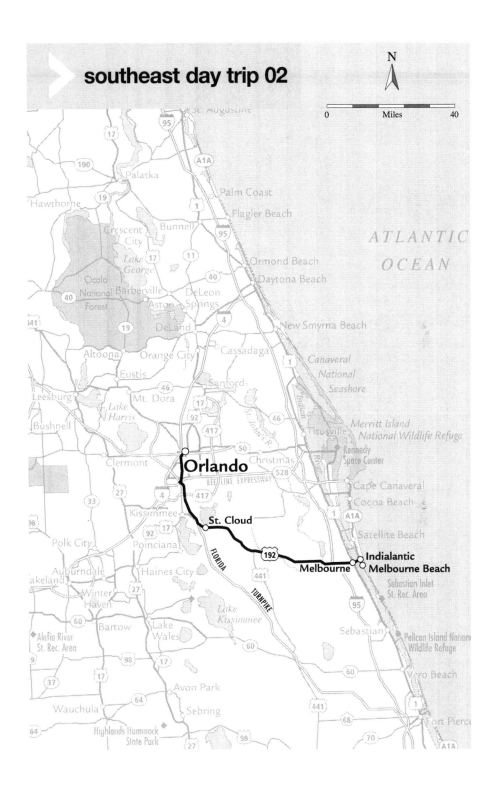

southeast day trip 02

N

0   Miles   40

the area next to the ranch as a nature refuge, and his father, Dr. William Broussard, has made that dream a reality. Take a nature tour. See ranch and farm animals up close. Take a bicycle or horseback tour. Eat native Florida foods in the Cypress Restaurant, then relax in a rocker on the veranda or, if the day is cool, warm up next to the stone fireplace. Shop for gifts and souvenirs, or book a coach or covered-wagon tour. In the Bio Park, nature species including the red wolf, otter, and Florida panther have a refuge. Activities are priced a la carte. Call for reservations and information.

melbourne

Even though it's part of the Space Coast tourism orbit, Melbourne is much more than rockets. It's the site of an international airport that is a good alternative to flying into Orlando and is a major community with its own identity. To reach Melbourne from St. Cloud, go southeast on US 192.

where to go

Archie Carr National Wildlife Refuge. 1300 Hwy. A1A, Melbourne Beach; (772) 562-3909; www.fws.gov/archiecarr. This refuge protects one of the best places in the Western Hemisphere for loggerhead turtles to nest. Call to see if any ranger-led excursions are planned during your visit. The refuge also offers spectacular bird-watching. It's open every day during daylight hours. Free admission.

Brevard Art Museum. 1463 Highland Ave.; (321) 242-0737; www.brevardartmuseum.org. The museum collects, displays, and interprets all aspects of the visual arts, Educational programming is at the core of the Brevard Art Museum's mission. They offer an extensive range of programs designed to appeal to the community. It's the only visual arts museum in Brevard County. Children and adults now have the opportunity to study and create art in the Museum School at the Renee Foosaner Education Center. Admission is $5 for adults, $3 for seniors, and $2 for children and students. Open Tues through Sat 10 a.m. to 5 p.m. and Sun 1 to 5 p.m. Closed Monday and major holidays.

Brevard Zoo. 8225 North Wickham Rd.; (321) 254-WILD; www.brevardzoo.com. The zoo is home to more than 400 animals representing 109 species from around the world. In the free-flight aviary, you'll see cockatoos, lorikeets, and a laughing kookaburra. In natural-appearing habitats see dingoes, red kangaroos, wallabies, llamas, and giant anteaters. Weather permitting, take a guided kayak tour of the zoo's wetlands area for $10 additional. Also extra is a ride on the train, and you'll need a few dollars to buy nectar to hand-feed the birds. Kids love the Paws-On learning center. Bring a picnic lunch (tables are provided), or eat in the snack bar. Admission is $12.50 for adults, $11.50 for seniors, and $9.50 for children ages two to twelve. Open daily 9:30 a.m. to 5 p.m. Closed some holidays, so call ahead.

where to shop

Orchid Beach Trading Company. 826 East New Haven; (321) 723-8008. This shop carries sunny and smart beachwear, casual resort togs, and cool, comfortable cottons for everyday wear. Open daily 9 a.m. to 5 p.m., Sun noon to 5 p.m.

Super Flea and Farmers' Market. Located off I-95 at exit 72 in Melbourne; (321) 242-9124; www.superfleamarket.com. More than 900 booths sell fresh produce and everything else under the sun, from shoes to sunbonnets. Choose from a variety of vendors in the food court, where beer and wine are also sold. There's plenty of parking in the ten-acre lot. Open Fri through Sun, rain or shine, 9 a.m. to 4 p.m.

where to eat

Bonefish Willy's Riverfront Grille. 2459 Pineapple Ave.; (321) 253-8888; www.bonefish willys.com. This spot offers a great view of the river, whether you're indoors or outside on the deck. Seafood is the star of the culinary show here, but landlubbers can choose beef or chicken. The beer is cold and the fritters crusty. Dress in casual resort duds, and enjoy the laid-back atmosphere. Open Mon through Sat 11 a.m. to 10 p.m., and Sun 11 a.m. to 9 p.m. $$.

Chart House. 2250 Front St.; (321) 729-6558; www.chart-house.com. This spot sits on the waterfront and offers beautiful views of the Indian River Lagoon. You may catch sight of a manatee while dining. Try the Snapper Hemingway or Shrimp Fresca. Beef is available as well. Top off your dinner with a Hot Chocolate Lava Cake. Sunday brunch is popular here. Open Mon through Thurs 5 to 9:30 p.m., Fri 5 to 10 p.m., Sat 4:30 to 10:30 p.m., and Sun 11 a.m. to 9:30 p.m. $$–$$$.

where to stay

Crowne Plaza Melbourne Oceanfront Resort and Spa. 2605 North Hwy. A1A; (321) 777-4100; www.cpmelbourne.com. Located directly on the Atlantic Ocean, the ocean villas create a welcoming environment. Take a long stroll along the beach or just watch the waves lap the shore from the pool deck. Unwind with a massage, or help your children discover lots of fun with the kid's activities. A fitness center, spa, Internet access, restaurant, and lounge are only some of the amenities offered. $$$.

Hilton Melbourne Airport. 200 Rialto Place; (321) 768-0200 or (800) 437-8010; www1 .hilton.com. This is the best place to stay before an early flight, but it's also a good *pied-à-terre* for touring the southern Space Coast, with all the hospitality bells and whistles to make up a carefree getaway they call a Hilton Bounceback Vacation. A full breakfast is included with room rates. The hotel is handy to the city's high-tech corridor and has business travel-er–friendly desks, data ports, and on-site car rental. The lobby, lush with greenery and waterfalls, is a good place to see and be seen. The hotel has a swimming pool, hot tub, restaurant, lounge, fitness center, and lighted tennis courts. $$–$$$.

Windemere Inn by the Sea. 815 South Miramar Ave., Indialantic by the Sea; (321) 728-9334 or (800) 224-6853; www.windemereinn.com. This dream of a bed-and-breakfast inn on the beach is elegantly styled and warmly traditional. Visit the Web site, look over the three Victorian-style rooms, and make your choice. Or just call for reservations and discuss the choices with the innkeeper. A gourmet breakfast comes with the deal.

south

day trip 01

south

>>> **florida's "hill" country:**
poinciana, lake wales

poinciana

Poinciana isn't found on all road maps, but follow our directions and you'll find a sprawling wilderness untouched by time—and just south of Orlando. Begin by taking US 17/92 south toward Haines City and turn east on Cypress Creek Parkway, SR 580.

where to go

Disney Wilderness Preserve. 6075 Scrub Jay Trail, Kissimmee; (407) 935-0002; www .nature.org. Follow SR 580 to Dover Plum, then right to the Conservation Learning Center. Off Pleasant Hill Road, Poinciana sets aside 12,000 acres at the headwaters of the Florida Everglades ecosystem to host rare scrub jays, bald eagles and their nests, bobcats, sandhill cranes, gopher tortoises, and lakes filled with largemouth bass. Walk the self-guided trail for a look at Florida wilderness with all of its beauties and surprises. Bring binoculars and walk the 2.5-mile hiking trail. Open daily 9 a.m. to 5 p.m. Call to confirm times for guides and rides. Hiking costs $3 for adults and $2 for children ages six to seventeen.

lake wales

One of the loveliest hamlets of Central Florida's hilly lake country, Lake Wales suffers growing pains but still retains much of the charm that brought tourists here generations ago. The

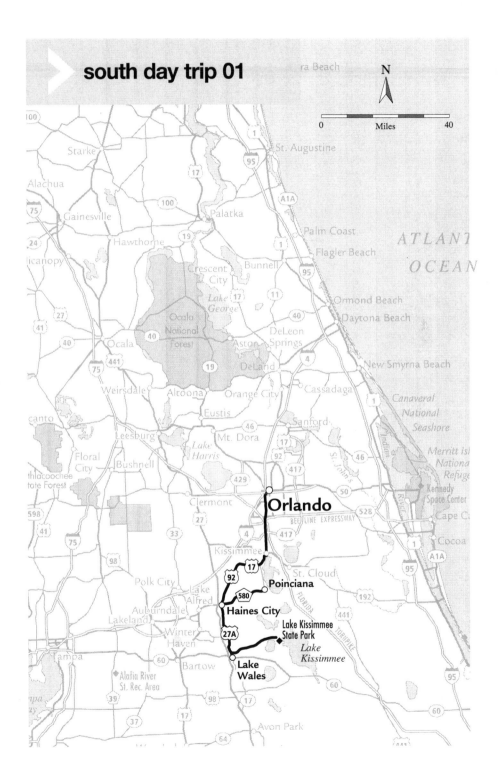

ra Beach

N

0   Miles   40

100
Starke
Alachua
75
Gainesville
24
Hawthorne
icanopy
27
41
40
Ocala
75
441
Weirsdale
canto
Leesburg
Floral
City
Bushnell
thlacoochee
tate Forest
598
41
75

1
95
St. Augustine
95
17
100
A1A
Palatka
19
Palm Coast
1
Crescent
City
Bunnell
95
Flagler Beach

ATLANTⁱ

OCEAN

Lake
George
17
11
Ormond Beach
Ocala
National
Forest
40
DeLeon
Springs
Daytona Beach
441
Aston
441
DeLand
19
New Smyrna Beach
Altoona
Orange City
Cassadaga
1
Eustis
Canaveral
National
Seashore
Lake
Harris
Mt. Dora
46
Sanford
Merritt isl
Nationa
Refuge
17
92
46
417
Kennedy
Space Center
429
Clermont
50
Orlando
528
Cape C
27
BEE LINE EXPRESSWAY
33
4
417
Cocoa
Kissimmee
1
98
17
St. Cloud
95
A1A
92
Poinciana
192
Polk City
Lake
Alfred
580
441
Auburndale
Haines City
Lakeland
Lake Kissimmee
State Park
Winter
Haven
27A
Lake
Kissimmee
Tampa
60
Bartow
Lake
Wales
95
Alafia River
St. Rec. Area
39
98
17
60
pa
ay
37
12
Avon Park
64
60

community is the home of time-honored Chalet Suzanne, and cattle graze miles of pastures in the surrounding countryside. From Poinciana, retrace your route west on SR 580 to US 27, then south to Lake Wales.

where to go

Bok Tower Gardens. 1151 Tower Blvd.; (863) 676-1408; www.boktowergardens.org. The gardens have been here for generations of tourists and loyal locals, who love the ever-changing gardens and the song of the sixty-bell carillon. Gardens are spectacular in Feb and March when the azaleas bloom, but something is alight here year-round, even on the most bleak winter day. Sit in the shadow of the tower, or explore woodland paths. Bring a picnic or eat in the cafe. Save time for the gift shop and ice-cream parlor. A half-mile trail leads through the Pine Ridge Preserve, a habitat of longleaf pine and turkey oak. Sometimes open to the public is the ravishing Pinewood House and Gardens, a textbook Mediterranean Revival home built in 1931 as the winter home of a steel magnate. Most furnishings are original to the house, which is a showplace when decorated for Christmas. Bok Tower Gardens admission is $10 for adults, $3 for children. Open daily 8 a.m. to 6 p.m., later when moonlight concerts are held. Additional charges may apply for Pinewood.

Lake Kissimmee State Park. 14248 Camp Mack Rd.; (863) 696-1112; www.floridastate parks.org/lakekissimmee. This is more than a great state park for hiking, fishing, camping, picnicking, boating, and wildlife watching. It's also the home of one of the most unusual living-history performances in the South. Held only on weekends, Cow Camp re-creates the way Florida wranglers lived in the mid-nineteenth century. They weren't called cowboys, because the term "boy" was considered an insult in the old South. They were "cow hunters" who used long braided whips to "pop" cattle out of the scrub. Western-style cattle drives were impossible in Florida, where cattle hid in thickets and swamps. As you walk down the path from the parking lot, a century slips away and you're in a time warp. Ulysses S. Grant is president, and these cow hunters can't discuss anything that isn't known in the times in which they live. Authentic Florida scrub cattle and stout marshtackie horses, both introduced by the Spanish to survive in the hot, buggy swamps of Florida, are usually seen in the camp. The park is open every day 8 a.m. to sunset.

where to eat

The Mill at Lake Hamilton. 823 US 27 South, Lake Hamilton; (863) 439-5075; www .themillatlakehamilton.com. Located north of Lake Wales, just south of Haines City, the Mill is a general store with an old-time soda fountain, a place to browse as well as dine or snack. Bread bowls are a specialty of the house, filled with your choice of salads or hot combinations such as Oozing Italian Meatballs, Sissy's Chicken Stew, or the Wot-Ever Daily Special. Children can get a Teenie Beanie Wienie bread bowl filled with beans and wieners or their choice from the grown-up menu. Have a hearty whole-meal salad or a sandwich platter. Desserts focus on homemade fruit pies, including an apple pie with no added sugar. Or you can have homemade ice cream in a dip, sundae, waffle cone, or Chocolate Volcano. Open Sun through Wed 8:30 a.m. to 3 p.m. and Thurs through Sat 8:30 a.m. to 8 p.m. $.

Scuttles New England Seafood. 343 West Central Ave., #9; (863) 676-7547. This is the place for New England–style seafood. Portions are huge, and most people will leave with some for a snack later. Scuttles has been serving food here for more than twenty years. It's not fancy. You'll be served with paper plates and plasticware, but the seafood is terrific. New Englanders will want the fried Ipswich clams or the broiled haddock for that taste of home that will put a smile on their faces. Open Tues through Sat 11 a.m. to 8 p.m. and Sun 11 a.m. to 6 p.m. $–$$.

where to stay

Camp Mack's River Resort. 14900 Camp Mack Rd.; (863) 696-1108 or (800) 243-8013; www.campmack.com. For the nature lover and angler, Camp Mack's is located right on the Kissimmee River and offers fishing, water skiing, nature tours, airboat rides, and rental boats. Both efficiency rooms and cabins are available. $–$$.

Chalet Suzanne Restaurant and Inn. 3800 Chalet Suzanne Dr.; (863) 676-6011 or (800) 433-6011; www.chaletsuzanne.com. This golden nugget of Florida history has a heart-warming story. During the Depression, Bertha Hinshaw was widowed with two children. She had a fine education for a woman of her time, had traveled abroad when her husband was alive, and was a sophisticated hostess and chef. So she hung out a shingle on US 27 and began offering meals. One of her early drop-ins was famous food writer Duncan Hines. He praised her in his column, and soon Chalet Suzanne became one of Florida's most sought-after dining rooms. Four generations later it is still family operated and still showered with awards, yet it hasn't lost the small-town friendliness that launched it. You've seen canned Chalet Suzanne soups in gourmet shops; buy them here by the case. Shop for antiques and visit the pottery. The traditional menu starts with the famous romaine soup and marches on through multiple courses. The wine cellar is outstanding. Open daily for breakfast, lunch, and dinner. Reservations are highly recommended. Each room in the inn is different. Guests can use the swimming pool, fish in the lake, and land their airplanes on the private airstrip. $$$–$$$$.

Green Gables Inn. 1747 North US 27; (863) 676-2511; www.greengablesfl.com. This is an old-fashioned "tourist court" motel, handy to the highway and smartly updated with a fitness center, guest laundry, in-room coffee, cable television, and phones with data ports. There's a swimming pool, tennis courts, hot tub, and on-site restaurant and lounge—and a private fishing dock just outside the door. $–$$.

A Prince of Wales Motel. 513 South Scenic Hwy.; (863) 676-1249. The Prince of Wales is an older but recently remodeled motel. All rooms have an in-suite bathroom, refrigerator, independent air-conditioning, cable television, and limited telephone service. They also have rooms with microwaves and coffeemakers, as well as "efficiency" rooms. Hair dryers and irons and ironing boards are also available. It's clean, comfortable, friendly, and moderately priced. $$.

day trip 02

south

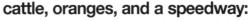

cattle, oranges, and a speedway:
avon park, sebring, lake placid

avon park

This sleepy village deep in Florida's belly hasn't changed much in decades, which makes it a tempting day trip away from the din of the city. Take I-4 southwest from Orlando to the US 27 exit, then turn south onto this historic artery that is still a pretty, interesting drive through cattle country past sparkling lakes and through unspoiled hamlets along the spine of a prehistoric ridge. US 98, and other roads running east and west through this area, was part of the original route used by Florida cow hunters to take cattle to Punta Rassa on the Gulf of Mexico for shipment to Cuba. Today it's known as the Florida Cracker Trail.

In a quest for snakes, alligators, and other swamp denizens to study, Connecticut native Oliver Martin Crosby came to this area in 1884, followed by others in search of winter warmth. An early British settler suggested the name Avon because the town reminded her of Shakespeare's birthplace on England's Avon River. Today's residents call it the City of Charm, a land of thirty lakes and enough wilderness to attract 30,000 hikers each year.

where to go

The Mile-Long Mall, a nickname for Avon Park's Main Street, is a swath of specialty shops and restaurants. Browse from one to the next, with a stop at the Hotel Jacaranda for lunch. www.apfla.com/main.htm.

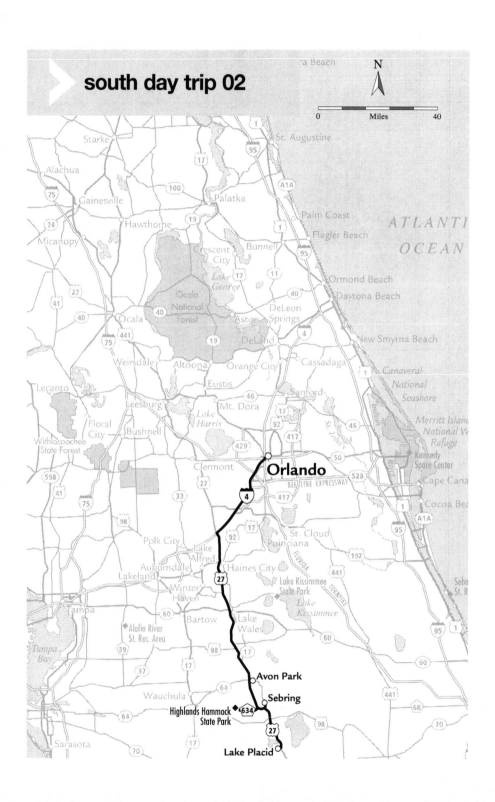

> ## driving along the lake wales ridge

Running north and south from Lake County, through Orange and Polk Counties and down into Highlands County, is the Lake Wales Ridge. Followed by US 27 for most of its length, the interested motorist can observe this line of ancient sand dunes as he travels the road. Scientists consider the Lake Wales Ridge precious because in its undeveloped stretches its ecosystems have remained essentially undisturbed since the Miocene Age.

The biological contrasts here are striking. Although in a typical year 50 inches of rain fall upon Lake Wales Ridge, it includes many desert-like habitats. It is the highest point in peninsular Florida, but only stands about 300 feet above sea level. Ancient seas deposited this enormous sand dune, then receded. Its scrub habitat is a miniature forest.

This scrub forest, in most places less than 10 miles wide, shelters one of the largest collections of rare organisms in the world. Sadly, its well drained sand attracts both citrus farming and housing developments.

While you motor down US 27, consider the following:

- *When falling sea levels exposed the Florida peninsula thirteen million years ago, giant ground sloths, horses, and saber-toothed tigers roamed the land.*

- *Two million to five million years ago, the sea rose again, depositing the sand that created the Lake Wales Ridge.*

- *20,000 years ago the seas retreated again, locked up in polar ice caps, and the Florida peninsula was twice its current size.*

- *120 years ago approximately 80,000 to 100,000 acres of native upland habitat thrived on the ridge.*

- *By 1990 about 85 percent of original Lake Wales Ridge upland habitats had been either cleared for agriculture and business or planned for residential use.*

where to eat

El Paso Tienda. 209 US 27 North; (863) 453-0400. This restaurant serves up a Mexican buffet *el grande* with familiar favorites, including tacos and tons of fillings, just like Mamacita used to make. Open every day 11 a.m. to 9 p.m. $.

Olympic Restaurant. 504 US 27 North; (863) 452-2700. This is a nice place for a quick lunch or an informal dinner. They have really good club sandwiches and excellent baked fish and fish fingers. The other thing you must try is their potato salad. Open daily 11 a.m. to 9 p.m. $.

where to stay

Hotel Jacaranda. 10 East Main St.; (863) 453-2211; www.hoteljac.com. This grand old hotel has been restored to its flapper-era look. It's owned by a hospitality school, which means affordable rates, great meals, and high service and housekeeping standards set by demanding teachers. The heated swimming pool is enclosed, and each room has individual climate control, television, and telephone. Master suites have bedroom, living room, and bath. Grand Suites have two bedrooms, living room, and two baths. The Sunday Grand Buffet is a stunner, prepared by culinary students who are learning all the latest techniques and tastes, and the everyday lunch buffet is boffo. $$.

Lake Brentwood Motel. 2060 US 27 North; (863) 453-4358; www.lakebrentwoodmotel .com. This property is rustic and plain, just the perch for anglers who like a lakefront location, a private dock, horseshoes, croquet, free use of boats and canoes, and picnic tables with grills. Take a room or an efficiency with cooking facilities. Golf, tennis, and restaurants aren't far away. $–$$.

Lake Verona Lodge Bed and Breakfast. 310 East Main St.; (863) 452-9940; www.way .to/LakeVeronaLodge. Nestled in the heartland of Florida amongst the orange groves, this beautiful 1925 lodge has spacious rooms, heart pine wood floors, beaded wood walls, period antiques, and breathtaking views and sunsets over Lake Verona. Rates include Continental breakfast. $–$$.

sebring

South of Avon Park is Sebring, a planned paradise laid out around a central circle with spokes/streets fanning out all around. It has been internationally famous for years as the home of the twelve-hour Sebring Grand Prix of Endurance auto race, but there's much ado here all year. For a really offbeat side trip from Orlando, come here by Amtrak and get a glimpse of Florida's vast cattle ranches and orange groves along the way. If you're a race fan, book early. If you're not, come at another time, when it's easier to get a room and restaurant reservations.

where to go

Chamber of Commerce. 227 US 27 North; (863) 385-8448; www.greatersebringchamber ofcommerce.org. This is a good place to stop for information and maps. Open Mon through Fri 9 a.m. to 5 p.m.

Highlands Hammock State Park. West of Sebring off Highway 634; (386) 386-6094; www.floridastateparks.org/highlandshammock. More than an awesome 3,800-acre wildlife sanctuary buzzing with birds and bugs, this is also Florida's first state park and home of the largest oak tree in Florida, the tallest sable palm in the country, some 1,000-year-old hardwoods, and a sweeping expanse of some of the last remaining hammock in the state. Walk eight nature trails, camp, picnic, take the catwalk across the swamps to watch for alligators, or take the tram tour for a modest fee. A horseback-riding trail is available to those who bring their own horses. (Horses must have a recent negative Coggins test.) Campground sites accommodate tents or RVs. Ask at the ranger station for a birder's list and perform your own survey. A museum honors Civilian Conservation Corps workers who created the park in the 1930s and 1940s. It's so lush and gentle a jungle, kids will see Fern Gully and grownups will see Bali Hai here. Admission is $4 per car. Camping is extra. Open 8 a.m. to sunset daily.

Lake Jackson. (863) 471-5100. An 11-mile trail circles this natural lake. Take your bicycle, baby stroller, in-line skates, or walking shoes. A good place to start is downtown at The Circle.

Skip Barber Racing School. Sebring International Raceway, 113 Midway Dr.; (863) 655-4437; http://skipbarber.com. This is a serious training ground for future race drivers, but anyone is welcome to take a one-, three-, or four-day course to improve his or her driving skills. If you meet SCCA requirements after your course, you'll be certified to drive in real races. Training is in cars designed specifically for high-speed race training. Courses are taught by top competitors in such leading series as Formula 1, NASCAR, SCCA, and British Formula 3. The one-day course, for those who just want a taste of the action, begins with classroom work, then an afternoon on the track. Longer courses provide classroom work, plenty of track time, lapping days, GT races, and other programs. Ask about packages that include accommodations. $$$.

where to eat

Andy's Hot Dog World. 340 East Interlake Blvd.; (863) 699-5577. Think inside the bun, and enjoy a classic American favorite at Andy's. Varieties include the Lake Placid Dog, the All American, the Kraut Dog, the Boston Dog, the Texas Chili Dog, the Italian Dog, and more. Have sides of curly fries or sweet potato fries and coleslaw or baked beans. Top it all off with a milk shake or a sundae. Lots of fun for the family! Open from 10 a.m. to 6 p.m. Mon through Fri and 10 a.m. to 3 p.m. on Sat. $.

Chicanes. 3100 Golfview Rd.; (863) 314-0348 for reservations (recommended); www .innonthelakessebring.com. Delight in romantic views of Lake Jackson as you enjoy one of a variety of entrees from Chicanes's eclectic menu. Breakfast is served each morning from 6:30 to 11 a.m., lunch is served daily from 11 a.m. to 4 p.m., and the dining room is open nightly from 5 to 10 p.m. Try the Moyers Flat Iron steak or mahimahi San Padre, and finish your meal with the Pile Up, a brownie sundae. $–$$$.

The Tea Room in Sebring Lakeside Golf Resort Inn. 500 Lake Sebring Dr.; (863) 385-7113; for inn reservations, call (888) 2-SEBRING. This is one of those charming lakefront places where you feel like an old friend, even if this is your first visit. The tearoom is open for lunch only, and reservations are suggested. $$

where to stay

Chateau Élan. 150 Midway Dr.; (863) 655-6252; www.starwoodhotels.com. This is a smart, modern boutique hotel in a patch of Florida outback that, until the hotel was built, sprang to life only during the famous twenty-four-hour Sebring auto races. It adjoins the track, so bookings are hard to get during race events. Accommodations are splendid, with coffeemakers in each room, satellite television, phone with data port, hair dryer, and iron and ironing board. Work out in the fitness room, play golf, attend auto-racing school, and pamper yourself in the European-style spa, where massages, facials, restorative body treatments, and hydrotherapy are on the menu. The restaurant is stellar and offers room service as well as breakfast, lunch, and dinner. The lounge and outdoor swimming pool overlook the track's famous hairpin turn. You can also drive into historic Sebring for dining and shopping. Ask about race school packages, golf getaways, and a day package that includes lunch and a tour of the track. $$–$$$.

Inn on the Lakes. 3100 Golfview Rd. at US 27 South; (863) 471-9400 or (800) 531-5253; www.innonthelakessebring.com. The inn is a modern lakefront resort offering water-ski and Jet Ski rentals, tennis, workout rooms, a lakeside restaurant with lounge, a coin laundry, swimming pool, and tempting golf packages. Suites have wet bars. $$–$$$.

Kenilworth Lodge. 836 Southeast Lakeview Dr.; (863) 385-0111 or (800) 423-5939; www.kenlodge.com. This eye-arresting Mediterranean Revival–style lodge opened in 1916 overlooking Lake Jackson. Centered by a massive lobby with a grand staircase, it offers efficiencies, apartments, villas, and rooms with a refrigerator in each unit. The swimming pool is 80 feet long, and there's a golf course with a choice of seven golf packages. Water-ski, play tennis, bicycle, and catalog the bird life. Pull up a rocker on the veranda to read the morning paper, and plan to come back to this spot in time for sunset over the lake. Dine in the lodge's restaurant; rates include breakfast. Weekly rates give you one night free. $–$$$.

Quality Inn. 6525 US 27 North; (863) 385-4500. This property is part of a reliable chain with an Olympic-size swimming pool, a tiki bar outdoors, and a lively lounge as well as a full-service restaurant. Ask about golf packages. Rooms have free premium movie channels, in-room coffee service, free local calls, pay-per-view movies, iron and ironing board, and a daily USA Today left at your door. Room service is available, and pets are welcome in some rooms. $$–$$$.

Sebring Lakeside Golf Resort Inn. 1062 Sebring Dr.; (863) 385-7113; www.2sebring .com. Visit the Tea Room for lunch, enjoy a round of golf on the executive-style course or just relax in one of the luxury suites. You'll find just the right balance between old-time southern charm mixed with the amenities you expect. If you're a golfer, you'll find a dozen courses within 15 minutes. Also available are a swimming pool, paddleboats, and rental bicycles. $$–$$$.

lake placid

Continuing south on US 27 from Sebring soon brings you to Lake Placid. The city claims to have been the largest town (in area) in the nation at one time, when it was a community named Lake Stearns after the U.S. surveyor general at the time. Dr. Melvil Dewey, inventor of the Dewey Decimal System, arrived in the 1920s and got behind efforts to promote the area as a winter resort with a new name. Growth has been slow but steady, allowing the area to retain its small-town flavor.

where to go

Henscratch Farms Vineyard and Winery. 980 Henscatch Rd.; (863) 699-2060; www .henscratchfarms.com. A certified "Florida Farm Winery," the property boasts ten acres of native southern muscadine and scuppernong grape varieties, a hydroponics growing system for strawberry production, and a highbush blueberry patch. Two hundred American breed laying hens range freely in the vineyard. They supply the country store with fresh eggs. Visit the farm, sample the "Country Style Wines," or just sit a spell on the Florida Cracker–style porch before wandering through the grounds to explore the unique projects in progress. Hours change seasonally, so call first. Tues through Sat 10 a.m. to 4 p.m., Sun noon to 4 p.m.

Historical Museum. 12 Park St.; (863) 465-1771. The museum is housed in the city's old rail depot. In addition to interesting antiques and local memorabilia, the museum contains an old caboose and the entire old jailhouse. Hours are 1 to 3:30 p.m. Mon through Fri; admission is free but donations are encouraged.

Murals are Lake Placid's claim to fame. It has more than two dozen eye-popping, master-fully done outdoor paintings that depict area history and culture in what is called "uptown." Bring a wide-angle lens, a tripod, and a time-delay camera so that you can put yourself in the picture with a cattle drive that comes complete with sound effects, an airboat, the caladium field, or one of the historic scenes. See the murals anytime on a self-guided tour, allowing plenty of time to shop uptown's interesting boutiques and crafts shops. A mural map can be picked up during business hours at the Lake Placid Chamber of Commerce, 18 North Oak St., Lake Placid 33852, or at most area merchants. Contact the Lake Placid Mural Society at (863) 531-0211.

Arriving in town on US 27, note the 360-foot-high **Placid Tower.** The tower is now closed, but the town is working on getting it listed as a historical monument.

where to eat

Heron's Garden. 501 U.S. 27 North; (863) 699-6602; www.heronsgarden.com. Heron's is famous for its Greek salad and shish kebab. Choose from a menu of steaks, chicken, fresh seafood, and a selection of pasta dishes. There's a lounge with full bar. Open from 11 a.m. every day. $$.

Main Street America, An Eatery. 15 South Main Ave.; (863) 465-7733. This popular establishment serves breakfast and lunch only. You're already familiar with the menu—eggs, omelets, pancakes, and French toast; burgers, chicken, salads, soups, and sandwiches. Open 7 a.m. to 2 p.m. Tues through Fri, 7 a.m. to noon Sat, and 7 a.m. to 1 p.m. Sun. $.

No Frills Grill. 1979 Placid Lakes Blvd.; (863) 465-1050; www.nofrillsgrill.net. Don't expect pretense here. You'll get good sandwiches, wraps, and burgers. Dinner favorites include Honey Pecan Chicken and Garlic Sautéed Alligator. Live entertainment every Wednesday night. Open Mon through Thurs 11 a.m. to 9 p.m., Fri and Sat 11 a.m. to 10 p.m., Sun 11 a.m. to 7 p.m. $–$$.

where to stay

Hotel Valencia. 2165 US 27 South; (863) 465-3133: http://hotelvalenciafl.com. This property is modern and comfortable with full hotel facilities, including a swimming pool, plenty of parking, a full-service restaurant, and a lounge with dancing. Breakfast is on the house. $$.

Valencia Suites. 1865 US 27 South; (863) 465-9200; www.valenciasuites.net. This homey place has one-bedroom suites. Kitchens are fully furnished, so bring supplies; there is no restaurant on-site. Rent by the night, week, weekend, or month, and bring your trailerable boat to launch from the motel's own ramp. $–$$.

southwest

day trip 01

southwest

a land of lakes:
polk city, lakeland

I-4 wanders southwest from Orlando toward Tampa. Just barely past Orlando's attractions area, you'll find a cluster of small communities that offer a Mayberry-like atmosphere. Don't blink as you go past it on I-4, or you'll miss the Polk City exit. It's the off-ramp to another world—a world of small towns with village squares surrounded by storefronts, once hardware stores and grocers, that are now boutiques and tearooms.

polk city

Venturing into the community itself, you'll find a charming village square surrounded by shops. However, Polk City's most impressive attraction is right at an interstate exit, well worth a stop on your way to somewhere else.

where to go

Fantasy of Flight. 1400 Broadway Blvd., Southeast Polk City; (863) 984-3500; www .fantasyofflight.com. Watch for the exit off I-4 to find one of the world's greatest aircraft collections as well as an attraction with plenty of punch. Start by going through a time tunnel into the history of aviation. Experience a jump into occupied France, see a World War I bunker, and visit an English airfield. Then come into the twenty-first century to fly a simulator and tour the restoration area, where interesting planes are always being worked on. See the back lot where movie props and bits and pieces are stored, and spend time in

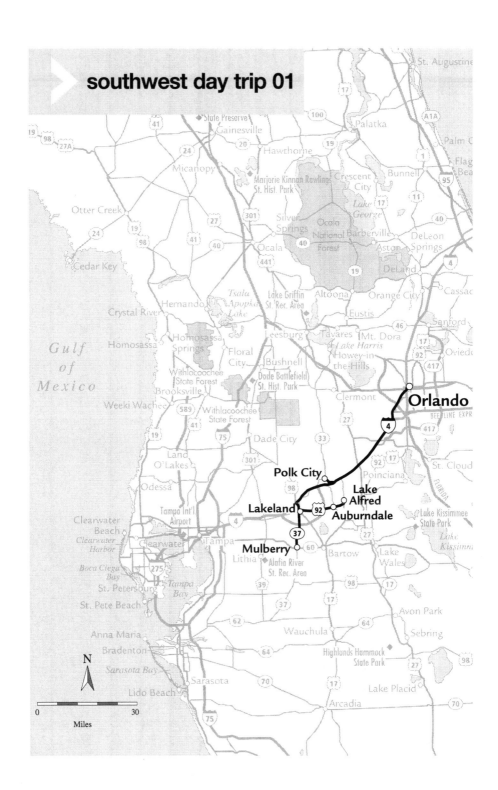

southwest day trip 01

a hangar filled with a fortune in antique airplanes. Many are one of a kind; most are flyable. No admission is required to eat at the Compass Rose, a delightful diner like those found in airports in the 1950s. The attraction is handy to I-4, with easy-off, easy-on access, so stop for breakfast or lunch and a look at the gift shop—even if you aren't staying to tour the attraction. Hours are 10 a.m. to 5 p.m. daily except Christmas and Thanksgiving. Fees are $28.95 for adults and $14.95 for children.

lakeland

Each April, Lakeland is abuzz with small planes as it hosts Sun 'n Fun, one of general aviation's most important annual events. Aircraft of all sizes and colors zero in on the airport here for contests, camping, and the kind of tale swapping known as "hangar flying." Even if you're not an aviation buff, you'll love the color and verve of it all. The community's other chief claim to fame is the Florida Southern College campus, the largest collection of Frank Lloyd Wright buildings in the world. Lakeland, located just off I-4 halfway between Orlando and Tampa, makes a good headquarters for exploring the surrounding small towns, including Auburndale and Lake Alfred, along Highway 600.

where to go

The Florida Air Museum at Sun-n-Fun. 4175 Medulla Rd.; (863) 644-0741; www.sun-n-fun.org. The museum is filled with sport airplanes and memorabilia, a must for aviation buffs—especially those who follow aviation as a competitive sport. You'll need up to three hours to see it all. Open daily but hours vary, so call ahead. Admission is $8 for adults, $6 for seniors, and $4 for children.

Florida Southern College. 111 Lake Hollingsworth Dr.; (863) 680-4111; www.flsouthern .edu. This active college is also the home of a dazzling collection of buildings designed by Frank Lloyd Wright. If you're a fan of this quirky architect, whose disciples forgive his leaky roofs and high-maintenance designs, the $10 per person walking tour of the campus is one of the state's great bargains. A two-and-a-half-hour, in-depth tour is available for $18 per person. These are available on Monday and Friday. Stop first at the visitor center for information and to shop at the gift shop. The visitor center is open Tues through Fri 10 a.m. to 4 p.m. The campus is open year-round, even when classes aren't in session, but not all buildings are open. It's best to phone ahead.

Mulberry Phosphate Museum. Route 60 at Route 37, Mulberry; (863) 425-2823; www .mulberrychamber.org/attractions.htm. Located just south of Lakeland, this is a surprise find. Florida is an archaeological treasure trove from stem to stern, and here is living proof. Thousands of creatures died here in the Cenozoic Era and were preserved in lands that were later mined for phosphates. See more than 3,000 specimens, including a whale vertebra with a shark's tooth imbedded in it, a prehistoric equus horse, and a five-million-year-old skeleton of a dugong, ancestor of the modern manatee. Admission is free, and special digs are arranged for kids. Open Tues through Sat 10 a.m. to 4:30 p.m.

Polk Museum of Art. 800 East Palmetto St.; (863) 688-7743; www.polkmuseumofart.org. At this small but important art museum, view changing exhibitions plus a sculpture garden, galleries filled with contemporary American works, an impressive collection of pre-Columbian artifacts, Asian arts, and a collection of European arts with a fine showing of Georgian silver and antique ceramics. From here you can walk to the Florida Southern campus or the city's antiques district. Open Tues through Sat 10 a.m. to 5 p.m. Closed major holidays. General admission is $5; $4 for seniors and free for students.

where to shop

The Barn Antiques; The Stable Gifts; The Back Porch Tea Room. Route 557, Lake Alfred; (863) 956-1362; www.barnantiques.biz. Located 4 miles north of Lake Alfred, this is a cheery, family-operated place where lunch is served in its own picnic basket. Shop for antiques, silk flowers, seasonal accessories, and gifts galore. Open from 10 a.m. to 4 p.m. Tues through Sat. $–$$.

Biggar Antiques. 140 West Haines Blvd., Lake Alfred; (863) 956-4853; http://biggar antiques.spaces.live.com. Biggar's has been family-run here for more than forty years. Their specialty is country-store antiques and memorabilia for private buyers as well as for decorators who furnish restaurants. Buy a poster, tin sign, or country furniture. Hours are Tues through Sat 10 a.m. to 4 p.m.

Brooke Pottery. 223 North Kentucky Ave.; Lakeland; (863) 688-6844; www.brookepottery .com. Works in clay, metal, glass, and wood by some of the best pottery artists in America are featured at this contemporary fine crafts shop that offers a wide selection of decorative and useful pottery pieces. Mon through Sat 10 a.m. to 6 p.m., Sun noon to 5 p.m.

International Market World. 1052 US 92, Auburndale; (863) 665-0062; www.intlmarket world.com. This big flea market lures visitors who are speeding by on the highway. See its 1909 carousel, shelves filled with crafts and art supplies, new and used oddments, and food concessions. Open Fri through Sun 8 a.m. to 4 p.m.

Lloyds Lakeland Antiques. 301 North Kentucky Ave., Lakeland; (863) 682-2787; www .lloydslakeland.com. This two-story antique mall, located in the historic district of Lakeland, features thirty dealers. Find antique and collectible items, art pottery, vases and glass, furniture, framed art, antique toys, stained glass windows, and more. Open Mon through Fri 11 a.m. to 5 p.m., Sat 10: a.m. to 5 p.m., or by appointment.

Magnolia Gift Shop and Tea Room. 212 Howard St., Auburndale; (863) 965-1684, www .magnoliatearoomandgiftshop.com. Pass a pleasant afternoon looking for antiques and collectibles and chatting over a steaming cup of good tea at this fine gift shop and tearoom. Open 11 a.m. to 3 p.m. Mon through Sat.

Second Hand Rose. 600 South Combee Rd., Lakeland; (863) 665-0755; http://mysecond handrosemall.com. A great collection of antiques, collectibles, and hobby items are available at this two-story antique mall that features over eighteen vendors selling high-quality merchandise. Open Mon through Sat 10 a.m. to 5 p.m., Sun noon to 5 p.m.

This Olde House. 1070 South Lake Shore Way, Lake Alfred; (863) 956-9433, www.this oldehousela.com. This six-room house is filled with gifts and antiques plus a selection of unfinished furniture. Shop for stuffed animals, unusual candles, frames, and furniture Tues through Sat 10 a.m. to 4 p.m.

where to eat

Black 'n Brew. 205 East Main St., Lakeland; (863) 682-1210. Count on B&B for a quick, delicious, and convenient lunch every time. The bistro atmosphere is very warm and inviting and there are few outdoor tables, too. The fare is consistently fresh and tasty, with salads, soups, sandwiches, wraps, and more. $.

Crispers. 217 North Kentucky Ave. (downtown); (863) 682-7708; or 3615 South Florida Ave. (Merchants Walk); (863) 646-2299; www.crispers.com. This is a popular lunch place as well as a favorite for takeout. Homemade soups are made fresh daily and available to eat in or take out by the bowl, pint, or quart. There's also a good choice of sandwiches, including a crunchy vegetarian selection on grainy bread, a hot Reuben, and breast of chicken with bacon. Sandwiches are available by the whole or half, and there are a dozen salads with a variety of dressings to make a meal or a side dish. In addition to punch, iced tea, and juices, there are frozen specialties such as Chocolate Monkey, Coconut Fantasy, and Caramel Chiller. Ice cream, cake, cheesecake, and cookies round out the desserts. Check out their menu online, then phone in your take-out order. Open daily 10:30 a.m. to 8 p.m., Sun 11 a.m. to 6 p.m. $.

Harry's Seafood, Bar, and Grille. 101 North Kentucky Ave., Lakeland; (863) 686-2228; www.hookedonharrys.com. One of a small chain of eight restaurants found throughout Florida, Harry's features a creative menu done with flair, reflecting the fun and ambience of New Orleans. Start your meal with a cup of gumbo. Then move on to the crawfish étouffée. If there's any room left, top it off with Lulu's Louisiana Mud Pie. Many other Louisiana specialties are available, as well as more traditional American fare. You'll think you're on Bourbon Street! $$.

Lavender & Lace Tearoom & Gift Shop. 430 North Lake Shore Way, Lake Alfred; (863) 956-3998 restaurant, (863) 956-2174 gift shop; www.lavenderandlacetearoom.com. This combination Victorian tearoom and shop sells everything you need to do a proper English tea at home. Sit down to an authentic English tea with little sandwiches or sweets, then shop for gifts for your Anglophile friends. Open daily, except Sun, 11 a.m. to 3:30 p.m.

Terrace Grille. 329 East Main St.; (863) 603-5400 or (863) 603-5420; www.terracehotel .com. It's worth a visit just to see this swank 1920s hotel, and the food keeps pace with your high expectations. Start with the soup of the day or spinach-and-artichoke fondue, macadamia-crusted brie, or fried oysters in a Creole remoulade. Main dishes include the chef's vegetarian plate, jumbo lump crab cakes, an oak-grilled pork chop with whiskey butter, grouper seared with wild mushrooms and topped with oyster stew, wood-grilled steaks or rack of lamb, mahimahi, and much more. Open daily for breakfast, lunch, and dinner. Reservations are recommended. $$–$$$$.

where to stay

Lakeland Terrace Hotel. 329 East Main St.; (863) 688-0800 or (888) 644-8400; www.terrace hotel.com. The hotel opened its doors in 1924, as one of the finest in something new to Florida: a year-round hotel. The boom was on, and this handsome high-rise went up in the heart of downtown, overlooking Lake Mirror. Today the courthouse and Amtrak station are within walking distance of the hotel. Dine in the Terrace Grille, or have a drink in the Terrace Bar. It's restful and refined, and renovated to take you back to another age. Choose one of the seventy-three guest rooms or one of the fifteen suites with separate bedroom plus a sleeper sofa. All units have in-room coffee, a working desk with data ports, cable television, individual climate control, and iron and ironing board. $$–$$$.

Lake Morton Bed & Breakfast. 817 South Blvd.; (863) 688-6788; http://lakemorton bandb.com. Continental breakfast is included in the rates at this four-room inn situated in a handy downtown location. Choose a room or a suite. $$.

Residence Inn Lakeland. 3701 Harden Blvd.; (863) 680-2323; www.marriott.com. Convenient to the interstate and close to major attractions such as Sun-N-Fun, Cypress Gardens, and Joker Marchant Stadium, home to the Detroit Tigers spring training. Guest rooms are 50 percent larger than the normal hotel room and feature separate living and sleeping areas. Amenities include free wireless Internet, fully equipped kitchen, queen-sized beds, and a free hot breakfast buffet. $$–$$$.

day trip 02

southwest

florida's first theme park:
winter haven

winter haven

Waterskiing was not invented here, but the sport owes much of its popularity to warm Florida waters, where it became a year-round passion. It's still one of the most important reasons to come to this hotbed of water-ski shows, schools, competitions, and even a water-ski hall of fame and museum. From Orlando, go west on I-4 then south on US 27 and west on US 17/92 into Winter Haven.

where to go

Cypress Gardens. 6000 Cypress Gardens Blvd.; (863) 324-2111; www.cypressgardens .com. This spot has been an evergreen oasis since the 1930s when a swamp was transformed into a garden showplace on the shores of Lake Eloise. Take an electric-boat tour past a floral spectacular that changes with the seasons. The cypress trees have been here since time began, and the show begins with them, followed by more trees, shrubs, topiaries, and waterfalls and climaxing in oceans of bright annuals that are changed each season. You could come here every week to soak up the beauty, sunshine, and sweet breezes off the lake, and it wouldn't get old. Bring your camera; southern belles in hoopskirts will gladly pose for your shots.

The gardens alone can occupy tranquil hours, but the park also offers rides, a water park, breathtaking ski shows, a flashy ice show, a butterfly conservatory, wildlife on display,

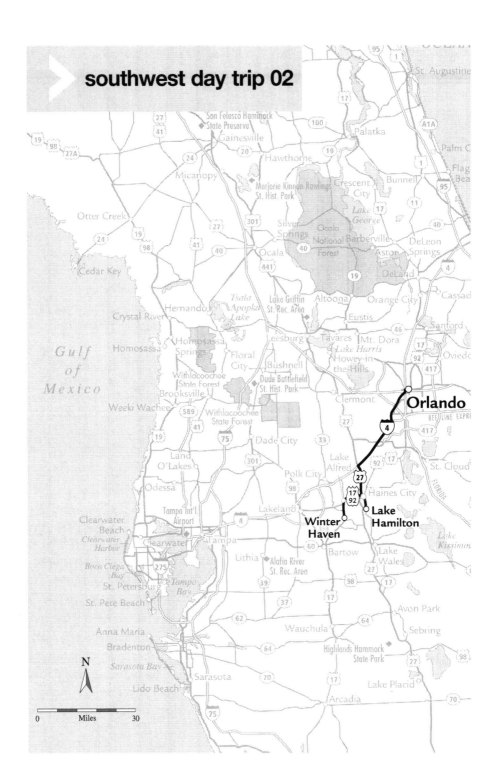

southwest day trip 02

a petting zoo, a radio museum, a paddle-wheel boat with lunch and dinner cruises, plenty of shops and snackeries, and a very good sit-down restaurant. Plan to spend all day and, during special events, into the evening. Special events include big-name concerts, Christmas lights, the annual Mum Festival, and much more. General admission to the gardens is $12.95; $9.95 for seniors age sixty and over and children ages three through nine. Parking costs $7 for cars, $9 for RVs. Admission to the water park is $23.95 for ages ten through fifty-nine; $17.95 for seniors ages sixty and over and children ages three through nine; plus parking. Ask about multiday, combination, and annual passes. The park opens at 10 a.m. year-round; check the Web site or call for closing times. Visitors can get a second day free for six days following their initial visit.

where to eat

The Mill at Lake Hamilton. 29400 US 27, Lake Hamilton; (863) 439-5075. A pleasant drive east from Winter Haven on the shores of one of the area's prettiest lakes, this homey place welcomes shoppers as well as diners, so make an afternoon of it. Dine on a bread bowl filled with a selection of hot delights (meatballs, chicken stew, chili, broccoli beef, the daily special) or a cold salad (crab and shrimp, Waldorf chicken, tuna). Dare the Dagwood Salad, a battleship-size bounty of meats, cheeses, and greens served with hot, buttered buns. Sandwich platters are a hearty meal. Kids like the Teenie Beanie Weenie Bread Bowl. For dessert, order from the old-fashioned soda fountain, which has a full menu of sundaes, sodas, dips, and floats; or have one of the homemade pies, including no-sugar-added apple. Finish with one of the gourmet coffees or teas. Ask about take-out picnics, whole meals, and whole pies. Open Sun through Wed 8:30 a.m. to 3 p.m. and Thurs through Sat until 6:30 p.m. $–$$.

where to stay

Cypress Inn. 5651 Cypress Gardens Rd.; (863) 324-5867 or (800) 729-6706; www .cypressinnusa.com. This AAA two-diamond inn is handy to Cypress Gardens, a good headquarters for visiting the gardens and local sightseeing. There's a choice of rooms, including some with kitchenette. The motel is set back from the noise of the highway and has a heated pool, laundry for guest use, and cable TV. Rooms have coffeemakers with coffee service, and a continental breakfast is included in the tab. Pets are welcome. If you're a member of AAA or AARP, ask about discounts. $$.

Holiday Inn Winter Haven. 200 Cypress Gardens Blvd.; (863) 292-2100; www.ichotels group.com. Located near Cypress Gardens and the downtown district of Winter Haven. The hotel's amenities include a business center, fitness center, bar, air-conditioning in public areas, lounge area, and breakfast daily. $$.

The Inn Place. 1150 Third St. Southwest (US 17); (863) 294-4451. This property's rooms have either two queen-size or one king-size bed, 27-inch television, coffeemaker, hair dryer, iron and ironing board, refrigerator, data ports, and voice mail. Swim in the outdoor pool while the kids splash in their own wading pool. Have a drink in the Club House Lounge, then dinner in the Country Kitchen, which can also provide room service if you prefer. The hotel is 3 miles from Cypress Gardens. $–$$.

Scottish Inns. 1901 Cypress Gardens Blvd.; (863) 324-3954. This clean, green, economical inn offers a refrigerator in each room, free HBO, a coin laundry, and a nearby restaurant. The location is handy for visiting Cypress Gardens, Walt Disney World Resort, and everything between. For a few dollars more, get an efficiency and do your own cooking. $–$$.

day trip 03

southwest

>>> **the city on the bay:**
tampa

tampa

Save this trip for a two- or three-day weekend because each of the theme parks—Busch Gardens Tampa Bay and Adventure Island—is worth more than one day. In fact, season passes are a good value if you live close enough to come here more than twice. Kids never tire of the water park, and adults love the ever-changing scene of birds, flowers, animals, and shows at Busch Gardens.

Tampa itself is one of Florida's most beguiling cities, from its Latin tempo to its fresh, youthful bustle. It's a major cruise port, has fine museums and shopping, hosts blockbuster events and festivals, and is the home of world-class resorts and spas. For Orlando residents, it's a second home where dining and shopping are world class, big-name artists play in concert, and an international airport sometimes provides better connections or rates than can be found at Orlando International Airport.

Early Native Americans called the area "Tanpa," or Sticks of Fire, but somewhere along the way the spelling was changed. Ponce de Leon was here in 1521, and Hernando de Soto sailed into Tampa Bay in 1539. But it wasn't until 1772 that Dutch mapmaker Bernard Romans recorded the Hillsborough River and gave it a name. Today's downtown was history's Fort Brooke.

Development began when Henry B. Plant arrived with his railroad, a steamship line ran to Havana, and a flamboyant $3-million hotel was raised to house rich tourists. In 1885 a

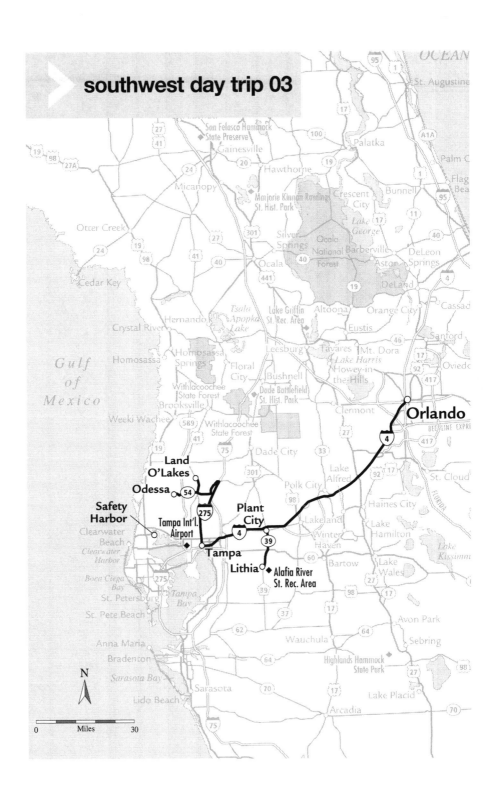

tract of land east of Tampa was opened by Cuban exile and cigar manufacturer Don Vincente Martinez Ybor. Soon the city swarmed with expatriate Spaniards, Cubans, Germans, and Italians, who made it the cigar capital of the world. To begin this Day Trip, head west from Orlando on I-4 to I-275 south into Tampa.

where to go

Adventure Island. 10001 McKinley Dr.; (888) 800-5447; www.adventureisland.com. Adjacent to Busch Gardens, this is the place to spend a torrid day splashing in cool waters. The thrill rides are as scary and exciting as the placid pools are relaxing and renewing. This thirty-acre tropic paradise has something for every age. Ride five-person rafts on Wahoo Run through one tunnel and four waterfalls. Dare the Splash Attack, where you'll be soaked. Ride through tubes and down slides. Float the wave pool and play volleyball. Eat at Mango Joe's Cafe, Surfside, or Gulfscream, or bring your own picnic. Lockers, showers, and changing facilities are here for your use. Admission is $39.95 for adults and $35.95 for children ages three to nine, plus $10.00 parking for a car or RV. Ask about combination tickets to Adventure Island and Busch Gardens. Hours vary seasonally, so check the Web site or call ahead.

Alafia River State Recreation Area. Mail address: c/o Hillsborough River State Park, 15402 US 301 North, Thonotosassa, FL 33592; (813) 672-5320; www.floridastateparks .org/alafiariver. Located in Lithia, 10 miles southeast of Tampa on Country Road 39, this 6,000-acre reclaimed phosphate mine is now a picnic place and playground, with the most rigorous mountain bike trails in the state. Or, bring your fishing tackle. The area has no admission charge.

Busch Gardens Tampa Bay. 3000 East Busch Blvd.; (888) 800-5447; www.busch gardens.com. This complex is more than a one-day wonder. In fact, every day is different. Plantings change, entertainers and shows are added or changed, and the wildlife never fails to delight and surprise. With the luxury of time, sit on a park bench and watch the passing Africa scene from the Casbah to the veldt. Browse shops for safari wear. Stalk a flamingo or a giraffe—with your camera, of course. Have lunch in old Africa. Schedule your time to see all the shows. Visit the nursery to watch newborn animals being fed. Sign up for a behind-the-scenes tour. Ride the roller coasters: Montu, Kumba, Gwazi, Python, and Scorpion. Retail admission is $69.95 for adults, $59.95 for children. Discounts are available if you purchase your tickets on-line. Parking is $6 for a car, $7 for an RV. Admission includes all attractions except the Serengeti Safari. Ask about multiday passes and combination tickets that include Adventure Island. Open daily; hours vary seasonally, so check the Web site or call ahead.

Canoe Escape Inc. 9335 East Fowler Ave.; (813) 986-2067; www.canoeescape.com. This company outfits you to explore the Hillsborough River through 16,000 acres of natural wilderness right at the doorstep of this pulsing city. Sign on for tours lasting from two hours to all day, and float downstream past a wildlife panorama starring turtles, alligators, and a world of birds. A variety of different adventures are available for a variety of prices, starting at $23.50 per paddler. Open daily 9 a.m. to 5 p.m., earlier on weekends. Kayak tours and rentals can also be arranged at various times and places.

Channelside Bay Plaza. 615 Channelside Dr.; (813) 223-4250; www.channelsidebay plaza.com. This $35-million festival shopping and dining center is located at the waterfront, adjacent to the Florida Aquarium. Come early and stay on for supper and the evening.

Cruise out of the Port of Tampa (www.tampaport.com), home to luxury cruise ships including Holland America's *Noordham,* Carnival Cruises' *Inspiration,* and Royal Caribbean Cruise Lines' *Rhapsody of the Seas.* Schedules, ships, and itineraries change throughout the year. Check with a travel agent who specializes in cruises; for information about Tampa Bay Port Authority, call (813) 905-7678 or (800) 741-2297.

Dinosaur World. 5145 Harvey Tew Rd., Plant City; (813) 717-9865; www.dinoworld.net. This place is a must if you have middle-schoolers. Walk through a jungle inhabited by one hundred life-size dinosaurs, each with a plaque explaining its life and times. It takes about two hours to see them all. Bring a picnic and spend the day. A playground, gift shop, and museum round out the experience. Open daily 9 a.m. to 6 p.m. Admission is $12.75 for adults, $9.75 for children, $10.95 for seniors.

Parrots of the Caribbean Trolley Boat Tours. Mail address: 5282 95th St. North, Tampa, FL 33688; (727) 391-7433; www.stpeteducktours.com. Catch the tour at The Hut at John's Pass Village and Boardwalk in Madeira Beach. These are authentic World War II DUKWs—a vehicle that is half boat, half truck, and all fun. You'll drive city streets for a narrated tour, then launch for a waterfront jaunt. You'll spend ninety minutes getting your bearings, so this is the tour to take before you take off on your own explorations. Adults tour for $29; seniors are $25; and children ages four to fifteen, $19. The ticket booth is open from 10 a.m. to 10 p.m. Tours run at noon, 2, 4:30, and 6:30 p.m. Reservations are strongly recommended.

Florida Aquarium. 701 Channelside Dr.; (813) 273-4000; www.flaquarium.org. Located downtown, this is one of the South's finest aquariums, a place to follow a drop of water from where it falls on upland Florida all the way to where it meets the sea. See creatures that live in fresh, brackish, and ocean waters; from shy manatees to sharks and rays in areas representing wetlands, bays and beaches, coral reefs, and offshore. Hands-on exhibits include a touch tank that delights children. This is just one of the attractions in the port area, so arrive early and spend the day here and in the area's shops and restaurants. Open daily 9:30 a.m. to 5 p.m. Adult admission is $19.95, $14.95 for children, and $16.95 for seniors. Parking is $6.00.

Glazer Children's Museum. 1107 East Jackson St., #200; (813) 277-3199; www.glazer museum.org. This new museum, scheduled to open in spring 2010, is located in the Curtis Hixon Waterfront Park. Designed to inspire children and families by creating learning opportunities around innovative play and discovery, the new 53,000-square-foot facility will have a combination of permanent and traveling exhibits, programs, and special events. Museum exhibits are interactive, engaging children's hands and minds. In an environment designed specifically for them, children will be in charge of their own experience. See the Web site for hours and admission prices.

MOSI. 4801 East Fowler Ave.; (813) 987-6000; www.mosi.org. MOSI is short for the Museum of Science and Industry, and everyone calls it by its nickname. Its IMAX Dome Theater shows awesome movies that put you right in the action, so fasten your seatbelt. Out of 450 hands-on activities, kids will find enough here to stay happy and involved all day. Interactive and interpretive exhibits are for every age, from young adults to seniors. Don't miss the hurricane exhibit, the Back Woods with its native plants and animals, Space Shuttle exhibits, and the chance to ride a virtual bicycle over the longest high-wire bicycle adventure in any museum in the nation. Outdoors, stroll the butterfly garden. Adult admission is $25.95, children $19.95, seniors $22.45. Open daily at 9 a.m.; closings vary seasonally.

Tampa Museum of Art. 600 North Ashley Dr.; (813) 274 8130; www.tampamuseum.com. This museum houses more than 4,500 objects in its permanent collection and exhibits the largest collection of Greek and Roman antiquities in the Southeast. The Center Gallery displays themed exhibitions from the permanent collection. For a look at nineteenth- and twentieth-century sculpture set against the backdrop of the Hillsborough River, visit the Terrace Gallery. Stroll through the Outdoor Courtyard featuring contemporary sculptures, fountains, and bronze work. For gifts, books, children's items, or home accessories, stop by the museum store. Open Tues through Sat, 10 a.m. to 4 p.m.; Thurs, 10 a.m. to 8 p.m.; and Sun 1 to 4 p.m. Admission is $5 for adults, $4 for senior citizens, and $3 for students.

Ybor City State Museum. 1818 East Ninth Ave.; (813) 247-1434; www.ybormuseum.org. This museum is housed in an old bakery, capturing completely the Spanish-Italian flavor of the old city, which was the cigar capital of the United States by 1900. See complete "shotgun" houses that were built for cigar makers, as well as memorabilia from throughout the area's history. The old Ybor City trolley line, stilled in 1946, runs again on a 2.3-mile track that is gradually being extended. Open Mon through Sun 9 a.m. to 5 p.m. Admission is $3 for adults, free for children under six.

where to shop

International Plaza. West Shore at Boy Scout Boulevard (next to the airport); (813) 342-3790; www.shopinternationalplaza.com. Opened in 2001, this is the largest and most fashionable shopping mall west of Tampa. Neiman-Marcus, Nordstrom, Lord & Taylor, and

Dillard's are the anchor stores, and more than 200 other shops and restaurants offer hours of shopping, dining, and people-watching pleasure. There's parking for 6,000 cars. Hours vary, but stores are all open by 10 a.m. and some restaurants stay open late.

Old Hyde Park Village. Located south of downtown at Swann and Dakota Avenues; (813) 251-3500; www.hydeparkvillage.net. This is a strolling village where you can browse among sixty upscale shops, stopping here for a glass of wine and there for dinner or coffee. Sidewalk cafes are fun for people-watching. Summer concerts are held the last Wed of the month.

where to eat

Ashley Street Grille. 200 North Ashley Dr.; (813) 226-4400. Located in the Sheraton Riverwalk, this restaurant has won accolades for its dashing cuisine, which starts with a surprise amuse bouche pre-appetizer as a gift from the chef. The house salad is greens in port wine vinaigrette with goat cheese, pears, and sun-dried cherries. Have the lobster strudel appetizer, blue crab and shrimp stuffed grouper, roast stuffed chicken breast, or a hearty porterhouse pork chop. For lighter dining (and pocketbooks), the chef offers grilled-chicken Caesar salad; green salad with gorgonzola cheese, tomatoes, and balsamic vinaigrette; or a sirloin burger with bacon. The wine list is extensive, with many fine vintages available by the glass as well as the bottle. Desserts are a triumph—from apple crumble torte with honey and vanilla ice cream to a trio of chocolate confections. Open nightly for dinner. Reservations are essential. $$–$$$.

Bern's. 1208 South Howard Ave.; (813) 251-2421; www.bernssteakhouse.com. Bern's has been a local institution forever, a dining experience like no other. It's best known for its homegrown vegetables and butter-tender steaks, hand-cut to the ounce and cooked to your taste—bloody, black, or anything in between. An elaborate chart on the menu helps you through the choices, from a small filet mignon at under $30 to a sixty-ounce strip sirloin priced at $233.42. Entrees come with French onion soup, baked potato, garlic toast, garlic butter, onion rings, and a sampling of fresh vegetables. Or order vegetables and side dishes a la carte: baked potato with sour cream and bacon, mushrooms, steak fries, Canadian wild rice, and much more. To order dessert, you leave your table and are reseated upstairs in a private booth with closed-circuit TV. By the time you make the change, your appetite is rekindled for tackling one of the house's memorable sweets. The wine cellar is one of the largest and most comprehensive in the South. Call for hours and reservations, which are essential. $$$–$$$$ plus 12 percent service charge.

Caffe Paradiso. 4205 South Macdill Ave.; (813) 835-6622. Caffe Paradiso is Italian to the core. The owner's father is from near Venice, and he knows his pastas and pancettas. You can't go wrong with the pasta of the day. Open daily, except Sunday, for lunch and dinner. Reservations are recommended. $$–$$$.

Capdevila's at La Teresita. 3248 West Columbus Dr.; (813) 879-9704; www.LaTeresita restaurant.com. This is a mouthful of a name for a simple hometown Cuban restaurant where a feast is made from black beans, white rice, and crusty Cuban bread. The roast pork is pull-apart tender; other Cuban classics include breaded steak, chicken with yellow rice, and fried plantains. $.

Columbia. 2117 South Seventh Ave.; (813) 248-4961; www.columbiarestaurant.com. This eatery is in the old section of town known as Ybor City, the place where Rough Riders mustered for the attack on San Juan Hill and where this restaurant was founded in 1912. The food takes you back to turn-of-the-twentieth-century Tampa, Havana, or Madrid. Desserts, coupled with flamenco dancing, are worth a special evening Monday through Saturday. Call ahead if you want the world-famous paella, which takes awhile to prepare. Although other Columbia restaurants in Florida serve much the same menu, this one demands a special visit to see the original tiles and decor. Call for hours and reservations. $$$.

Crazy Buffet. 2702 North Dale Mabry; (813) 998-9228; www.gocrazybuffet.com. Forget everything you ever thought you knew about buffet lines. This is an upscale Asian fusion buffet. You pick one meat item to go with your stir-fry for starters and the rest is unlimited. Visit the chefs at the hibachi grill, where your food is cooked to order. Then hit the buffet, which includes all the pertinent items plus steak, sushi, and seafood (on the weekend). It's tough to complain about all-you-can-eat snow crab legs, tuna, salmon, eel, oysters, fish, shrimp, crawfish, mussels, scallops, and more. Opens at 11 a.m. daily; closing hours vary with day of the week. $$.

Hungry Harry's. 3116 Land O' Lakes Blvd., Land O' Lakes; (813) 949-2025; http://hungry harrysfamousbbq.net. Harry's is north of Tampa, a half mile north of SR 54 and US 41. Take a ride in the country to find real wood-fired barbecue that has been famous in these parts since 1981, when Harry started his barbecue pit to make food for his friends. Order a slab of ribs, chicken by the whole or part, and trimmings such as garlic bread, corn on the cob, coleslaw, baked beans, and potato salad. Burgers and meatball and vegetarian subs are also good. Order your barbecue sauce mild, sweet and smoky, or what Harry calls hella-cious hot. Open for lunch and dinner every day. $–$$.

Mise en Place. 2616 South MacDill Ave.; (813) 254-5373; www.miseonline.com. This smart, sophisticated, locally popular bistro is best reserved for an unhurried dinner with a choice from the commendable wine list. Start with onion quiche with goat cheese or mussels in a tomato sauce scented with fennel. Your server can steer you to a fresh-fish dish, succulent chicken, a comforting ragout, or a veal concoction. Call for hours. Reservations are accepted only for parties of six or more, so get up a group—or be prepared for a long wait. $$–$$$$.

SideBern's. 2208 West Morrison Ave.; (813) 258-2233; www.sideberns.com. This place is kin to the famous Bern's Steak House next door. The menu is wildly eclectic, ranging from dim sum to pastas, curries, and whole-meal salads. If it's meat and potatoes you're after, go to Bern's. Both sites excel at desserts—they share a pastry chef. Call for hours; reservations are highly recommended. $$$.

***StarShip* Dining Yacht.** Channelside, downtown Tampa, no mail address; (813) 223-7999; www.yachtstarship.com. It's a yacht, not a cruise liner, which means an intimate setting for cruise-ship-style dining and entertainment. Lunch and dinner cruises leave port every day; meals are three courses. Bird-watching is great by day, but night cruises take in the breathtaking sparkle of the city's lights on the water. Reservations are essential. $$$.

where to stay

Chase Suite Hotel. 3075 North Rocky Point Dr.; (813) 281-5677; (877) 433-9644; www .chasehoteltampa.com. This property offers one- and two-bedroom suites for the price of an ordinary room, with continental breakfast included. Suites have separate bedroom(s), full kitchen, dining area, televisions, fireplace, hair dryer, ironing board, and all the comforts of home. It's on Rocky Point overlooking the bay, handy to shopping and attractions and not too far from the beaches. Swim in the heated pool, and soak your cares away in the hot tub. $$–$$$.

Days Inn Fairgrounds. 9942 East Adamo Dr.; (813) 623-5121; www.daysinn.com. This is a good choice if you want to stay on the east side of town, handy to I-75. The hotel has a pool, and continental breakfast is included in the modest prices. It can be hard to get a room here during special events at the state fairgrounds, so book early. $$.

Hyatt Regency Westshore. 6200 West Courtney Campbell Causeway; (813) 874-1234 or (800) 233-1234; www.westshore.hyatt.com. This is a full-service high-rise hotel with everything the leisure or business traveler could ask for in the heart of Tampa, yet it's on a spit of land that offers some of the best bird-watching in the county. Choose elegant or informal dining or room service, swim in the heated pool, and work out in the fitness center. The concierge can arrange any activity from downtown dining to golf to offshore fishing. $$$.

Safety Harbor Resort and Spa. 105 North Bayshore Dr., Safety Harbor; (727) 726-1161 or (888) 237-8772; www.safetyharborresort.com. This is one of the best spas in the state, providing a full menu of sophisticated spa and salon services as well as spa cuisine, golf, tennis, unlimited use of bicycles, and twenty supervised fitness classes daily. Rooms have coffeemakers, cotton robes and slippers, unlimited local calls and free access to long-distance services, and a daily paper. Valet parking is complimentary. Ask about singles, romance, and mother-daughter packages. $$$–$$$$.

Sheraton Tampa Riverwalk. 200 North Ashley Dr.; (813) 223-2222; www.sheratontampa riverwalk.com. Formerly the Radisson Riverwalk, this hotel overlooks the Hillsborough River in the heart of downtown. Walk to the Convention Center, Ice Palace, art museum, and the dazzling Performing Arts Center to see big-name concerts and Broadway shows. The Riverwalk is a 7-mile-long ribbon you can stroll, jog, bike, or in-line skate. The location is perfect for day trips, equally handy to Busch Gardens to the east and beaches to the west. $$$–$$$$.

day trip 04

southwest

>>> **a tropical delight:**
st. petersburg–clearwater

st. petersburg–clearwater

In the early days, the trip from Tampa all the way to St. Petersburg–Clearwater took an extra half day after passengers got off the train because they had to go all the way around Tampa Bay. They kept streaming westward, however, toward the Gulf of Mexico and its incomparable sunsets. For today's traveler, it means an extra forty-five to sixty minutes on the interstates to get here. It's fun to vary the trip by taking I-4/I-275 over the Sunshine Skyway Bridge southward, following SR 699 down the coast, then heading north from St. Petersburg on I-75 to connect with I-4 and the return to Orlando. Whatever route you decide to follow, you're sure to enjoy your day at the beaches.

where to go

Anclote Key State Preserve. Mail address: c/o Caladesi Island State Park, 1 Causeway Blvd., Dunedin, FL 34698; (727) 469-5942; www.floridastateparks.org/anclotekey. Located off Tarpon Springs, this cluster of sand spits in the Gulf of Mexico was chosen as the site of a lighthouse during the Grover Cleveland administration. Now a full-size key, it's protected from development by its remoteness—3 miles off the coast. Arrive in your own boat or rent a boat on the mainland. Bring everything you need, including food and drinking water. The beaches are superb for swimming and shelling. Watch for forty-three species of wildlife, including bald eagles and ospreys. Hike the island's diverse habitats, which include tidal

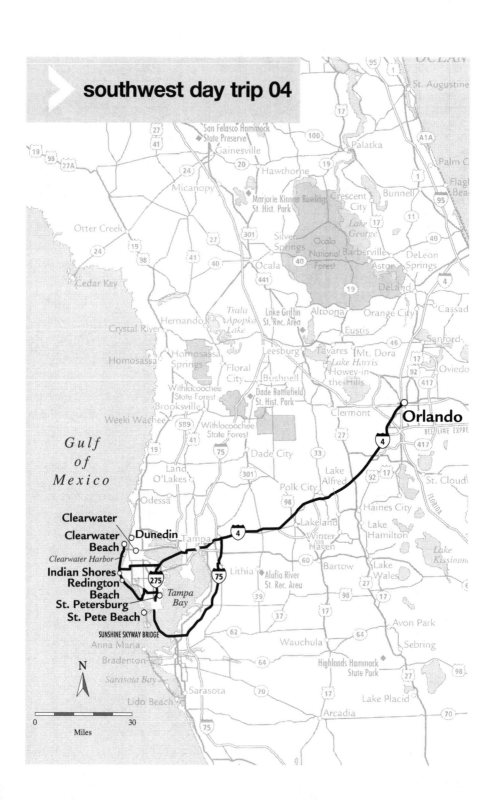

southwest day trip 04

marsh, maritime hammock, dunes, and swamps. There aren't any planned trails, so walk lightly with as little impact on the terrain as possible. Primitive camping is permitted in an area that has tables, grills, and pit toilets. The preserve is open 8 a.m. until sundown every day, and admission is free. Call ahead for more information.

Caladesi Island State Park and Honeymoon Island State Recreation Area. 1 Causeway Blvd., Dunedin; (727) 469-5918 or (727) 469-5942; www.floridastateparks.org/caladesi island. The sands are rearranged every decade or so by hurricanes, making them a new discovery with each visit. A scheduled passenger ferry runs to the islands from Clearwater, so advance planning is needed. A wonderland of wildlife, the islands are home to a long list of birds, marine life, small mammals, grasses, seashells, and vines. Stay at the marina onboard your boat, anchor off, or bring your backpack and take a primitive campsite. Trout, redfish, snook, tarpon, and kingfish are caught in season; cast-netting for mullet is popular. Overnight visitors must register before sundown and bring all their needs with them. Picnic tables, a snack bar, and showers are available. Fees are charged for day use or camping.

Canoe Escape Inc. 9335 East Fowler Ave., Thonotosassa; (813) 986-2067; www.canoe escape.com. Canoe Escape's trips run down the beautiful Hillsborough River through the 16,000-acre Wilderness Park. Trips range in length from two to six hours, and can be done as do-it-yourself trips, or as guided, interpretive affairs. You will see as much wildlife here as in any other area in Florida, including otters, deer, wild hogs, wild turkeys, and dozens of different bird species. The possibility of spotting an alligator always exists. Rentals start at $23.50 per person. The price of the interpretive guided trips depends on how many people participate. Canoe Escape is located only 12 miles from downtown Tampa.

Captain Memo's Pirate Cruise. Clearwater Marina, Clearwater Beach; (727) 446-2587; www.captainmemo.com. Go a-pirating on a playful ship where everyone gets to shoot water pistols, brandish cutlasses, and hunt doubloons. It's a family favorite. Sailings are four times daily, weather permitting. Fares are $33 to $36 for adults; $28 for children ages thirteen to seventeen and seniors; and $23 for children ages three to twelve. Call for reservations or book online.

Clearwater Marine Aquarium. 249 Windward Passage; (727) 441-1790; www.cmaquarium .org. This aquarium is less flashy than some others because it's also a rehabilitation and study center. That makes it all the more authentic and endearing. With reservations, join Marine Life Adventures, an interactive experience that takes you into the waters of Clearwater Bay. Admission is $11.00 for adults, $9.00 for seniors, $7.50 for children. Open Mon through Thurs 9 a.m. to 5 p.m., Fri and Sat 9 a.m. to 8 p.m., and Sun 10 a.m. to 5 p.m.

Gulf Coast Museum of Art. 12211 Walsingham Rd., Largo; (727) 518-6833; www.gulf coastmuseum.org. Nationally known and local Florida artists, sculptors, ceramists, and craftspeople exhibit their works here. For special exhibitions and the permanent collection, gallery talks and docent tours highlight features of the artists' works and lives. The museum store offers books, posters, toys, jewelry, and more. Admission is $5 for adults and $4 for seniors and students. Children under 10 are free. Open 10 a.m. to 4 p.m. Tues, Wed, Fri, and Sat; 10 a.m. to 7 p.m. Thurs; and noon to 4 p.m. Sun.

Museum of Fine Arts. 255 Beach Dr. Northeast; (727) 896-2667; www.fine-arts.org. This downtown landmark boasts a permanent collection consisting of classical and contemporary artistry in a variety of media. Monet, Renoir, Cezanne, Bellows, and O'Keeffe are a few of the greats in the rotating collection. Antiques, historical furnishings, crystal, timepieces, photography, and a sculpture garden—all combine to create a collection designed to appeal to a wide range of viewers. Lectures, concerts, guided tours, and even tea in the garden are available. Open 10 a.m. to 5 p.m. Tues to Sat, 1 to 5 p.m. Sun. Admission is $6 for adults, $5 for seniors, and $2 for students. Sunday admission is free.

Salvador Dalí Museum. 1000 Third St. South, St. Petersburg; (727) 823-3767; www .salvadordalimuseum.org. Salvador Dalí was the most famous of the surrealistic painters, and this spectacular museum showcases the planet's largest collection of paintings, sketches, and sculpture by the late artist. In addition to the continuing exhibits, a series of changing themed exhibits by Dalí and other surrealistic painters are also featured. At the museum store you can purchase that distinctive Dalí gift for the art lover at home. Admission is $17.00 for adults; $14.50 for seniors, military, teachers, and police; $12.00 for students age ten or older (eighteen or older with ID); $4 for children ages five to nine; and free for children ages four and under. The Web site has a discount coupon you can print out. Hours are Mon through Wed, 10 a.m. to 6 p.m.; Thurs, 10 a.m. to 8 p.m.; Fri and Sat, 10 a.m. to 5:30 p.m.; and Sun, noon to 5:30 p.m.

Sunken Gardens. 1825 Fourth St. North; (727) 551-3100; www.stpete.org/sunken/index .asp. Enjoy a "botanical experience" of tropical splendor, orchids, and bromeliads, featuring streams and pools adorned with colorful pink flamingos. There are special activities for children and wildlife presentations for everyone. Horticultural displays occur seasonally. A Rainforest Information Center here has exhibits of some of the eerier critters, including snakes and other reptiles, spiders, and scorpions. In the garden you'll also find a captivating butterfly aviary. Admission is $7 for adults, $5 for seniors, and $3 for children. Open Wed to Sun 10 a.m. to 4 p.m.

Ted Williams Museum and Hitters Hall of Fame. 1 Tropicana Dr.; www.twmuseum .com. This museum is a must-see for baseball fans and nostalgia buffs. Watch continuous videos of the Splendid Splinter and relive Ted's twenty-two-year-long career through displays that show his baseball career as well as his service as a Marine Corps pilot in World War II and the Korean Conflict. View an array of different artifacts and pictures of the "greatest hitter who ever lived." The great sluggers of all time are honored here, too: Babe Ruth, Lou Gehrig, Ty Cobb, Mel Ott, Ralph Kiner, and many more. The museum is open two hours before Tampa Bay Rays home games through the last inning, and is available exclusively to fans attending games. Admission is free.

Weedon Island Preserve Cultural and Natural History Center. 1800 Weedon Island Dr. Northeast, St. Petersburg; (727) 453-6500; www.weedonislandpreserve.org. You'll find a popular fishing and boating area at this park as well as a boardwalk over the tangled roots of mangroves. From the top of an observation tower see a great view of Tampa Bay and St. Petersburg's skyline. If you look, you're likely to spot a heron or egret and glimpse black crabs darting along mangrove branches. There's a fishing pier, picnic tables with charcoal grills, a canoe/kayak trail, and historical markers pointing out an Indian mound and an early airport ruin. Portions of the preserve are on the National Register of Historic Places. Open daily 7 a.m. to just before sunset. Admission is free.

where to eat

Frenchy's Rockaway Grill. 7 Rockaway St., Clearwater Beach; (727) 446-4844; www .frenchysonline.com. Frenchy's is so informal, all you need is a bathing suit cover-up and flip-flops to meet the dress code for dining on the wooden deck. Play volleyball on the beach to work up an appetite for jerk chicken or fish, quesadillas, calamari, Cajun special-ties, or a perky she-crab soup. Hours change with the seasons, so call ahead. $–$$.

Hurricane Seafood. 807 Gulf Way, St. Pete Beach; (727) 360-9558; www.thehurricane .com. The Hurricane has two floors of dining. The first floor has both an outdoor deck and inside dining. The second floor is a full-size restaurant that overlooks the Gulf, as well as a full-size veranda. Start with the fisherman's chowder, and follow it with a prepared-to-order grouper fillet that was caught within 100 miles of where you're sitting. They also feature hand-battered fried shrimp. Appetizers and drinks are still served up on the roof with live music featured seven days a week. $$.

Johnny Leverock's Seafood House. 840 Pasadena Ave. South; (727) 367-4588; www .leverocks.com. Seafood is king at this rock-solid local favorite. Shrimp is the house spe-cialty, served in a dozen ways from simply steamed to shrimp Diavolo to crusty, coconut-battered nuggets. The menu also features chicken, steaks, and plenty of fish choices with all the trimmings. Open Sun to Thurs 11:30 a.m. to 9 p.m., Fri and Sat 11:30 a.m. to 10 p.m. $$.

Patrick's Bayside Grill. 5007 Gulf Blvd., St. Pete Beach; (727) 363-4440; www.patricks baysidegrill.com. This lovely restaurant, once a 1940s home on St. Pete Beach, has a covered veranda, hardwood floors, vaulted ceilings, oak wainscoting, and a fireplace, all of which make it a wonderful place to visit. The seafood in particular is very fresh and very nicely done. You could start with the sashimi tuna, then follow it up with the seafood raviolis, which are unique and delicious. Or a gourmet pizza may be more to your liking. Whatever

a holy grail for art lovers

The white building, a former marine warehouse, sits on the waterfront in St. Petersburg, not particularly imposing in appearance. But for art lovers, especially those who appreciate surrealism, it's almost the Holy Grail. The Salvador Dalí Museum officially opened to the public on March 10, 1982, and since that time has attracted millions of visitors from around the world (six out of every ten come from outside the United States). This museum's collection consists of ninety-five oils, more than 100 watercolors and drawings, and over 1,300 graphics, sculptures, objects d'art, and photographs.

My most recent visit to the Dalí Museum was with my wife, son, and sister. While we were wandering through the galleries, amazed at the detail and complexity evident even in Dalí's early works, a docent tour began. Fortunately for our appreciation of Dalí's life and work and our own personal edification, we hooked up with the tour immediately.

The docent described to us young Dalí's life in Spain, spending summers in Cataques, experimenting, painting, and learning his craft. Many of these early paintings from his impressionistic period are on exhibit here. My favorite from this period was his Self Portrait (Figueres). It was painted during the time when the young artist began attending art school in Madrid. Dalí represented himself as a young dandy, wearing a large floppy hat, a black cape, and an audacious red scarf and sporting a pipe.

But Dalí did not smoke, and the clothing items were used in a local theatrical performance. That Dalí chose to use these props for this early self-portrait indicates that at the age of seventeen, he was already consciously building an eccentric public persona that became his calling card in later years.

One thing that surprised me was that in spite of the huge size of some of his paintings, especially those from his classical period, many of Dalí's best-known works are physically quite small. What is perhaps my favorite work in the entire museum is Geopoliticus Child Watching the Birth of the New Man. Unlike his surrealistic paintings, the imagery in this work doesn't require an interpreter to understand. But it still displays the brilliant technique and unusual symbolism for which Dalí is justly famous. If you find yourself in the vicinity of St. Petersburg, it's hard to imagine a more worthwhile place to visit.

your pleasure, be sure to save some room for dessert! Open Mon to Sun 5 to 11 p.m. Reservations recommended. $$–$$$.

Salt Rock Grill. 19325 Gulf Blvd., Indian Shores; (727) 593-7625; www.saltrockgrill.com. The grill is between Indian Rocks Beach and Redington Shores. Porous limestone "salt" rocks are heated in an open wood fire and used to quick-sear tuna, steaks, mahimahi, pork tenderloin, and vegetables, imparting an incomparable juiciness and flavor. Sunsets reflect beautifully in the Intracoastal Waterway, so arrive in time for cocktails at sundown followed by a leisurely dinner. $$–$$$.

where to stay

Don CeSar Beach Resort & Spa. 3400 Gulf Blvd., St. Pete Beach; (727) 360-1881 or (800) 282-1116; www.doncesar.com. For generations this has been the Pink Palace, an apparition that rises out of the white sand and glows like pink coals in the setting sun. In the Gatsby era, it was a hangout for the famous and infamous, including Lou Gehrig, Clarence Darrow, and Al Capone. The years caught up with "The Don" after World War II, when it saw service as a convalescent center, but relentless renovations have made it a showplace once again. Now a AAA four-diamond hotel, it's filled with luxuries, from the elegantly appointed guest rooms (Sealy 700 Posturepedic mattresses, goose down pillows and comforters, 220-thread Egyptian cotton sheets) to facilities such as in-room massage, an old-fashioned ice-cream parlor, world-class salon and spa, twenty-four-hour room service, an impressive lobby bar, and a variety of dining venues. Sup in grand style at the Maritana Grille or the King Charles Sunday Brunch, or go barefoot at the Beachcomber Bar. For casual dining, there's the Sea Porch Cafe.

Take afternoon tea, play golf or tennis nearby, swim in the heated plunge pool, relax in a whirlpool, parasail, snorkel, join in aerobics or aqua aerobics, and spoil yourself with a sea scrub or body masque. Water toys can be rented on the beach. Put the kids in the children's program, where they'll have fun while you shop the hotel's boutiques. A room fee applies per person per night to pay for shoe-shines, turndown, free local calls, long-distance access, parking, a choice of weekday newspapers, morning coffee in the lobby, and gratuities for housekeepers. $$$$.

Gulfside Resort. 565 Seventieth Ave., St. Pete Beach; (727) 360-7640 or (800) 823-9552; www.gulfsideresort.com. The Gulfside is a family-owned find, the kind of small, comfy place that people come back to every year. Units rent by the week and have cable TV, telephone with free local calls, and full kitchen with microwave. It's 200 yards from the Gulf beach, or you can swim in the heated pool. This is an affordable home base for anglers, golfers, water-skiers, or baseball fans who follow spring training (fifteen minutes away) as well as for those who simply want to stay beachside while they explore the area. It's a member of Small Superior Lodgings, a group that must meet its group's standards for facilities and cleanliness. Drive to nearby shopping and restaurants. $.

Marriott Suites Clearwater Beach at Sand Key. 1201 Gulf Blvd., Clearwater Beach; (727) 596-1100; www.marriott.com/hotels/travel/tpams-clearwater-beach-marriott-suites-on-sand-key. The Marriott is an all-suite resort located across the street from the beach. Visitors can swim under a waterfall in a heated pool, sign up for spa service, or work out in the fitness center. Enjoy coffee from Starbucks, fine dining at Watercolors, or just relax in the lounge. There are several supervised activities for the kids, too. $$$–$$$$.

Renaissance Vinoy Resort and Golf Club. 501 Fifth Ave. Northeast; (727) 894-1000 or (800) HOTELS-1; www.marriott.com/hotels/travel/tpasr-renaissance-vinoy-resort-and-golf-club. In the halcyon days between the world wars, a palace of a hotel was built here in the Mediterranean style that was so popular then in Florida. Now restored to its Gatsby-era splendor, the Vinoy is not just a plush place to stay, it's the handiest location for travelers who want to be in the heart of town. Visit the Pier, home of museums, shops, and restaurants and known for its spectacular, rooftop views of the sunset. Walk to museums and churches. Book a boating or fishing trip at the marina across the street. Shop, dine, and stroll peaceful parks and neighborhoods. The Sunday brunch at the hotel's Marchand's Grill is one of Florida's best, but anytime is a right time to dine in this handsome room. The resort also offers dining in the Terrace Room, Alfresco, the exclusive Fred's Bar (open only to members and guests), or in the Clubhouse at the eighteen-hole golf course. The hotel's standard rooms are spacious and pleasant, its suites are showplaces and its patio suites have private hot tubs. Don't miss the gift shop. Ask about packages and special events. $$$–$$$$.

Double Tree Beach Resort. 17120 Gulf Beach Blvd., North Redington Beach; (727) 391-4000; www.doubletreebeachresort.com. This property has a band of pure white beach where you can watch a Gulf sunset at the tiki bar before the torches are lit and the evening's pleasures begin. Each of the rooms has its own balcony. Dine on Florida-Caribbean cuisine in Mangos, then dance to live music. Swim in the ocean, rent one of the water toys, or float in the azure pool. $$$.

Tradewinds Beach Resorts & Conference Centers. Island Grand Beach Resort, 5500 Gulf Blvd., St. Pete Beach; (727) 367-6461 or (800) 360-4016. Sandpiper Hotel and Suites, 6000 Gulf Blvd., St. Pete Beach; (727) 360-5551 or (800) 360-4016; www.tradewindsresort .com. These are two different beach resorts with shared guest privileges—a unique and very pleasant touch—just steps apart on a long strip of Gulf beach. Catering to families, the Island Grand is indeed grand, with 585 newly renovated guest rooms and suites. At 159 rooms, the Sandpiper Hotel and Suites offers relaxed, tropical solitude in a somewhat smaller package. Both resorts carry four-star ratings. Bright, newly renovated rooms and suites offer a wide range of rates and accommodation choices. $$$–$$$$.

day trip 05

southwest

>>> **culture on the beach:**
sarasota, bradenton

sarasota

Long known as one of Florida's cultural capitals, little Sarasota shines. It has its own theaters, cabaret, dance companies, film festival, symphony, chamber music group, dinner theaters, chorale, jazz club, opera, ballet, dinner theater, and much more. Among its world-class attractions are the John and Mable Ringling Museum of Art, housing a host of masters, and the Asolo Theater, where you can see living productions in a thirteenth-century theater that was brought from Europe and reassembled here, piece by piece. See Regional Information at the back of this book for contacts, then plan an entire trip around the cultural offerings.

From Orlando, head west on I-4 and then south on I-75 to exits for Bradenton and Sarasota. You can work this Day Trip as a loop before heading back to Orlando.

where to go

Golden Apple Dinner Theater. 25 North Pineapple Ave.; (941) 366-5454 or (800) 652-0920; www.thegoldenapple.com. The Golden Apple is a longtime local fixture offering cocktails, a prime-rib dinner, then a popular Broadway show. Plan ahead to assure getting tickets for a show you want to see, then make it the focus of your day trip from Orlando. Tickets are $37 to $45. Reservations are essential.

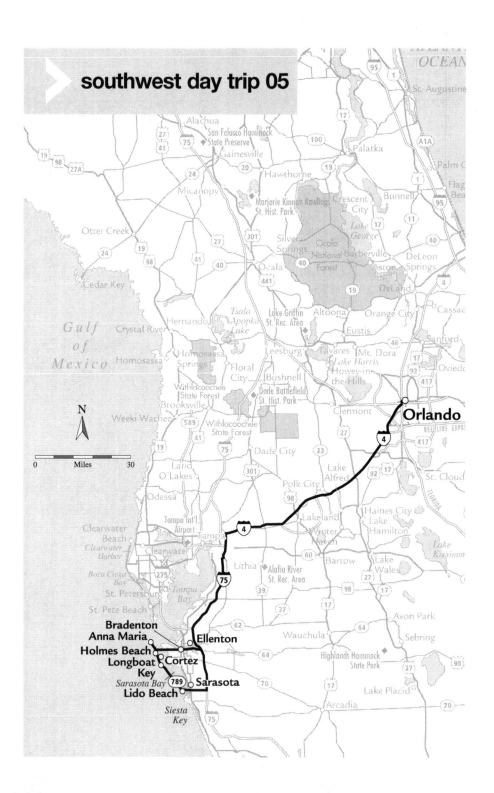

John and Mable Ringling Museum of Art. 5401 Bayshore Rd.; (941) 359-5700; www .ringling.org. The museum attracts visitors from all over the world to see one of the most impressive collections of baroque paintings on the planet. Painted between 1550 and 1775, the massive paintings were collected by Ringling in the 1920s and 1930s. They'd fallen out of fashion with wealthy Europeans, and he was able to amass a priceless collection at a fraction of what the paintings are worth today. See works by Franz Hals, Peter Paul Rubens, and other masters. The courtyard is filled with fine sculpture. Other collections take you through the entire world of fine art. Give the museum several hours, and all day if you're an art connoisseur. There's a restaurant and gift shop, plus the Ringling mansion, Cà d'Zan. Open every day 10 a.m. to 5:30 p.m. Admission is $20 for adults; $17 for seniors; $7 for students, teachers, military, and children ages six to seventeen; and free for children age five and under.

Marie Selby Botanical Gardens. 811 South Palm Ave.; (941) 366-5731; www.selby.org. The gardens are best known for their orchids, more than 6,000 of them, which are show-cased, studied, and propagated. Other rare plants, collected in the wild on research expeditions, are on view for the public and scholars alike. Once a private estate, the Selby home is surrounded by eight and a half acres of the bay, with sparkling water views to ponder while you relax on a comfortable bench in the breezes. See the butterfly garden, Bamboo Pavilion, koi pond, and special collections of succulents, banyans, bromeliads, and palms. The museum is devoted to botany of the eighteenth, nineteenth, and twentieth centuries. Adult admission is $17, $6 for children ages six to eleven. Open daily, except Christmas, 10 a.m. to 5 p.m.

Mote Aquarium. 1600 Ken Thompson Parkway; (941) 388-4441; www.mote.org. This is a working research facility, staffed by top professionals as well as dedicated volunteers who are glad to answer your questions about all the sea creatures you'll see, including a moray eel, manatees, sharks, rays, and huge turtles. Pet a stingray and a horseshoe crab. Ask about the boat tour schedule and reservations. The gift shop is the perfect place to buy fishy souvenirs and educational materials based on the sea. Admission is $17 for those over twelve, $16 for seniors, and $12 for students ages four to twelve. Open daily 10 a.m. to 5 p.m.

Sarasota Jungle Gardens. 3710 Bayshore Rd.; (888) 861-6547; www.sarasotajungle gardens.com. This botanical wonderland is also home to seventy species of reptiles, birds, and other animals. See five educational shows, have a snack, shop for souvenirs, stroll the shaded paths, or just pick a park bench and watch nature's show unfold as it has here for more than half a century. Stay as long as you like for one admission price. Open every day 9 a.m. to 5 p.m. Admission is $14 for adults, $13 for seniors, and $10 for children ages three to twelve.

where to shop

St. Armands Key. From I-75 take Sarasota exit 39, then go west on SR 780; or take US 41 to SR 780 west to St. Armands Key; (941) 388-1554. It's on the road to popular barrier islands, but don't rush through this planned shopping area with its smart shops, galleries, restaurants, sidewalk cafes, snacks, and services. You can easily spend days browsing, noshing, people-watching, and seriously shopping for fashions, unique souvenirs and gifts, books, beauty services, shoes, artworks, and everyday needs from medications to sunglasses. Hours vary. Follow signs to free parking.

Towles Court is an old neighborhood that has been transformed into a community of artist studios, art galleries, and art schools where the art lover can browse, tour galleries, and have lunch at the Continental Cafe. Call ahead (941-362-0960 or 941-955-0050) for tours that include lunch. Most of the galleries and studios are open Tues through Sat 10 a.m. to 4 p.m. The art colony is bounded by US 301, Adams Lane, Links Avenue, and Morrill Street, 3 blocks south of downtown Sarasota. For more information, visit www.towlescourt.com.

where to eat

Barnacle Bill's. This is one of the area's favorite seafood chains, with locations in Sarasota at 3634 Webber St. (941-923-5800), 1526 Main St. (941-365-6800), and 5050 North Tamiami Trail (941-355-7700); www.barnaclebillsseafood.com. You get all the ambience and great, fresh seafood tastes of the beach restaurants but without the long drive to the beach. Stop in for the catch of the day done to order, steak, shrimp, chicken, or a combination platter. It's casual enough for the family, but the food is also good enough to bring a date or a client. $$.

Columbia Restaurant. 411 St. Armand's Circle; (941) 388-3987; www.columbiarestaurant .com. This is a clone of the original Columbia, established in 1905 in Ybor City. Generations have loved this family-run chain for its enduring, endearing traditional recipes. They hark back to the old Cuba that had just won its independence from Spain. The paella takes extra time but can be the focus of a celebration evening. Or order one of the fish dishes, pork, chicken, steak, or meltingly tender beef done in "old clothes" style. Don't miss the special house salad or flan for dessert. Dine indoors or on the patio. Open daily for lunch and dinner. Reservations are recommended. $$–$$$.

Ruth's Chris Steak House. 6700 South Tamiami Trail; (941) 924-9442 or (800) 544-0808; www.ruthschris.com. This is one of Florida's favorite chains, known for succulent steaks done to perfection and brought to you sizzling hot from the oven that Ruth herself invented. There's also chicken, chops, and seafood, including fresh Maine lobster. For the ultimate feast, have surf and turf. There is an impressive wine list and valet parking. Dinner is served daily from 5 to 10 p.m. Call for reservations. $$$.

Sugar and Spice Family Restaurant. 4000 Cattlemen Rd.; (941) 342-1649. This eatery is one of Sarasota's delicious little secrets. You wouldn't expect to find an Amish restaurant in a Florida resort city, but long ago a colony of "Pennsylvania Dutch" settled here and spawned this and other great restaurants. Meals are hearty and home-style, such as meat-loaf and mashed potatoes, roasted turkey with all the trimmings, golden fried chicken, and liver and onions. The desserts, especially the pies, are sinfully good. The decor is rich in the crafts and symbols of the "plain people." Open daily 7 a.m. to 9 p.m., except Sun. $–$$.

Yoder's Amish Restaurant. 3434 Bahia Vista St.; (941) 955-7771; www.yodersrestaurant .com. Yoder's has been here long enough to be thoroughly Floridian, but the Yoders haven't forgotten their Amish roots. Everything is down-home delicious, brimming with old-fashioned flavor. Have crispy fried chicken with mashed potatoes, gravy, and fresh vegetables; or enjoy the juicy meatloaf. Save room for pie, especially one of the fruit pies made season by season as the harvests ripen. Open daily 6 a.m. to 8 p.m., except Sun. $–$$.

where to stay

Colony Beach & Tennis Resort. 1620 Gulf of Mexico Dr., Longboat Key; (941) 383-6464 or (800) 4-COLONY; www.colonybeachresort.com. This family-run resort enjoys a long list of loyal repeaters. It's best known for its fine tennis program, with play and instruction for all ages and all skill levels. Stroll the wave-washed Gulf beach, swim in the pool, take a fit-ness session with a trainer who can help you with your tennis game, or arrange a round of golf. Units have sleeping room for two to eight persons and full kitchens, but you can also call room service. Have at least one meal a day in one of the resort's outstanding, award-winning restaurants. The Colony is the home of the annual Hacker's Open for tennis buffs and an annual seafood-and-wine festival that brings in celebrity chefs. Children love the Kidding Around program for ages seven to twelve and Kinder Kamp for ages three to six. In addition to fun and creative activities, they'll be introduced to tennis. $$$–$$$$.

Coquina on the Beach. 1008 Ben Franklin Dr., Lido Beach; (941) 388-2141 or (800) 833-2141; www.coquinaonthebeach.com. The Coquina is just around the corner from chic, European-style St. Armands Circle. Beachfront and beach-view studios have two double beds and a full kitchen. Swim in the big pool or off the snow-white beach. Coffee is compli-mentary, but there's no restaurant on-site. Ask about senior rates. $–$$.

Helmsley Sandcastle Hotel. 1540 Ben Franklin Dr., Lido Beach; (941) 388-2181 or (800) 225-2181; www.helmsleysandcastle.com. The Helmsley sits on a long stretch of snowy beach on the Gulf of Mexico, offering panoramic views of the water and everything you could ask for in resort activities. Sail, fish, play beach volleyball, or just sun on the beach. Rooms have safes, complimentary morning paper, and a small refrigerator. Dine in one of the two restaurants or order from room service, then relax after dinner in the lounge to live music. $$$–$$$$.

Hilton Longboat Key Beachfront Resort. 4711 Gulf of Mexico Dr., Longboat Key; (941) 383-2451 or (800) 282-3046; www.longboatkey.hilton.com. This resort is a white vision rising from a white-sand Gulf beach. Every room has a private patio or balcony; ask for a Gulf-view room or suite so that you won't miss any of the famous sunsets. Every unit has nightly turndown, minibar, and in-room safe. Dine in the Sunset Grill, or have lunch or a frozen drink outdoors at the pool bar. Swim off the private beach or in the heated pool. Shop for sundries and beachwear in the Beach Hut. Rent cabanas and equipment for water sports. A free shuttle takes shoppers to St. Armands Circle. $$$.

Holiday Inn Lido Beach. 233 Ben Franklin Dr., Lido Beach; (941) 388-5555; www .lidobeach.net. This property brings you the allure of pristine Lido Beach and all the hotel amenities of a major, modestly priced chain. Spacious rooms are done in sea tones. Ask for a Gulf-front room with a balcony, where you'll have a private view of the sunsets with their legendary green flash. Rooms have a coffeemaker, TV, phone with voice mail and data port, ironing board and iron, and hair dryer. The hotel has a rooftop restaurant and pool bar, heated outdoor pool, fitness room, bicycle rental, gift and sundries shop, and a free airport shuttle. $$$.

Hyatt Sarasota. 1000 Blvd. of the Arts; (941) 953-1234 or (800) 233-1234; www.sarasota .hyatt.com. This sleekly modern downtown hotel has everything the business or leisure traveler could ask for, plus a yachty ambience thanks to its Boathouse restaurant overlooking the marina. Even if you're not staying here, it's worth a visit to sample the innovative New American cuisine. The Sunday brunch is dazzling. Walk to the concert hall and other city sights and parks. The hotel has a swimming pool, fitness equipment, cable television, and an airport shuttle. The concierge can arrange fishing, boating, sightseeing, golf, or a tennis match. $$–$$$.

The Resort at Longboat Key Club. 301 Gulf of Mexico Dr., Longboat Key; (941) 383-8821 or (888) 237-5545; www.longboatkeyclub.com. This AAA four-diamond resort sits on a wave-washed beach, with two championship golf courses, driving ranges, pro shop, clubhouse facilities including lockers and steam rooms, tennis courts, a children's program, a fitness center, swimming pool with Jacuzzi, captained sailing charters, charter fishing boats, and a choice of restaurants and lounges with live entertainment. Room service is also available. All the spacious, lavishly furnished guest rooms have a private balcony and refrigerator with ice maker. Also available are suites with up to two bedrooms. A 9.5-mile jogging path starts here and runs the length of the key. In-line skate rentals are available nearby. $$$–$$$$.

Ritz-Carlton Sarasota. 1111 Ritz-Carlton Dr.; (941) 309-2000 or (800) 241-3333; www .ritzcarlton.com. This property has been exciting news in downtown Sarasota since it opened late in 2001, looking right at home in this high-toned community. Walk to cultural attractions, shopping, and dining. All rooms have a view of the bay, marina, or skyline.

Book a superior room, suite, or Club Level accommodations that have a separate lounge, concierge, and complimentary food and beverage presentations. Rooms have private balconies, housekeeping twice a day with evening turndown, twenty-four-hour room service, multiple telephone lines, high-speed Internet access, and marble baths. Use of terry robes and a free daily newspaper are provided. Play tennis day or night, or have the concierge arrange a tee time at one of the nearby golf courses. The big full-service adjacent spa incorporates native Florida botanicals into its full menu of soothing treatments. Dine elegantly in the Vernona for Mediterranean fare or more casually in the Bay View Bar & Grill. The bar, which has a cigar bar and single malts, is called Cà d'Zan after the historic Ringling property. Take a wellness, training, or fitness program, or just be lazy at the Beach Club on Lido Key's powder-white beach. It's reached by a free shuttle and has information, a tiki bar, restaurant, beachside pool with hot tub, and programs for children. $$$–$$$$.

Sandpiper Inn. 5451 Gulf of Mexico Dr., Longboat Key; (941) 383-2552; www.sandpiper inn.com/FL. This homey little place is right on the beach and surrounded by lush green, with a full kitchen in each one- or two-bedroom apartment. It's one of a handful of spots in this tony area that fit our "$" rating. Pets are permitted, and there's a swimming pool. $.

Silver Sands Gulf Beach Resort. 5841 Gulf of Mexico Dr., Longboat Key; (941) 383-3731; www.resortquestswfl.com/silversands. This property puts you on the beach in a resort room, apartment, or villa with up to three bedrooms. Daily maid service is provided. Swim in the heated beachside pool, use complimentary chaises and beach umbrellas, take to the putting green, or play tennis or shuffleboard. Kitchens are furnished with everything you'll need to cook every meal, or you can drive to a good selection of restaurants nearby. $$–$$$.

Turtle Beach Resort. 9049 Midnight Pass Rd., Siesta Key; (941) 349-4554; www.turtle beachresort.com. Each quiet, secluded cottage at this romantic hideaway has its own hot tub. Massages are just a phone call away. Watch turtles nest on Turtle Beach, listen to the wild parrots, watch for dolphins and manatees, and dine in the area's best seafood restaurants just footsteps away. Children and pets are welcome. You can bring up to two pets for a 10 percent additional fee. Add $200 for a romance package that includes champagne, dinner for two, and a sunset cruise. Most units have a full kitchen. One- and two-bedroom cottages and studios are available. Use the resort's bicycles, kayaks, rowboat, paddleboat, canoe, and fishing poles. The spacious swimming pool is heated. $$$ plus maid service.

bradenton

The most direct route from Sarasota to Bradenton is I-75 North. Let's sort out the nomenclature. Bradenton area beaches are Anna Maria, Holmes Beach, and Bradenton Beach—reached from the mainland at Cortez. The entire island is Anna Maria Island, bordered by the Gulf of Mexico to the west and Tampa Bay to the east. The island cities are Anna Maria, Holmes Beach, and Bradenton Beach. The beach road is SR 789, known variously as Midnight Pass Road, Gulf of Mexico Dr., and Casey Key Road as it passes from island to island. Refer to a good map to decide what bridge is best for where you're going. One goes to Holmes Beach, one to Bradenton Beach, and then there isn't another until the US 41 bridge from Sarasota to Lido Key.

Calusa and Timucuan Indians inhabited these sands long before recorded history, feasting on the bountiful seafood and shellfish. Homesteaders began arriving in 1892 by boat, and by 1921 the island was hitched to the mainland by a wooden bridge. Today there's a better highway and bridge, but the old span is still used as a fishing pier. SR 84 enters the island at Holmes Beach, south of the city of Anna Maria. To reach Bradenton Beach, take SR 684 from the mainland.

where to go

Anna Maria Island Historic Museum. 402 Pine St., Anna Maria Island; (941) 778-0492; www.amihs.org. This small effort is worth visiting to see relics and records of the people and events that shaped this lonely barrier island. The museum's home was once an icehouse where sawdust-packed ice, sailed down from the frozen north, was sold through the summer until it was gone. Hours vary seasonally. Donations are appreciated.

Around the Bend Nature Tours. 1815 Palma Sola Blvd.; (941) 794-8773; www.around bend.com. Naturalist Karen Fraley will take you on walking tours, sunset cruises, a venturer's visit with a picnic, or a Backwaters History Cruise to Cortez Village, a working fishing village since 1889. There's a lot of variety and spontaneity here because it's the work of one dedicated woman, so call ahead to see what's on the schedule. Modest prices start at $20 and go to $60, including transportation and lunch.

Gamble Plantation State Historic Site. 3708 Patten Ave., Ellenton; (941) 723-4536; www.floridastateparks.org/gambleplantation. The plantation lies on the mainland just west of I-75 off US 301. Established along the Manatee River in the 1840s, this successful sugar plantation once covered 3,500 acres. The home of Major Robert Gamble here is the only antebellum plantation house that survives in south Florida. Tour the mansion, furnished in the style of the mid-nineteenth century, and note the Judah P. Benjamin Confederate Memorial, dedicated to the secretary of state for the South. When the Confederacy fell, Benjamin took refuge here until a boat could be found to take him across Sarasota Bay. Fleeing Union soldiers, he escaped via the Caribbean to England, where he became a leading member of the English bar. The site is open Thurs through Mon 9 a.m. to 5 p.m. The house is open to tours only, given on the hour until 4 p.m. except at noon. Admission is $5 for adults, $3 for children. Bring lunch; a shaded picnic area is provided.

where to shop

Everything Under the Sun. 5704 Marina Dr., Anna Maria; (941) 778-4441. Visit this farmers' market to stock your condo or picnic basket, order citrus to send to friends back home, sip a citrus drink, or select gifts and souvenirs. Hours vary seasonally, so call ahead.

Ginny's and Jane E's at the Old IGA. 9807 Gulf Dr., Anna Maria; (941) 778-3170; http:// annamariacafe.com. Ginny's is an Internet cafe serving fresh organic produce and juices, salads, soups, quiche, and freshly baked goods. All the furnishings in the store—vintage wicker and rattan furniture, tables and chairs, art, lamps, furniture, pottery, wind chimes, and more—are for sale. Do you like that vintage wicker chair you're sitting on? Take it home! They feature live music on Friday nights. It's a neat place. Ginny has a second location (without the refreshments) called Ginny's Antiques & Art a few miles down the road at 5602 Marina Dr. in Holmes Beach (941-779-1773).

The Sea Hagg. 12304 Cortez Rd. West, Cortez; (941) 795-5756; http://seahagg.com. This is a good place to stop on your way to or from Anna Marina Island. Buy nautical collectibles, antiques, art, and souvenirs as remembrances of your trip. Hours vary seasonally.

where to eat

Beach Bistro. 6600 Gulf Dr., Holmes Beach; (941) 778-6444; www.beachbistro.com. This is one of the island's smartest spots. Wear your best resort casual duds for an evening of fine Mediterranean cuisine with a good wine. Fresh seafood plays an important role, but you can also order a steak, rack of lamb, or a vegetarian dish. Reservations are essential in season. This is an award-winning restaurant, one of *Florida Trend's* Top 200 and a consistent favorite with Zagat voters. Open daily for dinner. $–$$$.

The Beach House. 200 Gulf Dr.; (941) 779-2222; www.beachhouse-restaurant.com. This establishment offers a lovely beach location with a covered area outside. For appetizers try the crab artichoke dip and sweet and spicy shrimp. Delicious entrees include sirloin steak, fettuccini Alfredo, Ybor Cuban Sandwich, and Beach Chicken. Their pina colada bread is not to be missed. Open 11:30 a.m. to 10 p.m. $$.

Cantina Toscana. 8203 Cooper Creek Blvd.; (941) 359-2500; www.cantinatoscana.biz. All the chefs at this establishment hail from Italy, so the food is authentic Italian. For appetizers sample the very aromatic and spirited tomato basil zuppa, the carpaccio marinated in lemon juice topped with parmesan, or the very tender calamari. For an entree the mussels, shrimp, and calamari sautéed in a tomato sauce over a bed of pasta or the fresh sea bass are both excellent. Or keep it simple and have a pizza and salad. The dessert selections are numerous, sweet, rich, and luxurious. Open for lunch and dinner. $$–$$$.

Euphemia Haye Restaurant. 5540 Gulf of Mexico Dr., Longboat Key; (941) 383-3633; www.euphemiahaye.com. This charming Longboat Key restaurant has been chef-owned and -operated since 1980. They offer a friendly atmosphere and an innovative menu featuring an eclectic, global cuisine, which has won the restaurant numerous awards. Unusual in modern restaurants, all of the breads, stocks, sauces, soups, desserts, and even the pastas are homemade on the premises. Enjoy one of the wonderful, original signature dishes: crisp roast duckling with bread stuffing and a seasonal fresh berry sauce is not to be missed. One of the area's most comprehensive wine cellars offers the perfect complement to your meal. After your entree move to the Dessert Room, where freshly prepared, award-winning desserts will tempt your palate, accompanied by the freshly brewed coffee of your choice. The Haye Loft upstairs features jazz seven nights a week and one of the largest Scotch selections in Florida. Reservations recommended. $$$.

Mr. Bones BBQ. 3007 Gulf Dr., Holmes Beach; (941) 778-6614; www.mrbonesbbq.com. Mr. Bones has an eclectic selection that includes baby back ribs, Indian specialties, vegetarian dishes, and whole-meal salads. End the meal with espresso or cappuccino. Mr. Bones is open Mon through Sat 11 a.m. to 9 p.m. and Sun 12 to 9 p.m. $–$$.

Rotten Ralph's. 902 Bay Blvd. South, Anna Maria; (941) 778-3953 and 200 Bridge St., on the pier at Bradenton Beach; (941) 778-1604; www.rottenralphs.com. These two locations specialize in British-style fish-and-chips, but there is also a big choice of other seafood as well as sandwiches, steaks, burgers, and pub grub in a salty, waterfront setting. Ralph is renowned for his escargot and key lime pie. Open every day for lunch and dinner 11 a.m. to 9 p.m. The pier location is also open for breakfast. $–$$.

The Sun House Restaurant and Bar. 111 Gulf Dr. South, Bradenton Beach; (941) 782-1122; www.thesunhouserestaurant.com. The Sun House Restaurant and Bar specializes in Floribbean cuisine featuring fresh seafood and award-winning salsas. Appetizers include such fare as jumbo lump crab cakes with mango-papaya salsa and camarones barracho. Entrees likewise emphasize seafood. Carnivores might prefer the Island Style Filet Mignon, or the Sundown Burger. The restaurant offers indoor and outdoor dining with sweeping views of the Gulf of Mexico and the Intracoastal Waterway. Open daily at 3 p.m. $$–$$$.

where to stay

BridgeWalk. 100 Bridge St., Bradenton Beach; (941) 779-2545 or (866) 779-2545; www .silverresorts.com. This property has Key West style and all the comforts of home. Choose a room, studio, or one- or two-bedroom suite with full kitchen, fireplaces, whirlpool bath in the master bedroom, and spacious screened veranda. Views are of the beach and Intracoastal Waterway. Swim in the heated pool, dine on-site, and walk to nearby shops, restaurants, and nightlife. $$$.

Harrington House Bed & Breakfast. 5626 Gulf Dr., Holmes Beach; (941) 778-5444 or (888) 828-5566; www.harringtonhouse.com. This B&B pampers guests with personal service delivered by caring owner-hosts. It's on a private Gulf beach and has a heated swimming pool. $$.

Sand Pebble Apartments. 2218 Gulf Dr. North, Bradenton Beach; (941) 778-3053 or (800) 500-7263; www.sandpebble.com. This is a tropical treat on the edge of the Gulf. Comb 7 miles of salt-white sand. Self-catering studios and one- and two-bedroom apartments are equipped for housekeeping in style. Splurge on a unit with private pool or private whirlpool, or use the complex's own pool. Rentals are by the week or month. $$.

Silver Surf Gulf Beach Resort. 1301 Gulf Dr. North, Bradenton Beach; (941) 778-6626 or (800) 441-7273; www.silverresorts.com. The resort sits on a private white-sand beach. Get a room, studio, or suite—all with daily maid service. Suites have a full kitchen, and studios have a microwave, coffeemaker, and minirefrigerator. Walk to restaurants, swim in the heated swimming pool, or book a sportfishing charter. Parasailing and bridge fishing are nearby. $$–$$$.

Tradewinds Resort. 1603 Gulf Dr. North, Bradenton Beach; (941) 779-0010 or (888) 686-6719; www.tradewinds-resort.com. The Tradewinds offers island living in laid-back style. It's on the bay side of the island, across the street from a private beach. Small and intimate, it has a Superior Small Lodging rating and three diamonds from AAA. Rentals are by the day, week, or month. $$.

west

day trip 01

west

sleepy little towns:
clermont, bushnell, dade city

clermont

As the sprawling shadow of Orlando spreads over it, Clermont, just west of Orlando on SR 50, is quickly losing its identity as a separate community. Still, Clermont is in pretty lake country, with open spaces that call for a special visit. Because it's an old crossroads dating back to long before the turnpike or interstates were built, you'll see vestiges of the old, pre-Disney Florida. Roadside stands sell oranges, grapefruit, goat milk fudge, and orange blossom honey. You'll see motor courts that were forerunners of modern motels and cornball attractions that continue to rope in road-weary visitors.

where to go

CFT Sommer Sports. 1271 Commons Court; (352) 394-1320; www.sommersports.com. This company organizes bicycle rides within Lake County, including a triathlon. Call to see what's scheduled and when.

Citrus Tower. 141 North US 27; (352) 394-4061; www.citrustower.com. The tower is one of the tourist attractions your grandparents visited on their trips to Central Florida, and somehow it has survived into the interstate era. US 27 is no longer the main artery through the heart of Florida, but it continues to pump tourists into an area that still has the tower, but little citrus. Today's view from the twenty-two-story tower is of increasing urban sprawl, but

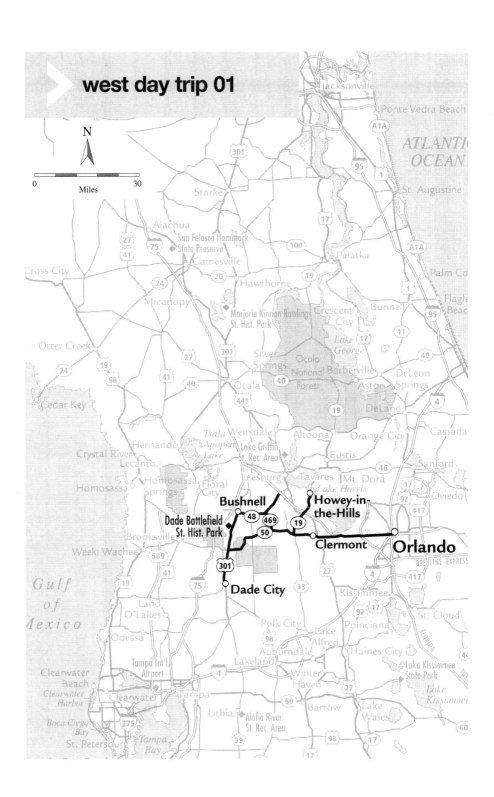

west day trip 01

the tower is worth visiting for its nostalgic exhibits as well as for the 225-foot elevator ride. Except Christmas and Thanksgiving, hours are 9 a.m. to 5 p.m. Mon through Sat. Admission is $4 for adults and $2 for children ages three to eleven.

Lake Louisa State Park. 12549 State Park Dr.; (352) 394-3969; www.floridastateparks .org/lakelouisa. The park is 10 miles south of SR 50 off CR 561. This 4,372-acre park is on the shores of Lake Louisa, one of a chain of lakes formed by the Palatlakaha River. Come here to fish, swim, picnic, canoe, exercise your horse on miles of equestrian trails, or train your binoculars on red foxes, bobcats, white-tailed deer, pocket gophers, marsh rabbits, and a swirl of bird life. Open 8 a.m. to sundown. State park fees apply.

Lakeridge Winery. 19239 US 27 North; (800) 768-9463; www.lakeridgewinery.com. Lakeridge is a beautiful botanical site where sixty-seven acres of vineyards grow hybrid grapes that were developed especially for the hot, humid, grape-hostile Florida climate. Varieties including Blanc de Blanc have come a long way from the syrup-sweet muscadine and scuppernong wines that the South was once known for. Take the one-hour tour anytime, but the winery is especially lively at harvest times, mid-June and late Aug, with live jazz entertainment. The winery is open Mon to Sat 10 a.m. to 5 p.m. and Sun 11 a.m. to 5 p.m.; free except during concerts and special events.

where to eat

Akina Sushi. 4300 South SR 27; (352) 243-8988. Akina offers a wide variety of sushi as well as other Asian fusion dishes including noodles, meat dishes, soups, and more. The Singapore Rice Noodles with tofu is very good. Be sure to try a salad, as the dressing is excellent. You may want to sample a bottle of the house sake as well. $$.

Chef's Table. 796 West Minneola Ave.; (352) 242-1264; www.clermontchefstable.com. This traditional deli serves up typical hearty breakfast and lunch fare. Some creative sandwiches are available too, like the Roma and the Crabby Patty Po Boy. They also serve paninis wraps, salads, and more. Open Tues to Sat 8 a.m. to 3 p.m. $–$$.

Outback Steak House. 1625 East US 50; (352) 243-0036; www.outback.com. No rules, just right! The Outback chain is deservedly popular for their fine steaks and chops. The salmon and shrimp dishes likewise are excellent. Never a bad choice, the Outback in Clermont is particularly popular due to the general lack of other good eateries. $$.

Stromboli's. 1042 East SR 50; (352) 242-4800. If you need a pizza or a sub sandwich just like up north, Stromboli's is the place. It doesn't look like anything special on the outside, but inside there is a very nice dining room where they serve good pastas and other Italian specialties, too. $–$$.

where to stay

Howard Johnson Express Inn. 20329 US 27 North; (352) 429-9033; www.hojo.com. This sixty-five-room roadside motel is near everything and priced to please. There's a swimming pool and guest laundry, but otherwise this is a plain-Jane place for overnighting in a basic motel room. Parking is plentiful. Restaurants aren't far away. $. (352) 429-9033.

Mission Inn Golf & Tennis Resort. 10400 County Rd. 48M, Howey-in-the-Hills; (352) 324-2350 or (800) 874-9053; www.missioninnresort.com. This resort is a groomed, green oasis halfway between Clermont and Tavares. Built in Spanish Mission style with red-tile roofs and graceful archways that frame views of the golf courses, the resort has courtyards with fountains; winding pathways to its 187 rooms, resorts, and villas; twenty-four-hour room service; two eighteen-hole golf courses; tennis; and boating out of a full-service marina; croquet; bicycling; jogging; and fishing. Shop in the arcade and dine in El Conquistador. $$$.

Mission Park Florida Vacation Homes. 9550 US 192; (800) 311-7105; www.ipgflorida.com. This is a gated community with a mix of permanent residences and vacation home rental villas. There is a community swimming pool and children's play area with basketball. Accommodations range from three- to six-bedroom homes complete with fully equipped kitchen. The community is situated near Champion's Gate and Reunion Golf Courses. Nearby there are many lakes and canals and the "Rails to Trails" bike trail that extends from Clermont to Ocoee. $$$.

The Old Bicycle Inn. 931 West Montrose St.; (352) 394-6944; www.theoldbicycleinn.com. This is an elegant guesthouse, a 1920s California bungalow that's been converted into a bed-and-breakfast. The Old Bicycle Inn offers three private rooms, a comfortable two-bedroom apartment, and a full two-bedroom, one-bathroom guesthouse. It's popular with the athletes training at the USAT or triathletes participating in the Greater Floridian Iron Man and Half Iron Man competitions. $$–$$$.

Summer Bay Resort. 25 Towne Center Blvd.; (352) 242-1100 or (888) 742-1100; www.summerbayresort.com. This is a popular destination for tourists because it's centrally located to sightseeing in the Tampa and Orlando areas and has all the resort bells and whistles—swimming pool, children's program, fitness center, and boat dock. Every unit has a kitchen. Restaurants are nearby. $$–$$$.

bushnell

From Clermont, stay with SR 50 through Mascotte, watching for a right turn (north) onto Route 469. This becomes Route 48 as you go through the community of Central Hill. Stay with US 301 toward Dade Battlefield State Historic Site.

Although this day trip goes only as far as the Dade Battlefield south of Bushnell, the town itself has motels, a campground, and places to eat.

where to go

Dade Battlefield State Historic Site. Mail address: 7200 CR 603 South Battlefield Dr., Bushnell, FL 33513; (352) 793-4781; www.floridastateparks.org/dadebattlefield. The battlefield is just southwest of Bushnell off SR 476 (Seminole Avenue).

One of the most poignant battles in American history took place in the lonely pinewoods here in 1835 during the Seminole Wars. Major Francis Dade and his force of 108 marching men were suddenly attacked by Indians, who had shadowed them for five days. Because the most suspect ambush points were behind them, Dade hadn't posted scouts. Worse still, it was raining, so the men's muskets and ammunition were covered with their coats. Half were killed or wounded with the first volley. With no shelter, the soldiers quickly felled a few pines to create meager breastworks, but still they died one by one. Two wounded soldiers made it to Fort Brooke to tell the tale, but it was almost two months before a party arrived at the scene of the massacre to bury the dead.

The scene is reenacted each year on the weekend closest to Christmas, but the site is worth visiting anytime. Bring a picnic, walk the trail, and see exhibits in the visitor center, which has restrooms. Open Thurs through Mon 9 a.m. to 5 p.m.

dade city

Dade City was named for the major who, with 108 men, was ambushed north of here during the Seminole Wars. The community thrived in old Florida, but the interstates stole its thunder and downtown faded—only to be reborn as a chic center for antiques shops, boutiques, and trendy restaurants. Write ahead for a map (see Regional Information at the back of this book) showing historic homes, and take your own walking or driving tour to see more than sixty historic sites, including the old hospital, Victorian homes, and the stately courthouse with its charming band shell. Ask, too, for the *Historic Downtown Dade City Shopping* guide, showing the locations of more than sixty antiques and specialty shops, galleries, and restaurants, most of them on or just off US 301. From Bushnell follow US 301 south to Dade City. After your visit, hop back on US 301, this time heading north, back to SR 50 and Orlando.

where to go

Pioneer Florida Museum. Mail address: P.O. Box 335, Dade City, FL 33526; (352) 567-0262; www.pioneerfloridamuseum.org. Located north of Dade City off US 301, this is an entire village of buildings, including a shoe shop, a house dating to the mid-1860s, a 1913 depot with steam engine, a restored one-room schoolhouse, and much more. A variety of collections are shown in the main museum building and barn. Special events held here throughout the year include a quilt show and sale, magnolia show, pioneer craft days, and more. Hours are Tues through Sat 10 a.m. to 5 p.m. A modest admission is charged.

where to eat

Kafe Kokopelli. 37940 Live Oak Ave.; (352) 523-0055; www.kafekokopelli.com. This building was the original Ford agency, built to sell and service Model Ts and all the cars that came later. Its tools were served by a pulley system that's now in the Smithsonian, but the remains can still be seen in the rafters. Burgers are served all day, and there are also hot and cold sandwiches, quesadillas, fried fish, vegetarian selections, snacks such as wings and nachos, and a killer raspberry–key lime cheesecake. House wines, sangria, and specialty coffees finish the meal. Open for lunch and dinner Tuesday through Saturday. $.

Lunch on Limoges. 14139 Seventh St.; (352) 567-5685; http://lunchonlimoges.com. Located on the old courthouse square, this eatery actually serves your lunch on Limoges china. A chalkboard shows daily specials, such as pecan grouper, chicken salad on a croissant, shrimp salad with fresh fruit, or poached salmon. Reservations are suggested. Open Tues through Sat 11:30 a.m. to 2:30 p.m. $–$$.

A Matter of Taste. 14121 Seventh St.; phone/fax (352) 567-5100. The restaurant is upstairs, with a nice view of the passing scene below. Choose from a tempting list of soups, salads, quiches, cold plates, and sandwiches or hot dishes, including a country skillet of vegetables, béarnaise sauce, and rice. The Tarpon Springs Greek salad is made with Greek potato salad and a homemade Greek dressing. The building dates to the early 1920s, when it was the headquarters of the city's telephone company. Call ahead for takeout. $.

where to stay

Pasco Motel. 18051 US 301; (352) 567-6220. This is a simple, clean, no-frills motel run by nice people, a true mom-and-pop operation. $–$$.

St. Charles Inn Bed and Breakfast. 12503 Curley Rd., San Antonio; (352) 588-4130; http://stcharlesinnbedandbreakfast.com. This inn was built in 1913. After a number of years of sitting idle, the hotel was purchased by Ted and Anne Stephens, who have restored the grand structure to its original glory. With many of the original antiques and many they have added, the inn has become a gracious bed-and-breakfast. Guests can enjoy impeccable decorating touches or just rock away on one of the porches and smell the aroma of the many fragrant plants and flowers. $$–$$$.

day trip 02

west

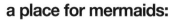

>>> **a place for mermaids:**
brooksville, weeki wachee

brooksville

Brooksville was a hotbed of blockade-runner activity during the Civil War, when Confederate troops counted on it to supply them with beef, pork, and salt. Each year in January, the Brooksville Raid Civil War reenactment is one of the city's biggest tourism events. The historic hamlet is a good place to headquarter while you explore the springs, coasts, and forests of this area. Take SR 50 west from Orlando; it joins US 98 and takes you into Brooksville.

where to go

Hernando Heritage Museum. 601 Museum Court; (352) 799-0129; http://hernando historicalmuseum.com. The museum houses one of the state's best collections of Civil War relics, including a complete doctor's office and 6,000 antiques dating to the mid-nineteenth century. Admission is $5 for adults and $2 for children. Hours are noon to 3 p.m. Tues through Sat. Ask about the Brooksville Raid, which is organized by the museum.

where to shop

Rogers' Christmas House and Village. 103 South Saxon Ave.; (352) 796-2415 or (877) 312-5046; www.rogerschristmashouse.com. The complex of shops is housed in five quaint old houses from the early 1900s. Shop all year for Christmas gifts and decorations in one

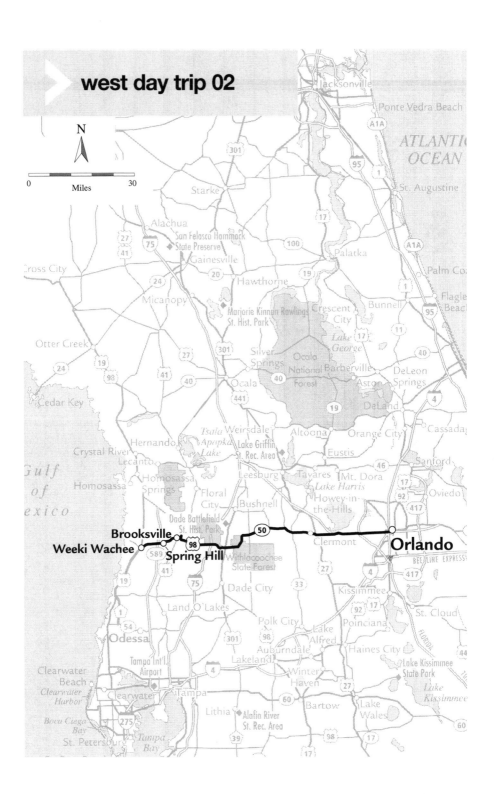

west day trip 02

of the Sunshine State's oldest and most popular Christmas stores. Open every day but Thanksgiving, Christmas, and Easter, 10 a.m. to 5 p.m.

where to eat

Coney Island Drive Inn. 1112 East Jefferson St.; (352) 796-9141. For forty-three years Coney Island has been serving hot dogs, corn dogs, burgers, chicken, and fish to Brooksville. If you're a hot-dog fan, this is a must stop. $.

Deep South Family Bar-B-Que. 7247 Cedar Lane; (352) 799-5060. At this very informal, laid-back, and small restaurant, Clay, the owner, does all of the cooking. He makes you feel at home with personal attention and conversation. The menu features barbecued pork, ribs, and chicken as well as steak, meatloaf, pork chops, and sausage. There is a large side menu featuring barbecued beans, fried okra, fried green tomatoes, and many more. It just don't get mo' better than this! $.

Mykonos II. 1740 East Jefferson St.; (352) 799-3154. This place specializes in a Greek combination dinner, but Italian and Cuban dishes are also available. The Cuban sandwich makes a great lunch, but go Greek with the baklava for dessert. Call ahead for hours. $–$$.

where to stay

Lakewood Retreat. 25458 Dan Brown Hill Rd.; (352) 796-4097; www.lakewoodretreat .org. As you might guess, the eleven cabins at the Lakewood are located on St. Clair Lake. The kids can play in the playground, or you can stroll the walking trails. $$.

Mary A. Coogler Cottage. 114 South Brooksville Ave.; (352) 796-6857. Located downtown, this two-bedroom guesthouse is named for an artist who once lived here. $$. Through the same telephone number, you can arrange to stay at the **Amapola Guest House** (238 North Lemon Ave.), a more than fifty-year-old duplex. $$.

weeki wachee

The ancients gathered here for the sweet, healing waters, and it has been a landmark since before European settlement. To reach Weeki Wachee from Brooksville, head west on SR 50.

where to go

Weeki Wachee Springs State Park/Buccaneer Bay Water Park. 6131 Commercial Way; (352) 596-2062; www.weekiwachee.com. This is one of Florida's oldest attractions, still quaint, unique, and bubbling with charm. Real "mermaids" swim a lithe ballet, staying underwater for the entire show because they take discreet breaths of air through tubes. Two shows are given every day, but call ahead because times vary. Admission to the springs is $13.95 for adults, $10.95 for children. Admission to Buccaneer Bay is $24.95 for adults and $16.95 for children; yearly passes are an excellent value. Restaurants and snack bars serve a good choice of menus, but you're also welcome to bring a cooler (no glass, please). Hours change seasonally, so either call ahead or visit the Web site.

where to stay

Quality Inn Weeki Wachee. 6172 Commercial Way; (352) 596-2007 or (800) 490-8268; www.qualityinn.com. Located across the street from the springs, this property has a swimming pool, playground, and lounge. Lodgings are basic but comfortable. Spend a weekend at the water park and fishing in the Gulf of Mexico. Ask about fisherman's rates. $$.

day trip 03

west

This area is bordered to the west by the Withlacoochee State Forest and to the east by sprawling Tsala Apopka Lake. Ten thousand years ago, Paleoindians thrived along the warm, life-giving waters of the Withlacoochee River. Later, Seminoles settled in, and by 1836 white settlers began eyeing these moist woodlands north of Tampa. After the Civil War, settlement began in earnest. From Orlando, go northwest on the Florida Turnpike to where it joins I-75 at Wildwood. At the next exit, go west on SR 44 to Inverness. From Inverness you can go north on Route 45 to Hernando. Or head 9 miles west to Lecanto. From there, head south on US 491, east on US 480, and north on US 41 to reach the Withlacoochee State Forest and then into Floral City.

inverness

The earliest burials in Magnolia Cemetery date to 1869, when settlers streamed into Florida to make new lives after the War between the States. In time the stagecoach route was replaced by a railroad, which in turn gave way to highways—and the motorcar changed everything. The original county seat, Mannfield, became a ghost town after the government moved to Inverness. Today historic sites and the outdoors are still drawing visitors to this quiet, less-discovered part of Florida.

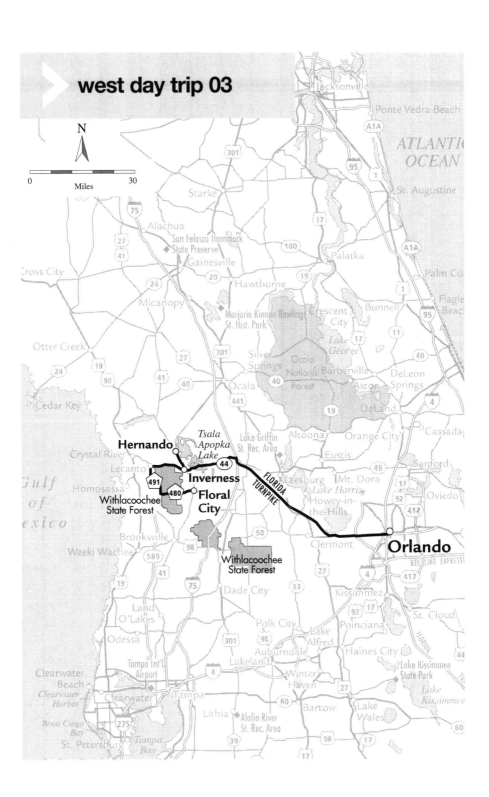

N

0   Miles   30

where to go

Citrus County Heritage Tour. Call or visit the Web site for information (see below) on the historic highlights of the county and set out to see them on a series of pleasant, country drives through Crystal River, Inverness, Lecanto, Ozello, Homosassa, and Floral City; (352) 341-6427; www.cccourthouse.org. The Old Courthouse on the square in Inverness dates to 1911 and is one of only twenty-five historic courthouses remaining in the state. It's now a museum open weekdays and on Saturday morning. Shop the museum store for educational toys and unusual gifts. The neoclassical revival Masonic Temple dates to 1910, the Crown Hotel to the 1920s, and the Kelley House to 1903. The Atlantic Coast Line Railroad Depot was built in 1910 in the Prairie style introduced by Frank Lloyd Wright. In Florida City see Pleasant Hill Baptist Church, founded in 1895 by African Americans who came to the area to work the phosphate mines. Follow the history of Florida architecture from the years before World War I through the colonial revival craze of the 1920s and the ever-present practicality of Florida Vernacular, with its wide verandas.

Fort Cooper State Park. 3100 South Old Floral City Rd.; (352) 726-0315; www.florida stateparks.org/fortcooper. Located 2 miles southeast of town, this park is home to Lake Holathikaha, the spring-fed waters that hosted battle-weary soldiers of the First Georgia Battalion of Volunteers in 1836 during the Second Seminole War. General Winfield Scott had marched to Tampa, leaving his sick and wounded behind to drink the healing waters and hold off the Seminoles as best they could. They held their own for sixteen days until Scott returned with supplies and reinforcements.

The remains of the old fort weren't excavated until the 1970s. Now the fort is the scene of reenactments featuring volunteers from all over the South. Walk 5 miles of nature trails looking for deer, fox, rabbits, owls, and herons. Swim, rent a canoe, or fish in the clear lake. Break out a picnic. Play volleyball or horseshoes. There's a primitive camping area, restrooms, parking, and picnic tables. The park is open during daylight hours. State park fees apply.

Old Courthouse Heritage Museum. One Courthouse Square; (352) 341-6428; www .cccourthouse.org. Once the courthouse for Citrus County, this museum houses a courtroom as it looked in 1912, rotating exhibits, galleries for local history and prehistory, and a museum store. There's plenty of parking east of the museum and room for a picnic on the grassy grounds. Wallace Brooks Park, 0.75 mile northeast of the museum at Dampier Street and Martin Luther King Drive, has picnic tables and a playground. The museum is open weekdays 10 a.m. to 4 p.m. and Sat 10 a.m. to 2 p.m. Admission is free, but donations are appreciated.

Withlacoochee State Trail. Mail address: 12549 State Park Dr., Clermont, FL 34711; (352) 726-0315; www.dep.state.fl.us/gwt/state/with/default.htm. The trail runs from Trilby to just below Dunellon along an old railway. It's paved in asphalt for 46 miles, a trail to hike, bike, or—if you stay off the paving—ride horseback. Write ahead for a map, then leave the car at one of the parking areas, such as the Inverness Depot listed above, and plan an excursion of a few hours or an entire day; or stay with the path, which is part of the Florida Trail and Croom Mountain Bike Trails, and end up miles away. The trail has a number of points of interest, access points, parks, and picnic areas, including one in Fort Cooper State Park.

where to shop

Accents by Grace and Friends. 106 North Pine Ave.; (352) 860-1990. Accents is a collection of delightful shops selling custom crafts, clothing, bears, old linen, sculpture, hand-blown glass, baubles, and bangles. Everything is imaginative and fun, and Grace will be glad to turn your purchases into a gift basket for any occasion. Hours vary, so call ahead.

Connors Gifts. 218 Tompkins St.; (352) 344-9790. This shop is perfectly placed across from the Crown Hotel, handy for shopping for collectibles and just the right gifts to take home with you. Among the specialties are Lladro porcelains and Zingle-Berrys figurines.

Country at Home. 101 West Main St.; (352) 637-6621. This place is all about country and quaint, so shop here for candles, fragrances, frills, and fripperies. In stock is what proprietors claim is the largest collection of Boyds Bears in the South, so add to your collection of the bears and their pals. Hours vary seasonally, so call ahead.

Ferris Groves. 7607 South Florida Ave., Floral City; (352) 860-0366; www.ferrisgroves .com. This is the kind of highway stop our grandparents looked for as they drove the country roads of Florida. Buy for yourself or have citrus shipped for you. There's a luscious array of strawberries and tomatoes in season; freshly squeezed juice; seasonal citrus including red grapefruit, oranges, and short-season Honeybells; homemade pies; and a selection of jams and candies with or without sugar. Open daily in season, except Sun, 9 a.m. to 5 p.m.

where to eat

Cinnamon Sticks Restaurant and Bakery. 2120 West SR 44; (352) 726-8800. Cinnamon Sticks features good, simple, hearty fare for breakfast, lunch, and dinner at very reasonable prices, with luscious, made-on-site pastries and desserts. Their pies, cinnamon rolls, and cobblers are local favorites. $.

Fisherman's Restaurant. 12311 East Gulf to Lake Highway; (352) 637-5888. Located on the river at the County Line Bridge in an area of the Withlacoochee known as a mini-Everglades, this is a classic Florida seafood shop with a huge choice of seafood plus steaks, chops, burgers, and side dishes. A specialty is grouper, prepared your way and served with all the trimmings. Shrimp, lobster, scallops, oysters, clams, crab cakes, and farm-raised catfish also highlight the menu. The fisherman's platters are belt-busters, especially the Shipwreck Special, consisting of a half-pound sirloin steak, a lobster tail, and tons of trimmings. Order a round of gator bites with tangy mustard sauce for the table. For dessert, have the lime pie. Hours are Sun noon to 8 p.m. and Tues through Sat from 11 a.m. $–$$$.

La Luna Italian Restaurant. 859 S US 41; (352) 344-1111. A typical Italian restaurant with good food and good service. Try the spaghetti with white clam sauce. You'll enjoy the plentiful clams and big chunks of garlic. $–$$.

Rutabagas Etc. 299 South Croft Ave.; (352) 341-0042. Rutabagas Etc. is a full-service health-food store, with a full-service cafe featuring homemade meals, juices, and frosties. Salads, sandwiches, wraps, and entrees are all delicious and certified organic. $.

Tijuana Willie's. 724 US 41 South; (352) 344-8476. This Tex-Mex restaurant's menu features unusual items including bison steaks and quail, along with beefsteaks, pork chops, and more typical Tex-Mex fare. Enjoy a golden margarita with your meal. $$.

Van der Valk Lakeside. 4555 East Windmill Dr.; (352) 637-1140; http://valkusa.com/restaurant/42. Fine dining featuring a touch of Europe. Many of the employees at Van der Valk's are Dutch, and the menu, serving both lunch and dinner, reflects a strong European influence. Try Giuseppe's Carpaccio as an appetizer, or the *soupe a l'oignon gratine.* For entrees, beef, lamb, chicken, pork, seafood, and pasta are all likewise served with a very continental flair. For example, the *Poulet Italien* is a juicy roasted and Italian-seasoned chicken breast stuffed with mozzarella cheese and salami, served with a tomato-basil sauce. For dessert enjoy a sorbet or crème brûlée. $$–$$$.

where to stay

Citrus Hills Lodge. 350 East Norvell Bryant Hwy., Hernando; (352) 527-0015; www .magnusonhotels.com/34442. This is a quiet country spot where you'll find reliable Magnuson quality. Stop for the night in a standard or deluxe room with Jacuzzi, take a swim in the heated pool, have your hair done or get a massage in the salon, and go on your way after a free continental breakfast. Every room has a coffeemaker; a microwave or refrigerator is available. The concierge can arrange tennis or a round of golf nearby. $$.

Van der Valk Inverness. 4555 East Windmill Dr.; (352) 637-1140; www.valkusa.com. Van der Valk offers spacious three-bedroom vacation homes with luxury appointments. Amenities include two bathrooms, screened lanais, a swimming pool, cable television, and more. Kitchens are fully equipped, and all towels and linens are included. Van der Valk's Lakeside Restaurant provides fine European dining. Be sure to ask about the unlimited four-golf-course plan. $$$–$$$$.

northwest

day trip 01

northwest

>>> **climb mount dora:**
mount dora, tavares, leesburg

Leave Orlando headed northwest on US 441, or the Orange Blossom Trail, through Apopka to Mount Dora. Continue west on US 441 to Tavares, then Leesburg. Return the same way, or check a map for alternative routes such as SR 48 around Lake Harris or US 27 south out of Leesburg to Route 50, then east into Orlando.

Sample an area that is filled with lakes, miles of green countryside, and still enough rural flavor to give you a rest from city life. Stay in a highway motel, an upscale hotel or inn, or a rustic fish camp.

mount dora

Even though it has been gripped by the giant tentacles of Orlando, Mount Dora still has an old-fashioned downtown and the quaint, quiet charms of the village it once was. Relive the past by booking a room at the Lakeside Inn and walking the shaded streets to shop and dine. In the old days, visitors arrived on the train and walked to the hotel, only a few footsteps away, while hand wagons followed with their mountains of baggage. Northerners (including President Calvin Coolidge, who spent a month here in 1930) came to stay the season, complete with their servants and all the steamer trunks it took to keep them in fashion for weeks. The yacht club on the lake is Florida's first, dating to 1913 and rebuilt after a fire in 1966. It's the scene of periodic antique boat shows and daily boat rides aboard the *Mount Dora Star.*

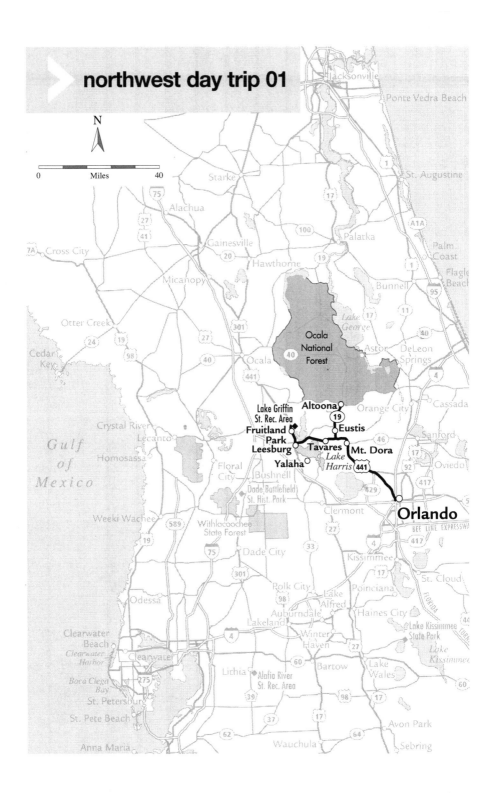

N

0   Miles   40

Jacksonville

Ponte Vedra Beach

St. Augustine

Starke

Alachua

Gainesville

Cross City

Hawthorne

Palatka

Palm
Coast

Micanopy

Bunnell

Flagler
Beach

Otter Creek

Lake
George

Ocala
National
Forest

Aston

DeLeon
Springs

Cedar
Key

Ocala

Altoona

Orange City

Cassada

Crystal River

Lake Griffin
St. Rec. Area

Eustis

Sanford

Lecanto

Fruitland
Park

Gulf
of
Mexico

Leesburg

Tavares

Mt. Dora

Homosassa

Yalaha

Lake
Harris

Oviedo

Floral
City

Bushnell

Dade Battlefield
St. Hist. Park

Clermont

Orlando

Weeki Wachee

Withlacoochee
State Forest

BEE LINE EXPRESSWAY

Dade City

Kissimmee

Odessa

Polk City

Lake
Alfred

Poinciana

St. Cloud

Auburndale

Haines City

Lakeland

Lake Kissimmee
State Park

Clearwater
Beach

Winter
Haven

Lake
Kissimmee

Clearwater
Harbor

Clearwater

Lithia

Alafia River
St. Rec. Area

Bartow

Lake
Wales

Boca Ciega
Bay

St. Petersburg

St. Pete Beach

Anna Maria

Wauchula

Avon Park

Sebring

Downtown is bordered by Clayton, Liberty, McDonald, and Tenth Streets. To browse the antiques district, you'll find most shops between Alexander and Tremain Streets on Third through Seventh Avenues. The city has more than a dozen individual shops, a nice contrast to the enormous antiques-fest at Florida Twin Markets, also known as Renninger's Antique Center, on US 441, which is also a must for serious antiquers.

There really is a Lake Dora, although the "mount" is a local joke celebrated in T-shirts that proclaim, I CLIMBED MOUNT DORA. The lake sits below the lawns of the Lakeside Inn, a sparkling expanse of sweetwater that is still a paradise for boating, fishing, and nature and sunset watching.

where to go

Central Florida Kayak Tours. (352) 589-7899; www.centralfloridakayaktours.com. If you're ready to get away from civilization for a while, paddling is a fun way to do so. Some of the nicest streams in Florida are found near Mount Dora. These folks offer two-hour beginner's tours to all-day photographer's expeditions. Prices start at $59 per person.

Chamber of Commerce. 341 Alexander St.; (352) 383-2165; www.mountdora.com. Located in the old train depot, the chamber provides a window on quaint yesterdays, when Florida visitors came by rail. Pick up brochures and ask friendly locals where to dine, shop, and sleep. One brochure describes a self-guided 3-mile driving tour past green parks and historic mansions dating to the 1880s and early 1900s. Another lists and maps the antiques shops and boutiques. Hours vary, but the depot is usually open business hours.

Premier Boat Tours. Docked at the Lakeside Inn, 100 Alexander St.; (352) 434-8040. Savor the charm of Mount Dora. Dine and relax at the historic Lakeside Inn and then see the "real Florida" aboard the twenty-one-passenger luxury pontoon cruiser, the *Captain Doolittle*. Adults, $22; children ages three to ten, $10. Call for times and reservations.

Palm Island Park. Tremain Street; (352) 383-2165. Located between Third and Fourth Avenues, this park covers twelve acres of wetlands accessed by boardwalks. You'll probably see alligators, otters, herons, ospreys, coots, ducks, woodpeckers, and much more wildlife among the cypress, oaks, maples, and palms. The park also has mulched nature trails, picnic areas, and a picturesque lighthouse. Open from 7:30 a.m. to a half an hour after sunset. Free admission.

where to shop

Country Cottage Crafts. 334 North Donnelly St.; (352) 735-2722 or (800) 735-2735; www.countrycottagecrafts.com. You'll find Country Cottage Crafts in the heart of downtown Mount Dora. The shop contains the labors of more than seventy crafters dispersed through twenty-one different rooms—over 4,000 square feet of merchandise. Each room has a different theme, and some of the rooms are rented by the crafters whose work is displayed here. In addition, they carry Willow Tree Angels and Hadley Pottery. Open Mon to Sat 10 a.m. to 5 p.m., Sun noon to 5 p.m.

The Olive Branch. 418 Donnelly St.; (352) 383-3333; www.theolivebranch-earthenwares .com. This store specializes in hand-painted, lead-free ceramics from Spain and Portugal. It's full of beautiful and colorful items, including fountains, house numbers, frames, hand-painted window boxes, and flowerpots of all sizes and shapes. Open from 10 a.m. to 5 p.m. daily.

The Painter's Daughter. 331 Donnelly St.; (352) 735-3470; http://paintersdaughter.com. In this eclectic boutique you'll find unique clothing and shoes, fine art and antiques, jewelry, and accessories. View creations from well-known designers as well as up-and-coming artists. Open Tues through Sat 10 a.m. to 5 p.m.

Renninger's Antique Center. 20651 US 441; (352) 383-8393 or (800) 522-3555; www .renningers.com. The center is one of the largest gatherings of antiques dealers in the state, with 180 (give or take a few) different dealers. Shop for antiques, collectibles, and rarities in every category from soup tureens to nut bowls. A farmers'market is also held here every weekend. Open Sat and Sun, 9 a.m. to 5 p.m.

where to eat

Beauclaire Restaurant. 100 North Alexander St.; (352) 383-4101. Located in the Lake-side Inn, the Beauclaire is sedate and lovely in its Gatsby-era garb. It's a favorite for its Sunday brunch as well as for elegant dinners, lingering lunches, and pleasant breakfasts. Start dinner with a dozen steamer clams in a succulent broth or the hearts-of-palm salad with shrimp. From the list of seafood, pasta, poultry, and meat entrees, try the chicken Georgia with peaches and pecans, seafood St. Jacques, grilled swordfish, or rack of lamb. Lunch-time favorites include chicken potpie, hot roast beef sandwich, and corned beef Reuben. Other choices range from soup to the vegi-sandwich. Open daily for breakfast, lunch, and dinner. Reservations are suggested at any time and are essential for Sunday brunch. $–$$.

Fifth Avenue Café. 116 East Fifth Ave.; (352) 383-0090; www.5thavenuecafe.com. The owners take great pride in their work and offer only the purest, freshest natural ingredients in all their offerings. Lunches range from "small plates" (soup and sandwich, shrimp skewers) to salads, burgers, paninis, quiches, and more. Dinner offerings are similar, with salmon, lamb, lasagna, and flounder in the mix. $–$$.

Goblin Market. 331 North Donnelly St.; (352) 735-0059; www.goblinmarketrestaurant .com. The Goblin is a tiny, bookish place with fewer than a dozen tables and personal service from the owners and chef. Start with a fragrant soup or the escargot en croute, followed by fresh grouper in potato crust, roasted chicken, or one of the chef's daily specials based on the best of what the marketplace offered that morning. Beer and wine are served, and the restaurant is smoke-free. Open daily, except Sunday, for lunch and dinner. $$$.

where to stay

Fiddlers Green Ranch. 42725 West Altoona Rd., Altoona; (352) 669-7111 or (800) 94-RANCH; www.fiddlersgreenranch.com. The ranch is located north of Mount Dora on the southern border of Ocala National Forest. Rent a cabin or villa with up to three bedrooms. Bring groceries; every unit has a full kitchen, laundry room, and living/dining room. Vacation dude-ranch style with trail rides into the forest, overnight campouts with a barbecue dinner, campfire entertainment, and chuck wagon breakfasts. The ranch also has a swimming pool and gift shop. Bring your pet if you like. $$–$$$.

Heron Cay Lakeview Bed and Breakfast. 495 Old Hwy. 441; (352) 383-4050 or (888) HERONCAY; www.heroncay.com. The Heron Cay looks like a Queen Anne mansion, but its modern touches have won it an AAA four-diamond rating. Five suites all have private baths; two have fireplaces. Watch sunsets on the lake, explore the area, go antiquing, seek out the area's smart restaurants, or play golf at one of Mount Dora's two country clubs. Tea and a country breakfast are included in rates. $$–$$$.

Lakeside Inn. 100 North Alexander St.; (352) 383-4101 or (800) 556-5016; www.lakeside-inn.com. The inn is in the heart of town, a few blocks from the main street overlooking the lake that attracted wealthy northerners to winter here more than a century ago. Headquarter here while you "do" the antiques district, stroll streets straight out of yesteryear, and try the town's trendy restaurants. Dine in the inn's restaurant, snack at the pool bar, enjoy happy hour in the lounge, enjoy live entertainment after dinner some nights, play tennis day or night, and bring your boat if you like. Dockage is free to hotel guests. Rooms and suites are available in the main hotel, which has a spacious front porch with rockers. Or stay at Lakeside Landings Bed & Breakfast, where guests take breakfast at the inn. Ask about packages. $$–$$$.

Magnolia Inn Bed and Breakfast. 347 East Third Ave.; (800) 776-2112; www.magnolia inn.net. The Magnolia Inn Bed and Breakfast is a historic estate built around 1926. Centrally located, it is an easy stroll for shopping and eating on the main street. Magnolia Inn has been voted as one of the best bed-and-breakfasts and country inns throughout the United States. The owners are constantly striving to maintain their high standards in service, food, and comfort. You'll start the day with a gourmet breakfast, accompanied by a selection of specialty coffees and teas. $$–$$$.

Mount Dora Historic Inn Bed & Breakfast. 221 East Fourth Ave.; (352) 735-1212 or (800) 927-6344; www.mountdorahistoricinn.com. The Mount Dora Historic Inn features beautifully appointed rooms, each with a private bath and decorated with individuality and an emphasis on comfort and tranquility. Amenities include cable television, DVD player, Internet access, and more. Located in the heart of Mount Dora. $$$.

tavares

Early settlers stopped short when they saw the beauty of this area, surrounded by lakes that are still the star of the tourism show here. A number of operators offer sightseeing, dinner, and luncheon cruises on the lakes and old canals that were dug generations ago for the lumber trade. Driving through on US 441, you'll see signs offering a number of cruises and boat rentals, or stay at the Mission Inn (see West Day Trip 01) and cruise Lake Harris aboard their antique yacht, *La Reina.*

where to go

Discovery Gardens. 30205 SR 19; (352) 343-4101; http://discoverygardens.ifas.ufl.edu. Discover nine gardens in a parklike setting. The goal is to teach visitors about horticulture and landscape design, but there's also pleasant self-guided strolling in a fragrant setting that changes day by day, season by season. Open every day 9 a.m. to 4 p.m.

Tavares Heritage Ecotours. 901 Lakeshore Blvd.; (352) 343-0200. Enjoy a one-and-a-half-hour ecocruise aboard a silent electric boat through the scenic canals and lakes surrounding Tavares. The cost is $22 per person. Reservations are a must, so call ahead.

where to stay

Lake Harris Lodge. 119 Lake Park Rd.; (352) 343-4111; www.lakeharrislodge.com. This is nothing fancy, just an RV park where you can rent a space for your RV or stay in a cottage that has all the basics for eating and sleeping after a day on the lake. All the fish-camp basics are here: boat rental, bait and tackle, a store selling basic supplies, and a launch ramp you can use for a fee. Fishing guides are available. $–$$.

leesburg

where to go

Lake Griffin State Recreation Area. 3089 US 441/27, Fruitland Park; (352) 360-6760; www.floridastateparks.org/lakegriffin. The park is 2 miles north of Leesburg, an ancient oak hammock where city-weary folks can fish, canoe, launch a boat, picnic, or camp in developed sites that have water and electric hookups. A 1,000-foot canal connects the recreation area to Lake Griffin. The area is open 8 a.m. to sunset every day. State park fees apply.

where to shop

Morning Glori Antique Mall. 1111 South Fourteenth St., Leesburg; (352) 365-9977. This is the largest antiques collection in Leesburg, with booth after booth and row after row of antiques. You will ask yourself, do I have enough time in one day to see it all? They claim to have over a million items, from dolls and sewing items to World Fair collectibles. Every dealer has his or her own personal taste in the items they collect or accumulate, and with over sixty dealer booths, you will probably find something that strikes your fancy. Items range in price from $2 to thousands of dollars.

where to eat

Yalaha Country Bakery. 8210 County Rd. 48, Yalaha; (352) 324-3366; http://yalaha bakery.com. The bakery is southeast of Leesburg, perfectly situated for a country drive into a slice of Bavaria. The bakery and restaurant are German to the core, serving sandwiches on crusty European-style breads. Buy breads from the wood-fire brick oven to take home. Open Mon through Sat 7 a.m. to 5 p.m., Sun 10 a.m. to 3 p.m. Check the Web site for news of Saturday concerts, usually jazz or big-band sound. Sandwiches are sold until 4:30 p.m. $.

where to stay

EconoLodge. 1308 North Fourteenth St.; (352) 787-1210; www.econolodge.com. This is one of EconoLodge's large chain of hotels. It's centrally located to many of Leesburg's attractions and shopping. Continental breakfast is included. $$.

day trip 02

northwest

>>> **the home of tarzan:**
ocala, silver springs

Today it's a busy crossroads city, growing explosively with modestly priced retiree developments, but just a generation ago, Ocala was a small town serving the dozens of sprawling horse farms stretching from one county line to another. Its neighbor, Silver Springs, has been inhabited since long before European settlement. Most forests with their chattering monkeys and lush, green tangle look like a movie set and, in fact have been used repeatedly by Hollywood. Take the Florida Turnpike north to Wildwood, then I-75 to Ocala.

ocala

where to go

Appleton Museum of Art. 4333 Northeast Silver Springs Blvd.; (352) 291-4455; www .appletonmuseum.org. Located on SR 40, this is an outstanding museum, starting with the stately building, grounds, and fountains. Collections are a mixture of this and that but are dazzling and unique. See African pieces, pre-Columbian art, and masterworks from all eras and media. Special exhibits and visiting shows are seen throughout the year. The gift shop alone is worth the trip. Adult admission is $6; hours are 10 a.m. to 5 p.m. Tues to Saturday, Sun noon to 5 p.m. Closed during Aug.

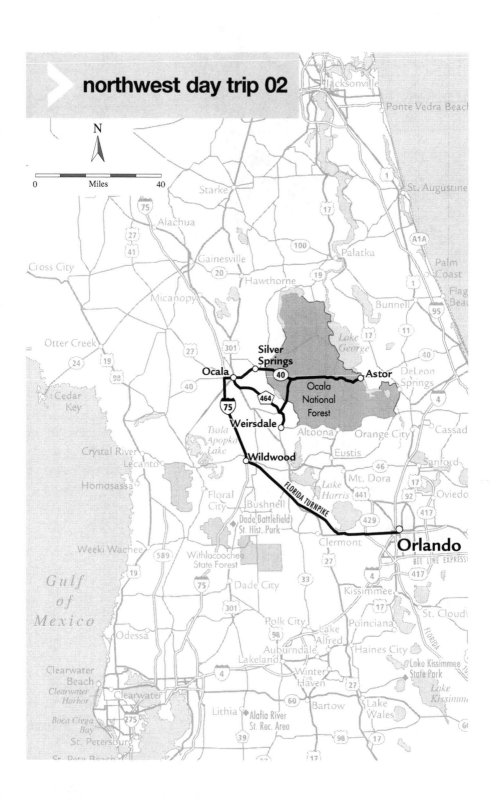

Don Garlits Museum of Drag Racing. 13700 Southwest Sixteenth Ave.; (352) 245-8661 or (877) 271-3278; www.garlits.com. This museum is a project of the "Big Daddy" of drag racing, whose enormous collection of classic and vintage cars is on display here. In the museum see memorabilia depicting the history of drag racing. Open daily 9 a.m. to 5 p.m. Adult admission is $15.

Marion County Museum of History. 307 Southeast Twenty-sixth Terrace; (352) 629-2773. This museum showcases Seminole Indian clothing and artifacts, a 1,500-year-old canoe, artwork, and other displays depicting the history of this ancient area. Hours vary, but it's usually open Fri and Sat 10 a.m. to 2 p.m. Admission is $2.

Silver River State Park. 1425 Northeast Fifty-eighth Ave.; (352) 236-1827; www.florida stateparks.org/silverriver. Located on SR 35 at the headwaters of the Oklawaha River, this park is one of the state's great wilderness reserves. It's the home of fourteen different habitats, laced with trails and dotted with clear, cold springs. Visit the pioneer park and museum, hike trails, or canoe the river. There are no other facilities. The museum and education center are open only on weekends and some holidays 9 a.m. to 5 p.m. State park fees apply.

where to eat

Arthur's. 3600 Southwest Thirty-sixth Ave.; (352) 854-1400. Located in the Hilton, Arthur's is worth a special trip for an intimate dinner or a memorable Sunday brunch. When you make reservations, indicate whether you want a quiet booth or a table overlooking the pool and gardens. Fine cuts of beef are a house specialty, but everything is done with a knowing touch for seasonings, herbs, and a hint of Haiti—or is it New Orleans? There's always a fresh catch of the day, salmon, and a good choice of dishes for carnivores and vegetarians alike. Desserts are showy and delicious. Open for dinner daily and brunch on Sunday. Reservations are strongly recommended. $$$.

BageLicious Bakery & Cafe. 2459 Southeast Twenty-seventh Ave.; (352) 237-6511. Located in Shady Oaks Mall, this is a handy place to grab a quick breakfast or a bag of sandwiches to take on a picnic or trail ride. Or stop here for lunch while you're shopping the mall. Nosh on New York–style bagels, pastries, a burger, a salad, or a sandwich. $.

Bella Luna Cafe. 3425 Southwest College Rd.; (352) 237-9155; http://bellalunacatering .com. This eatery is Italian to the core. Start with bruschetta, snails, or mussels, followed by the chef's special pasta e fagioli soup and one of the crisp salads. Choose your main dish from a long list of pastas, risotto, chicken, fish, beef, or veal dishes. There's also pizza and a nice choice of children's favorites. Call for hours and reservations. $$–$$$.

Blackwater Inn. SR 40 at US 17, Astor; (352) 759-2802; www.blackwaterinn.com. The Blackwater is a country inn overlooking the St. Johns River, well worth the forty-five-minute excursion out of Ocala because the drive takes you across the entire waist of the Ocala National Forest. The waterfront tables are hard to get, but every table has a good view of the river, bridge, and colorful parade of passing boats. Seafood is the star of the extensive menu, with a huge choice of ocean and freshwater fish, crab, oysters, and shrimp prepared many ways, with all the trimmings. The choice of soup, salads, chicken, steak, and other dishes is very good, and the big salad bar provides plenty of choices for those who want to pick and choose. Williams Landing, upstairs over the inn, is best for burgers and snacks. Both have a full bar. Note the location at Routes 17 and 40, because the inn is also handy when you are day-tripping north or northeast out of Orlando. Just east of the inn, note the large live oak tree and a marker at the site where naturalist William Bartram landed in the eighteenth century. Open for lunch and dinner daily except Monday. Reservations are highly recommended. $–$$$.

Harry's Seafood, Bar, and Grille. 24 Southeast First Ave.; (352) 840-0900; www.hooked onharrys.com. Harry's serves authentic New Orleans cuisine for both lunch and dinner, right in Ocala. Try the fried oysters or catfish, or have some étouffée or jambalaya. And that's just for lunch! Additionally, there is the more usual fare—steaks, burgers, salads, pasta, po' boys (can't forget the po'boys!). Top it off with a slice of Louisiana mud pie. $$.

where to stay

Ocala Silver Springs Hilton. 3600 Southwest Thirty-sixth Ave.; (352) 854-1400; www .hilton.com. This property is the city's best business hotel, a high-rise with a marble lobby and a piano bar for a romantic pre- or post-dinner drink, a superb restaurant, a business center, and a good location handy to both downtown and the interstate. Order from room service, use the putting greens or tennis courts, swim in the pool, or play volleyball. Some rooms have a minibar, refrigerator, and/or a whirlpool bath.

Seven Sisters Inn. 820 Southeast Fort King St.; (800) 250-3496; www.sevensistersinn .com. This Victorian showplace in Ocala's historic neighborhood has been showered with awards and honors. The inn serves a bracing breakfast filled with gourmet scents and new tastes and does all the things that B&B lovers dote on. Upstairs, a loft is roomy enough for a family. Special events include the occasional murder-mystery weekend or cooking class. Ask about special packages such as a candlelight dinner. $$–$$$.

Shamrock, Thistle & Crown. Mail address: P.O. Box 524, Weirsdale, FL 32195; (352) 821-1887 or (800) 425-2763; www.shamrockbb.com. This property is located on CR 42, 3 miles east of US 441/27 between Ocala and Leesburg. Sleep in a romantic three-story Victorian mansion built around 1887. Stay in a whirlpool suite with fireplace or the Victorian cottage. All rooms have private bath, coffeemaker, and TV with VCR. Included in the rates are a full breakfast, cider or hot drinks, shortbread, chocolates, and a morning newspaper. $$–$$$.

silver springs

To get to Silver Springs, travel east of Ocala on SR 40.

where to go

Silver Springs. 5656 East Silver Springs Blvd.; (352) 236-2121; www.silversprings.com. Located on SR 40, this is Florida's oldest theme park, dating to 1878 when the first glass-bottom boats began providing tourists a glimpse of a pristine underwater world of grottos, silvery fish, and artesian springs that spill millions of gallons of water every day into the Oklawaha River. There is still plenty here for the nostalgia buff who mourns the old Florida. Take a glass-bottom-boat tour. Stroll unspoiled footpaths lined with native plants and brilliant annuals. See alligators, gars, turtles, manatees, Florida panthers, native and imported bears, and wild monkeys that still roam free in the forests along the "lost river." Kids can play in Kids Ahoy! Playland. Movie fans can spend a cool, quiet hour in the museum, where movie clips show dozens of scenes that were shot here. They range from commercials to Tarzan movies and snippets of *Creature from the Black Lagoon.*

You'll really need more than one day to take all the cruises and the Jeep Safari, see the shows, watch the wildlife, shop the stores, and try the restaurants. Hours are limited in winter, so call ahead. Admission is $34.99 for adults and $24.99 for guests under 48 inches tall. Children ages two and younger are free. Ask about a combination ticket for Silver Springs and Wild Waters, and the twelve-month OnePass, which is a sensational deal because it covers not only unlimited general admission but also concerts and special events. Concerts, scheduled late March through Sept, feature top stars and groups such as Tanya Tucker, Glen Campbell, Roy Clark, and the Guy Lombardo Orchestra. There's an annual Corvette Show in Nov and a monthlong Festival of Lights in Dec.

Wild Waters Water Park. 5656 East Silver Springs Blvd.; (352) 236-2121; www.wild waterspark.com. Another attraction on SR 40, Wild Waters invites the family to dare the 60-foot-high Twin Twister flume and seven other thrill slides and rides. For little ones, the Caribbean Sprayground provides gentle fountains and mists; the Tad Pool is for wading. Splash in the wave pool, play volleyball, or dry out in a giant video arcade and game room. Lockers, restrooms, and a kennel for the dog are available. Three restaurants serve burgers, pizza, hot dogs, and the like, and the Shiver Shack has ice-cream treats. Suntan products, swimwear, and beach togs are sold in the shop. Make a day of it April through Sept 10 a.m. to 5 p.m., sometimes later during special events. Adult admission is $25.99, children ages three to ten pay $22.99, and parking is $5.00 unless you have a pass. There's a $2 discount if you purchase tickets on-line. Ask about annual passes and combination tickets for Wild Waters and Silver Springs.

where to stay

Days Inn Silver Springs. 5751 East Silver Springs Blvd.; (352) 236-2575 or (800) 329-7466; www.daysinn.com. This is a plain-Jane inn, clean and comfortable, across the street from Silver Springs attractions. It's an ideal headquarters for a weekend at the theme park and water park, especially during the blockbuster country concerts staged regularly. The twenty-four-hour restaurant is a plus, and the inn is kept up-to-date with data ports, cable TV, microwaves and refrigerators, and a business center.

Seven Sisters Inn Bed and Breakfast. 820 Southeast Fort King St., Ocala; (352) 867-1170 or (800) 250-3496; www.sevensistersinn.com. Guests here can experience light-houses of Cape Cod, a Safari Bengal room, gilded treasures and Egyptian artifacts, stone spa showers, a sultan's bed in mysterious India, imported French fabrics from Paris, and Zen-like harmony of the Orient. Jacuzzi, Victorian soaking tubs, spa showers, fireplaces, and heated towel bars are available in most rooms. A gourmet breakfast and afternoon tea are included. In-room coffee service, luxurious bathrobes, newspapers, free bicycles for use, candlelit dinners, and murder mysteries are available. $$$.

day trip 03

northwest

outdoorsman's paradise:
ocala national forest

ocala national forest

This is such a vast area with so many recreation opportunities, you could come here time and again and never tire of the nature show, crystal springs flowing into narrow rivers, spring-fed swimming holes, and miles of woodlands abuzz with birds and insects. Ocala National Forest consists of swamp, acres of prairie and pinewoods, countless springs, plus lakes, rivers, streams, hunting reserves, and a 66-mile portion of the Florida Trail. This wilderness is highly sensitive to nature's whims, so be aware of water levels, fire danger levels, winds, and currents.

There will be times when some lands aren't accessible due to flooding, some waterways too rough (especially Lake George, which is very large, shallow, and subject to quick buildups in high winds), or campfires not permitted because of the fire hazard. This is an ever-changing, ever-evolving landscape—always new, always exciting, always challenging. To the casual visitor, especially one who expects the towering trees and mountains of western forests, the flat sameness of this national treasure might seem featureless. Listen and watch. Let it reveal itself to you, and you'll find a natural drama that is filled with beauty and excitement.

SR 40 runs through the middle of the national forest between Barberville and Ocala. Much of its western border is the Oklawaha River. Just east of Ocala on SR 40, the Ocala National Forest Visitor Center offers information, souvenirs, and invaluable advice. Countless

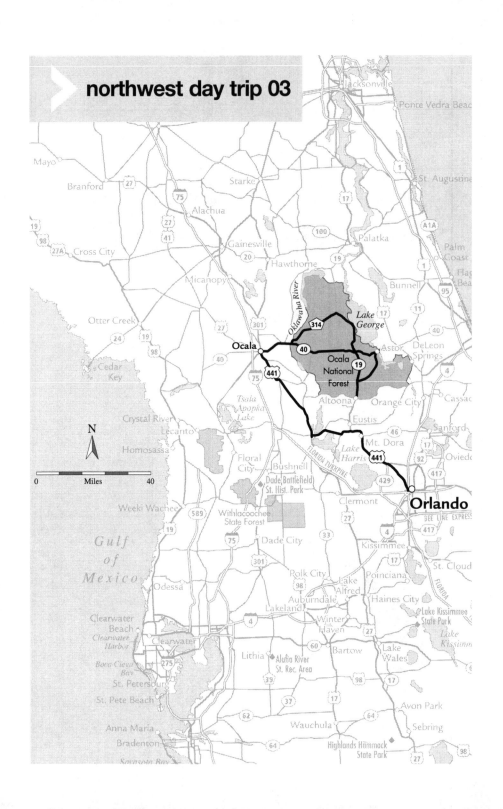

spots in the forest offer fishing, and many areas are set aside for hunting in season. Myriad rules apply throughout the forest, most of them based on respect for the environment and common sense in regard to personal safety. Leave a trip plan with someone at home. Familiarize yourself with the area's hazards, including poisonous snakes, insects, and plants. Keep small children well in hand. Bring a camp stove, since firewood may be in short supply. Be especially vigilant about cooking fires. If you start a forest fire, you are financially liable.

For information, write the Seminole Ranger District, 1551 Umatilla Rd., Eustis, FL 32726 (352-357-3721), or the Lake George Ranger District, Route 2, Box 701, Silver Springs, FL 32688 (352-625-2520). Many areas are free. Fee areas include Fore Lake, Mill Dam, Juniper Springs, Alexander Springs, Clearwater Lake, Lake Dorr, and Salt Springs. For more information on Florida's national forests, check out www.fs.fed.us/r8/florida.

where to go

Alexander Springs Recreation Area. This area is off SR 445, which runs south off SR 40 at Astor Park. Launch a canoe to float the spring run, camp in a developed campground with restrooms and a dump station (no hookups), swim off the salt-white beach, and hike the Timucuan Indian Trail along waters that were sacred to the ancients. A concession stand sells ice and staples and offers rental canoes.

Big Scrub is in the southwest corner of the national forest. A campground offers drinking water and restrooms.

Clearwater Lake is on the southern edge of the national forest off Route 42 near Paisley. It's a campground where you can also swim, walk an interpretive trail, and launch a boat. Restrooms, drinking water, and a dump station are available.

Johnson Field is east of Rodman Dam on the northern border of the national forest. Come here to camp, picnic, or launch a boat. There are restrooms but no showers.

Juniper Springs and **Fern Hammock Springs** are on SR 40 just west of Route 19. Swim in the springs and canoe the spring "run" at Juniper Springs, which also has camping, restrooms and showers, and a barrier-free nature trail.

Lake Dorr is on Route 19 just north of Route 42 in Lake County in the southern half of the national forest. The recreation area has campsites, drinking water, swimming, a picnic area, restrooms, a boat launch, and showers.

Lake Eaton Sinkhole Trails are found south of Route 314 off Road 79. Leave your car in the parking area and walk the half-mile loop to the sinkhole, which is 450 feet around and 80 feet deep, or add the 1.2-mile longer trail that reaches the sinkhole then joins the shorter trail. A boardwalk and stairs let you hike to the bottom of the sink.

Mill Dam Lake off SR 40 is a popular fishing hole offering camping, drinking water, swimming, a picnic area, boat launch, and restrooms. Hike the interpretive trail.

Salt Springs Recreation Area is just north of the intersection of Routes 19 and 314. Camp, swim, picnic, or launch a boat. The site has drinking water, restrooms, showers, and a dump station.

day trip 04

northwest

gator country:
micanopy, gainesville, hawthorne

The fastest way to get to this area from Orlando is on the Florida Turnpike north, then I-75 north to Micanopy off US 441 into Gainesville. From Gainesville, drive southeast on Route 20 to Route 2041 and Route 325 and watch for the Marjorie Kinnan Rawlings site on the way to Hawthorne.

micanopy

You'll think you're in another time zone when you drive into Micanopy (say mick-an-oh-pea), named for an Indian chief. Timucuan Indians had a thriving community here before Europeans arrived, and it's said to be the oldest continuously occupied inland settlement in the state. When naturalist William Bartram visited here in 1774, he found a Seminole village. Not long after Florida became a U.S. territory, a trading post was established here. Browse the antiques centers and have a meal in one of the restaurants or a picnic on a park bench in the grassy median that divides the main street.

Driving through, note the Town Hall, which is also the public library. It was built as a schoolhouse in 1895. Note old homes that were built in Victorian times, some of them elegant, others simple and utilitarian, suited to frontier life. You'll pass the Presbyterian Church, built in 1870 for a congregation established in 1854, the Herlong Mansion, now an inn, and the line of old banks and mercantiles that are now occupied by restaurants and antiques shops. If you have time, ask the way to the cemetery, where the oldest grave was dug in 1826 for a man born in 1737.

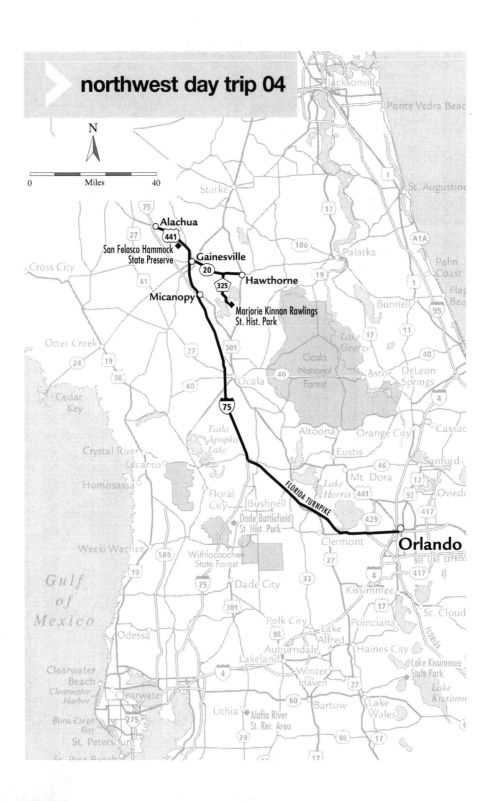

northwest day trip 04

N

0   Miles   40

Jacksonville

Ponte Vedra Beach

St. Augustine

Starke

75

27

Alachua
441

San Felasco Hammock
State Preserve

Gainesville
20

325 **Hawthorne**

Micanopy

Marjorie Kinnan Rawlings
St. Hist. Park

Cross City

41

100

Palatka

A1A

Palm
Coast

19

1

Flag
Beac

Bunnell

95

Otter Creek

24

19

98

27

301

40

40

Ocala

Ocala
National
Forest

40

Lake
George

Astor

17

11

DeLeon
Springs

40

4

Cedar
Key

75

Crystal River

Lecanto

Homosassa

Tsala
Apopka
Lake

Floral
City

Bushnell

Dade Battlefield
St. Hist. Park

Altoona

Eustis

Lake
Harris

Orange City

Mt. Dora

441

FLORIDA TURNPIKE

46

17

92

Sanford

Oviedo

Cassac

417

Weeki Wachee

589

Withlacoochee
State Forest

19

75

Dade City

301

Floral
City

33

Clermont

27

Kissimmee

4

429

17

Orlando

BEE LINE EXPRESS

417

St. Cloud

Gulf
of
Mexico

Odessa

Clearwater
Beach

Clearwater
Harbor

Clearwater

275

Boca Ciega
Bay

St. Petersburg

St. Pete Beach

Lithia

Polk City

98

Auburndale

Lakeland

4

Winter
Haven

60

Bartow

39

Alafia River
St. Rec. Area

Lake
Alfred

Poinciana

Haines City

27

Lake
Wales

98

Lake Kissimmee
State Park

Lake
Kissimm

FLORIDA

17

where to go

Micanopy Historic Society Museum. Cholokka Boulevard at Early Street; (352) 466-3200; www.afn.org/~micanopy. Located in the old Thrasher Warehouse, built in 1890, this collection takes you back through the history of a busy little country town that has changed little with the centuries. The Coca-Cola sign on the north wall was painted in the 1920s. The bookstore alone is worth a special visit. Open daily 1 to 4 p.m. for a modest admission.

Paynes Prairie State Preserve. Route 2, Box 41, Micanopy, FL 32667; (352) 466-3397; www.floridastateparks.org/paynesprairie. The preserve is 10 miles south of Gainesville on US 441; watch for signs off I-75. Within this 20,000-acre world of wildlife and lakes, you can boat, hike more than 20 miles of trails, fish, picnic, camp, or train your binoculars on the abundant bird life. Many migratory birds winter in this natural paradise, so dedicated bird lovers come back time and again to add to their lists. Herds of horses and American bison roam the land. Climb the observation tower for the best vista. The visitor center is open every day 9 a.m. to 5 p.m.; the park is open every day 8 a.m. to sunset. Call ahead for a schedule of ranger-led activities. A small admission is charged.

where to stay

Herlong Mansion. 402 Cholokka Blvd.; (352) 466-3322 or (800) 437-5664; www.herlong .com. This is a Greek Revival mansion surrounded by live oak trees dripping Spanish moss where hosts offer a variety of accommodations in rooms, suites, and cottages decorated in Victoriana. Ask for a fireplace, whirlpool tub, kitchenette, or refrigerator, and specify whether you want a TV and/or VCR. Not every room has electronic intrusions. Borrow a book from the home's library and relax on the veranda or in the garden. Breakfast is included. $$-$$$.

Shady Oak. 209 Cholokka Blvd.; (352) 466-3476; www.shadyoak.com. This three-story mansion has a wide wraparound porch to catch the breezes. The most romantic room is Victoria's Suite. Some rooms have a hot tub, TV, and/or VCR. Call at least three days in advance and hosts will serve a candlelight supper in your suite, make dinner reservations at a nearby restaurant, or have a picnic hamper ready for your local explorations. Breakfast is included in the rates. $$-$$$.

gainesville

The University of Florida is the elephant in the living room, the city's blessing and curse. Football games bring in 85,000 fans for big weekends, and the city's population swells and sinks by more than 30,000 depending on whether classes are in session. When fans and students are in town, it's hard to get restaurant and hotel reservations—and impossible to find a parking space. On the other hand, the university is a travel destination in itself—a world of museums, cultural events, and exciting, youthful action.

For a quiet walk that costs nothing, write ahead (see Regional Information at the back of this book) for a free walking-tour map through the Northeast Historic District. You'll see a timeline of southern architecture from the 1880s through the 1930s, including the Murphree House, where William Jennings Bryan was entertained, and Gracy House, where prohibitionist Carrie Nation stayed. She gave the children little wooden axes as souvenirs of her crusade to destroy saloons. From Micanopy follow US 441 north to Gainesville.

where to go

Devil's Millhopper State Geological Site. 4732 Millhopper Rd.; (352) 955-2008; www .floridastateparks.org/devilsmillhopper. Located on SR 232, this is like no other locale in the state. A 120-foot-deep, 500-foot-wide sinkhole opened here eons ago, allowing species that are found nowhere else in Florida to live in the cool, dark depths. In fact, the name of the county, Alachua, is Native American for sinkhole, or "large jug." Walk down the 232 steps to the bottom of the sinkhole, observing waterfalls and rare plants along the way. Guided walks are offered at 10 a.m. on Sat. Displays in the visitor center explain this geological phenomenon. Bring a picnic to enjoy on the grounds. It's generally open 9 a.m. to sunset but closes at 5 p.m. Oct through March. A small admission is charged. Just west of here a few miles is **San Felasco Hammock State Preserve,** almost 7,000 acres of pine and hardwood forest with sinkholes, creeks, wildlife, rare plants, and 10 miles of marked hiking and horseback-riding trails. (352) 462-7905; www.floridastateparks.org/sanfelascohammock.

Florida Museum of Natural History. Mail address: P.O. Box 112710, Gainesville 32611; (352) 846-2000; www.flmnh.ufl.edu. Located at Southwest Thirty-fourth Street at Hull Road, this museum is a star in the state's tiara, a repository of natural treasures native to Florida. More than twenty-five million specimens are in the collection. See fossils, skeletons of prehistoric creatures, rare plants, seashells, butterflies, and much more. The Collectors Shop offers scientific games for children and nature-related souvenirs for adults. Admission is free. Open Mon through Sat 10 a.m. to 5 p.m. and Sun and holidays 1 to 5 p.m. Closed Christmas and Thanksgiving.

Matheson Historical Center. 513 East University Ave.; (352) 378-2280; http://matheson museum.org/index.html. The center is of interest to all history buffs and a must for postcard collectors. In the center's collection are more than 18,000 postcards, 1,200 stereo-view cards, and 2,500 books about Florida history. See rare old maps and prints. Admission is charged. Open Tues through Fri 9:30 a.m. to 1:30 p.m. and Sun 1 to 5 p.m. Closed Saturday and Monday.

Mill Creek Farm. CR 235-A, Alachua; (386) 462-1001; www.millcreekfarm.org. The farm is a retirement home for horses, a labor of love in a beautiful setting. Learn about the volunteers who work so hard to make a home for more than eighty horses whose working life is over and the ten dogs, all of them with their own hard-luck stories, who stand guard over them. Admission is two carrots, but bring a whole bag if you can. You get to feed them to the horses, so the more carrots, the more friends you'll make. Open Sat 11 a.m. to 3 p.m.

Morningside Nature Center. 3540 East University Ave.; (352) 334-2171; www.nature operations.org. The nature center is a 278-acre living-history farm, operating just as it might have in North Carolina a century ago. You'll see a cabin dating to 1840, farm buildings, an heirloom garden, barnyard animals, a barn, and a schoolhouse. Seven miles of trails and boardwalks lead through the woods and sand hills, where you'll see more than 130 species of birds, 225 wildflower species, and countless critters to watch at the animal observatory. Every day is different, depending on what's going on in the farmer's life and what special programs or exhibits are on the schedule. Open every day 9 a.m. to 5 p.m. Free.

Samuel P. Harn Museum of Art. Hull Road at Southwest Thirty-fourth Street, University of Florida; (352) 392-9826; www.harn.ufl.edu. This is one of the state's largest art museums. It's filled with changing exhibits and permanent collections of American masters, African arts, and pre-Columbian works. One visit isn't enough because something is always going on, from lecture series to films and performances. Admission is free. Hours are Tues through Fri 11 a.m. to 5 p.m., Sat 10 a.m. to 5 p.m., and Sun 1 to 5 p.m. The gift shop closes at 4:30 p.m., and no one is admitted after 4:45 p.m.

Santa Fe Community College Teaching Zoo. 3000 Northwest Eighty-third St.; (352) 395-5604; www.sfcollege.edu/zoo. This is the only community teaching zoo in the nation that houses mammals, reptiles, amphibians, birds, and endangered species from all over the world. Zookeepers lead the tours, so it's a great place to bring children who are seriously interested in animals, endangered species, or animal husbandry. During the week visit by appointment, or come on Sat and Sun 9 a.m. to 2 p.m. Admission is $4 for adults, $3 for children and seniors.

The University Galleries at the University of Florida. (352) 392-0201, ext. 228; www.arts.ufl.edu/galleries. Three art galleries make up the University Galleries: the University Gallery, the Focus Gallery, and the Grinter Gallery. The University Gallery features contemporary art of all types, and hosts six exhibitions per year. The University Gallery is located in Building B of the Fine Arts complex. The Focus Gallery is a small space that presents exhibitions or works by both students and invited artists. Every month a new exhibit is featured. These exhibits typically "push the envelope," displaying radical new work. The Focus Gallery is located in the main lobby of Fine Arts Building C. Grinter Gallery of International Art presents exhibitions created by international students and area artists, as well as traveling exhibits of internationally based art. Exhibitions are installed for several months at a time. Grinter Gallery is located on the first floor of Grinter Hall, just east of the University Auditorium. Guest parking permits and maps for directions may be obtained from the campus main entrance.

where to eat

Ale House & Raw Bar. 3950 Southwest Archer Rd.; (352) 371-0818. This is an old-fashioned sports bar where you can watch the games on forty TVs while scarfing down a hearty burger and crispy fries. Do serious damage to a big steak, a bowl of pasta, or a platter of wings or seafood. Have one of the twenty-five draft beers, or try one of the bartender's daily drink specials. Open Mon through Sat 11 a.m. to 2 a.m. and Sun noon to 11 p.m. $–$$$.

Banyan's Restaurant. 7417 West Newberry Rd.; (352) 332-7500. Banyan's is revered for its all-you-can-eat seafood buffet on Friday and its prime-rib specials on Saturday. Stop in for the breakfast and lunch buffets, the weekend brunch, or dinner followed by the 9 or 10 p.m. show at Coconut's Comedy Club, which has its own telephone (352-332-2224). Open daily 4 a.m. to 10 p.m. $–$$.

BJ's Brewhouse. 6611 Newberry Rd.; (352) 331-8070; www.bjsrestaurants.com. Visit BJ's Brew House if you enjoy good food and great, full-flavored beer. The Mediterranean deep-dish pizza is some of the best pizza you'll ever have. Beer aficionados will want to try the seven-beer sampler. Open 11 a.m. to midnight Sun to Thurs, 11 a.m. to 1 a.m. Fri and Sat. $–$$.

Cabana Cove Caribbean Grille. 2410 Northwest Forty-third St.; (352) 377-3278; http://cabanacove.net. The mouth-watering menu items here are inspired by the fruits, flavors, and spices of the Caribbean. Tempting tastes like fresh mango, spicy jerk, and savory curry will transport you to the tropics with every bite. Start your meal with some conch fritters, then move on to the Voodoo Grouper. Top your dinner off with a rum-drizzled Cabana Banana. Open Mon to Thurs 11:30 a.m. to 10 p.m., Fri and Sat 11:30 a.m. to 11 p.m., Sun 10 a.m. to 4 p.m. $–$$.

Calico Jack's. 3501 Southwest Second Ave.; (352) 371-1675; http://calicojacks.net. This is a college hangout with a sports bar ambience and special prices on beer and seafood. Order crawdads by the pound, oysters, sandwiches, wings, shrimp, crab, or burgers. If you're headed for a game, call ahead and they'll pack up everything you need for a tailgate party. Live music plays Fri night. $–$$. Open every day 11:00 a.m. to 2 a.m., Sun noon to 11 p.m.

David's Barbecue. 5121 Northwest Thirty-ninth Ave.; (352) 373-2002; www.davidsbbq.com. Where there's smoke, there's great barbecue, so pull into the Timber Village Shopping Center for a pig sandwich, barbecued chicken with all the fixings, or a big barbecue dinner platter with ribs, chicken, beef, or a combination. Portions are massive, which makes the place popular with football players. Breakfasts are quick, hot, and sized for fullbacks. Open every day 7 a.m. to 9 p.m. $–$$.

Farah's. 1120 West University Ave.; (352) 378-5179; www.farahsontheavenue.com. Farah's has a Mediterranean look and feel, with a menu to match. In 2003 Farah's added a hookah lounge, so smokers, for the most part persecuted elsewhere, can find a haven here. Have one of the wraps, a gourmet hamburger, a Black Angus steak, pasta, fresh seafood, or the chef's special of the day. There's a full bar, and live jazz plays on weekends. Ask for a table in the enclosed patio overlooking the avenue, or get out of the spotlight for an intimate meal in the back of this attractive room. Open Mon and Tues 11 a.m. to 10 p.m., Wed and Thurs 11 a.m. to midnight, and Fri and Sat 11 a.m. to 2 a.m. $$–$$$.

Francesca's Trattoria. 4410 Northwest Twenty-fifth Place; (352) 378.7152; www.francescas trattoria.com. This is a northern Italian restaurant where the pastas, sauces, soups, and garlic bread are made from scratch on the premises. Try the hot antipasto appetizer and the shrimp Parmesan. You can't go wrong with the baked ziti or the linguini and clam sauce. There's live entertainment, too. Check the schedule on the Web site. Open Mon to Thurs 11 a.m. to 10 p.m., Fri 11 a.m. to 11 p.m., Sat 4 to 11 p.m., Sun 4 to 9 p.m. $$.

Harvest Thyme Cafe. 2 West University Ave.; (352) 384-9497; www.harvestthymecafe .com. These folks serve healthy foods prepared fresh daily, including salads, wraps, sandwiches, smoothies, freshly baked breads, and more. Peruse their display cooler full of chicken salad, dressings, spreads, sauces, and to-go items for people in a hurry. They feature daily luncheon specials. Open 8 a.m. to 5:30 p.m. Mon through Fri, 11 a.m. to 3 p.m. Sat. $.

The Melting Pot. 418 East University Ave.; (352) 372-5623; www.meltingpot.com. This spot is best known for its fondues—a good spot for family and friends to stick a fork in it together and have a leisurely, fun-filled meal. Order one of the main dish fondues with chicken, beef, cheese, or seafood, all served with fresh vegetables, then wade into the chocolate fondue for dessert. Reservations are recommended. Open Sun through Thurs 5:30 to 10 p.m., Fri and Sat to 11 p.m. $$.

Publix Supermarket. 3720 Northwest Thirteenth St.; (352) 335-3785. This supermarket has a sushi bar, where you watch as chefs create wonderful sushis in many flavors, then pick up a package to take to your hotel room or picnic. Everything is natural and ready to eat. If you have a special request or want a large quantity, call ahead. The supermarket also has a deli with hot and cold take-out dishes. $.

Yamato Japanese Restaurant. 526 Northeast Sixth St.; (352) 332-4466; www.yamato japaneserestaurant.com. Yamato features Teppanyaki tables that have a special grill built into them. The chef comes to your table and puts on a show as he prepares the vegetables, chicken, shrimp, beef, lobster, or whatever else you prefer to eat. In addition, traditional Japanese dishes, prepared in the kitchen, can be ordered from the full menu. Enjoy tempura as an appetizer, or choose from twenty varieties of sushi. Open for lunch Monday through Friday and for dinner every day. Dinner reservations are recommended. $$–$$$.

where to stay

America's Best Value Inn. 1900 Southwest Thirteenth St.; (352) 372-1880, (888) 502-8722; www.abvifl.com. This ninety-one-room lodge is large enough to offer services and small enough to provide special touches such as a free continental breakfast daily. Ask about weekly, monthly, and senior rates. Transportation to the campus, hospitals, and airport is offered. There's a swimming pool but no restaurant. Pets are permitted. $$.

Best Western Gateway Grand. 4200 Northwest Ninety-seventh Blvd.; (352) 331-3336 or (800) 528-1234; www.bestwestern.com. Reserve a room, minisuite, executive suite, or the presidential suite at this three-story inn. Every room has data ports and cable TV; some have refrigerator and microwave. Dine in the Key West Grill & Lounge, swim in the pool, soak in the outdoor whirlpool, and get your workout in the fitness room. Meadowbrook Golf Club is next door, so ask about golf packages. Ask, too, about special rates for seniors, groups, military and hospital personnel, or those on university business. Business and laundry services are available. $$.

Cabot Lodge. 3726 Southwest Fortieth Blvd.; (352) 375-2400 or (800) 843-8735; www.cabotlodge.com. This lovely property features a warm, inviting atrium with a large central fireplace and chandeliers made from antlers, all surrounded by comfortable furniture. They want you to feel at home, so much so that your stay includes a complimentary continental breakfast that features fresh fruit, a variety of pastries and breads, beverages, and, of course, the morning newspaper; then they offer a complimentary two-hour hospitality reception with cocktails every evening. After the eating and drinking, you can use the exercise room to work off the calories! $$–$$$.

EconoLodge. 2649 Southwest Thirteenth St.; (352) 373-7816 or (800) 446-6900; www.econolodge.com. This property is a 6-block walk from the campus and is within walking distance of several restaurants. There's a swimming pool, data ports in every room, and cable television as well as a complimentary continental breakfast. Pets are welcome. $.

Hilton University of Florida Conference Center. 1714 Southeast Thirty-fourth St.; (352) 371-3600 or (800) 695-8284; www.hilton.com. This is a full-service hotel with everything convenient for the business or leisure traveler. Swim in the pool, eat in the restaurant, order from room service, relax in the lounge, and shop for souvenirs and sundries in the gift shop. Data ports are in every room. The hotel also has suites, including a luxurious presidential suite. Ask the concierge about transportation to the campus, airport, hospitals, and business center. Hilton's trademark is the freshly baked chocolate chip cookies that greet every guest on check-in. $$–$$$.

Holiday Inn University Center. 1250 West University Ave.; (352) 376-1661 or (800) 465-4329; www.ichotelsgroup.com. Located on US 441, this is a reliable choice for business or vacationing with its restaurant, lounge, twenty-four-hour coffee shop, barber and beauty shops, and central location. The rooftop swimming pool is Olympic size and is surrounded by a football field–size sundeck. Rooms are attractively appointed with desks, user-friendly desk chairs, and data ports.

Magnolia Plantation Bed & Breakfast. 309 Southeast Seventh St.; (352) 375-6653; www.magnoliabnb.com. This B&B offers five rooms in a romantic Victorian mansion, plus three cottages. Have wine and cheese with the host each afternoon. You will be sent on your way the next morning with a grand breakfast. Rooms are all different, so discuss the choices when you reserve. Some units have a fireplace, VCR, refrigerator, and/or telephone. With restrictions, pets are allowed. If you want a massage, one can be arranged. $$$.

Red Roof Inn. 3500 Southwest Forty-second St.; (352) 336-3311 or (800) 843-7663; www .redroof.com. This popular chain motel is conveniently located at exit 75 East off I-75. It's a good spot for a comfortable room or suite, a swim, and a comfortable price. Pets are welcome. Restaurants are nearby. $$.

Reitz Union Hotel. Mail address: P.O. Box 118505, Gainesville, FL 32611; (352) 392-2151; www.union.ufl.edu/hotel. Stay in the heart of the University of Florida campus in this handy hotel on Museum Road. The hotel offers thirty-six rooms and suites, free continental breakfast, and that precious commodity on campus—free parking. $–$$.

Residence Inn by Marriott. 4001 Southwest Thirteenth St.; (352) 371-2101 or (800) 331-3131; www.residenceinn.com. This is an up-market hotel with touches of home. Ask for a one- or two-bedroom suite with or without a fireplace. Kitchens are fully equipped, pets are allowed on payment of a fee, and breakfast and hospitality hour are included in the price. Work out in the fitness center, and enjoy the pool and whirlpool. Walk to Bivens Nature Center, or drive to most points of interest in less than fifteen minutes. $$–$$$.

Sweetwater Branch Inn. 625 East University Ave.; (352) 373-6760 or (800) 595-7760; www.sweetwaterinn.com. This is an elegant Victorian palace, where fourteen rooms have been filled with antique furnishings and groomed for the fussiest business or pleasure visitor. Some rooms have hot tubs; most have a fireplace and plush Oriental rugs. $$$.

Super 8 Motel. 4202 Southwest Fortieth Blvd.; (352) 378-3888 or (800) 800-8000; www .super8.com. This no-frills motel offers a complimentary continental breakfast. Weekly rates are available; transportation to the university, hospitals, and the airport can be requested. If you're in town on university or hospital business, ask about discounts. $.

hawthorne

From Gainesville, take Route 20 east into Hawthorne.

where to go

Hawthorne Museum and Cultural Center. Johnson Street at Southeast Fourth Avenue; (352) 481-1491; www.hawthorneflorida.org/museum.htm. This museum once housed the New Hope United Methodist Church. Built in 1907, the building now showcases the works of local artists and artisans, as well as relics of the community's past. A modest admission is charged. Open Wed through Sun.

Marjorie Kinnan Rawlings Historic State Park. 18700 South CR 325, Cross Creek; (352) 466-3672; www.floridastateparks.org/marjoriekinnanrawlings. Beloved author of *The Yearling,* Marjorie Kinnan Rawlings lived and worked in the rural community of Cross Creek. Her "Cracker"-style (a Florida native) home has been restored and turned into a museum at this state park. Paths through gardens and citrus groves invite visitors to explore the property and immerse themselves in another era. Rangers, dressed in period costume as Rawlings herself dressed, are available to answer questions about her life and times. Rawlings's farmyard, grove, and nature trails are open 9 a.m. to 5 p.m. daily throughout the year. Visitors may tour the house with a ranger from Oct through July, Thurs through Sun five times daily, except Thanksgiving and Christmas. Picnic facilities are located in the adjacent county park. State park fees apply.

day trip 05

northwest

>>>

the nature coast:
homosassa, crystal river, cedar key

Gushing springs, ancient Indian relics, seas of manatees floating freely in pristine waters. They add up to a part of Florida unlike any other. From Orlando, take the Florida Turnpike north to I-75 and jog north for just one exit, then turn west on Route 44 to Lecanto. Turn south on Route 490, crossing US 19/98, and into Homosassa and Homosassa Springs. Returning, you might leave Cedar Key on SR 24 to Alternate 27, which joins I-75 just north of Ocala.

This Day Trip covers a lot of territory. You'll enjoy it much more with an overnight in one of these lovely towns.

homosassa

Homosassa and Homosassa Springs are just south of Crystal River, close enough to combine in one weekend.

where to go

Homosassa Springs State Wildlife Park. 4150 South Suncoast Blvd.; (352) 628-5343; www.floridastateparks.org/homosassasprings. This park showcases native Florida wildlife from manatees to alligators and crocs. It's one of the few places in the state where you're sure to see a manatee any day of the year. Some are here for rehab before their return into the wild; others will spend their lives here, unable to fend for themselves. Stroll nature trails

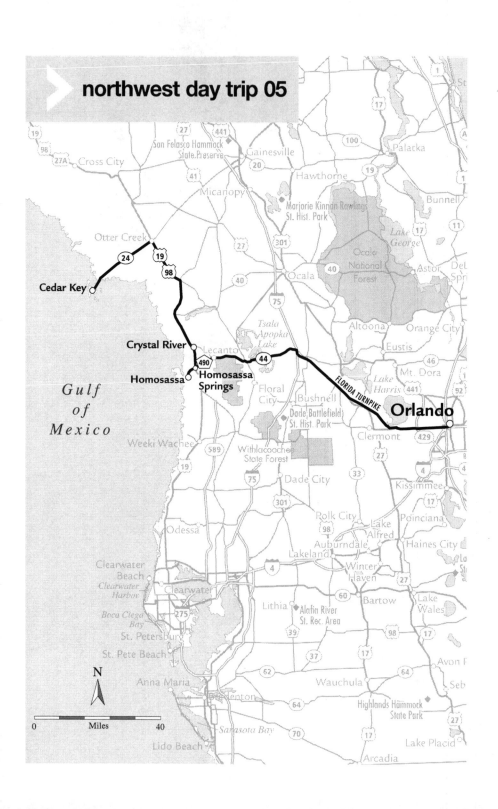

19
98
27A Cross City

27
441
San Felasco Hammock
State Preserve
Gainesville
100
Palatka
1

17

41
Hawthorne
19

20
1

Micanopy

Marjorie Kinnan Rawlings
St. Hist. Park
Bunnell

Otter Creek

27
301
Lake
George
17
11

24
19
Ocala
National
Forest
Astor
Del
Spri

98
40
Ocala
40

Cedar Key
75

Tsala
Apopka
Lake
Altoona
Orange City

Crystal River
Lecanto
Eustis

490
44
46

Homosassa
Homosassa
Springs
Mt. Dora
1
92

Gulf
of
Mexico
Floral
City
Bushnell
Lake
Harris
441
FLORIDA TURNPIKE

Dade Battlefield
St. Hist. Park
Orlando

Weeki Wachee
589
Clermont
429

19
Withlacoochee
State Forest
27
4

75
Dade City
33
Kissimmee

301
17

Polk City
98
Lake
Alfred
Poinciana

Odessa
Auburndale
Lakeland
Haines City

Clearwater
Beach
Clearwater
Harbor
Clearwater
4
Winter
Haven
27

Boca Ciega
Bay
275
Lithia
Alafia River
St. Rec. Area
60
Bartow
Lake
Wales

St. Petersburg
39
98
17

St. Pete Beach
17
Avon P

N
Anna Maria
62
Wauchula
64
Seb

Bradenton
64
Highlands Hammock
State Park
27

0   Miles   40
70
17
Lake Placid

Sarasota Bay

Lido Beach
Arcadia

to look for deer, black bears, bobcats, river otters, and cougars, plus bird life ranging from colorful flamingos to majestic birds of prey. See the museum, the gift shop, and the underwater observatory. Programs are scheduled throughout the day, so arrive early and plan to spend all day. Food is available at the Wildside Cafe, or bring a picnic to eat in the Garden of the Springs. The park is open daily 9 a.m. to 5:30 p.m.; tickets are sold until 4 p.m. Admission is $9 for adults and $5 for children ages three to twelve. A kennel is available for pets.

The Manatee Connection. (352) 697-0220; www.manateeconnection.com. Swim with manatees on these tours led by Coast Guard–licensed captains. Tours leave from various locations around Homosassa and Crystal River, depending on where the manatees are located. Gear rental available. Tours start at $30 per person.

River Safaris and Gulf Charters. 10823 Yulee Dr.; (352) 628-5222 or (800) 758-3474; www.riversafaris.com. This outfit is owned by Captain Dennis Lowe, a fifth-generation west coast Florida fishing guide, and his family. Let them plan your trip on Crystal Springs or Blackwater Rivers, sunsets on the Gulf, fishing expeditions to all the captain's secret hot spots, or an airboat ride through wetlands alight with wildlife. Or take the family to the St. Martins Keys for the wildlife sightings. In Homosassa Springs, take Yulee Drive off US 19 (by the Burger King), then go 2 miles to the stop sign, then left for 1 mile. The Lowes offer a variety of boat tours and fishing trips, all led by licensed captains, and they also have canoes, johnboats, and pontoon boats for rent. Bait, tackle, snacks, and supplies are sold here; there's an art gallery and gift shop, too.

Yulee Sugar Mill Ruins State Historic Site. 3400 North Museum Point; www.florida stateparks.org/yuleesugarmill. This was once the site of a thriving sugar plantation owned by David Levy Yulee, who was born in the West Indies and became a powerful politician in Florida. When the Civil War broke out, he chose to throw in his lot with the Confederacy. His mansion was burned by Union forces, and his mill fell to ruin. Today the imposing limestone mill has been partially restored to serve as the focal point of a picnic site and a pleasant roadside stop. Open 8 a.m. to sundown daily. Admission is free.

where to eat

Riverside Crab House. 5297 South Cherokee Way; (352) 628-2474 or (800) 442-2040; www.riversideresorts.com. Located at the Homosassa Riverside Resort (see Where to Stay), this place is famed for its Maryland-style crab cakes, grouper, prime rib, sirloin, daily pasta specials, and Dirt Pie for dessert. They'll also be glad to cook your catch for you. Call or check the Web site for hours. $$.

Seagrass Pub & Grill. 10386 Halls River Rd.; (352) 628-3565; www.seagrasspub.com. If you're arriving by boat, this eatery is at Marker #7 on the river. Make a meal out of the big choice of appetizers, or order them all in a sampler that serves up onion rings, mozzarella sticks, poppers, and beer-battered vegetables. Have a whole-meal salad with chicken or

> ## the springs at homosassa

We're fortunate in Florida to have a large number of state parks. I, for one, would much rather visit a state park than a theme park, and one of my favorite state parks in Florida is located at Homosassa Springs.

If you've grown up in a place where rivers start as trickles in the hills and get larger as they get closer to the sea, seeing a full-blown river come out of a hole in the ground will always amaze you. When that river consists of crystal-clear, fish-filled water, and when an underwater viewing room makes it possible to view the finned and flippered denizens residing there without so much as stepping into a puddle, that's what I would call a must-see.

While the park has other attractions, including trails for watching wild birds and a small zoo of native Florida wildlife, the underwater viewing room is what really sets it apart. You can observe all kinds of wild fish: snapper, mullet, snook, and jack crevalle. There are almost always manatees here, too, and they will stick their noses right on the glass. They're huge!

The entry fee for this park is higher than most other state parks in Florida, but it offers a unique experience that's truly not available anywhere else. If you enjoy the beauty of nature, this is a great place to experience it.

shrimp or a garden salad to go with a basket filled with your choice of foods. Choose the Black Angus burger, grilled chicken, shrimp, grilled kielbasa, fried ravioli, clam strips, or a prime-rib sandwich with fries or macaroni salad. Hours vary, so call ahead. $–$$.

where to stay

Homosassa Riverside Resort. 5297 South Cherokee Way; (352) 628-2474 or (800) 442-2040; www.riversideresorts.com. The resort sits on serene waters where you can while the day away doing absolutely nothing. Or fish, dive, take a river tour, swim with manatees, rent a pontoon boat or canoe, take an airboat ride, or sign on for a sunset cruise. This isn't the Ritz, but it's comfortable and homey, with standard and king rooms overlooking the Homosassa River. Efficiencies have a microwave and refrigerator. Kitchenette suites have a full kitchen. All units have cable television and telephone.

Hang out in the Monkey Bar, a tiki bar that overlooks Monkey Island, or the Yardarm Lounge with its floor-to-ceiling window on the river. Dining is in Riverside Crab House (see Where to Eat). Shop in a cluster of boutiques selling toys, gifts, candles, silks, jewelry, and home accessories. Only a mile away, the wildlife park at Homosassa Springs is one of the state's best manatee sanctuaries, where you can watch them from an underwater room.

Ask at the resort about the canoe and kayak trails that stretch from Crystal River to Chassahowitzka. $$.

MacRae's of Homosassa. Mail address: P.O. Box 318, Homosassa, FL 34487; (352) 628-2605; call between 7 a.m. and 6 p.m.; www.macraesofhomosassa.com. Located at 5300 South Cherokee Way, on the Homosassa River, MacRae's is a fish camp that has been here since 1917. Book a motel room or fully equipped apartment, and slip back a century or two while you explore this primeval paradise. Fish inshore or in the Gulf, dive with manatees, paddle waters filled with bird life, or call for a tee time at a nearby golf course. Boats, canoes, paddleboats, and pontoon boats are available for rent. Seafood restaurants are within walking distance; Crumps, known for its seafood and spirits, is just across the river. $–$$.

Seagrass River Resort. 10386 West Halls River Rd.; (352) 628-2551; www.seagrasspub .com. This resort is located directly on the Homosassa River, and offers a variety of lodging to fit the needs of families and friends. One-, two-, and three-bedroom villas, cottages, and efficiencies are available, and are decorated and equipped to give all the comforts of home. Boat rentals and dockage are available. $$.

crystal river

Crystal River is on the Gulf, west of Inverness. From Homosassa, return to US 19/98 for the trip north to Crystal River. Sweetwater springs boil up into the bay, creating a habitat that is irresistible to manatees. It's a unique destination for scuba divers, and the Indian mounds make it a unique destination for history hunters, too.

where to go

Aardvark's Florida Kayak Company. 707 North Citrus Ave.; (352) 795-5650; www.florida kayakcompany.com. These folks specialize in kayak rentals and tours in Crystal River and the surrounding coastal waters. They have guided manatee kayak tours, too. Kayak rentals start at $35, tours from $40.

Coastal Heritage Museum. 532 Citrus Ave.; (352) 795-1755; www.cccourthouse.org/ crystalriver.html. The picturesque building housing this museum was originally a Works Projects Administration structure built in 1939. It was listed on the National Register of Historic Places in 1998. The Museum features an array of exhibits, artifacts, furniture, and photographs of the early history of the west side of Citrus County. This building once housed the jail, and a unique feature is one of the original jail cells. Open Tues through Sat 10 a.m. to 2 p.m. Admission is free but donations are welcomed.

Crystal River National Wildlife Refuge. 1502 Southeast Kings Bay Dr.; (352) 563-2088; http://crystalriver.fws.gov. The refuge covers Kings Bay, where 72-degree spring waters flow twelve months of the year. Manatees can be found during the coldest months, generally Dec through Feb. Dive trips, snorkeling, and boating have to be arranged through private companies nearby. Canoeing the Crystal River is also popular; a number of outfitters rent canoes, or bring your own, which can be launched at most canoe liveries for a fee. Admission is free. The refuge is open during daylight hours.

Crystal River State Archaeological Site. 3400 North Museum Point; (352) 795-3817; www.floridastateparks.org/crystalriver. This site is steeped in mystery. Who were the people who lived here? How and why did they build these mounds? What happened to them? What is the meaning of the carved stones they left behind? Archaeological excavations have been going on here since 1903, so allow several hours for hiking the nature trail; touring the midden, ceremonial, and burial mounds; and seeing the displays in the visitor center. State park admissions apply. Call ahead or check the Web site for open times.

where to shop

The Back Porch Garden and Tea Bar. 639 North Citrus Ave.; (352) 564-1500; www .backporchgarden.com. Tea aficionados will want to visit to sample and purchase some of the finest teas available, as well as peruse the teakettles, teapots, teacups, and other tea accessories. Open Mon to Sat 10 a.m. to 5 p.m.

The Shoppes of Heritage Village in historic downtown Crystal River are clustered around US 19 at Citrus Avenue; (352) 302-3026; http://theshoppesofheritagevillage.com. Browse shops selling toys, custom jewelry, collectibles, antiques, gifts, apparel, and party supplies; have lunch at the cafe. Hours vary shop to shop, season to season, so call ahead.

where to eat

Charlie's Fish House Restaurant. 224 Northwest US 19; (352) 795-3949. This fixture in the Crystal River dining scene has been serving fresh, local Gulf seafood for forty-five years. Watch the sunset while enjoying a seafood platter, fried mullet, broiled grouper, or freshly made crab or grouper cakes. Charlie's also features stone crab claws in season. $$.

Cracker's Bar & Grill. 502 Northwest Sixth St.; (352) 795-3999; www.crackersbargrilland tiki.com. This spot overlooks Kings Bay. Laze away an hour or two in the Tiki Hut, then dine on sumptuous seafood platters or a grilled rib-eye steak. Start with a soup or chowder, or nosh on alligator chunks, deep-fried mozzarella, stuffed shrimp, or calamari. Choose from a cornucopia of side- and main-dish salads plus burgers and hot and cold sandwiches. Kids can choose clams with french fries, a hot dog, chicken fingers, spaghetti, or grilled cheese. Have a brownie sundae or peanut butter pie for dessert. Open for lunch and dinner every day, or ask about carryout. $$.

Cravings on the Water. 614 Northwest US 19; (352) 795-2027; www.cravingsonthewater .com. Enjoy the tropical atmosphere with the flavor of Cuban food while overlooking the Gulf. Cravings starts serving breakfast at 7 a.m. and stays open until the last patron leaves. Have a Cuban sandwich stuffed with shredded pork or chicken, or picadillo, beans, and rice. Finish your meal with a serving of flan. All foods are made on-site, and they do not accept credit cards. Open Sun to Thurs 7 a.m. to 8 p.m., Fri and Sat 7 a.m. to 9 p.m. $.

where to stay

Best Western Crystal River Resort. 614 Northwest US 19; (352) 795-3171 or (800) 435-4409; http://crystalriverresort.com. The resort offers rooms and efficiencies handy to the waters and wiles of Kings Bay. Every room has a coffeemaker, clock radio, iron and ironing board, hair dryer, safe, and data-port telephone. Swim in the pool, soak in the whirlpool, have a drink in the tiki bar, shop in Cabbage Palm, book an airboat ride or a scuba expedition in the full-service dive shop, and dine casually in the waterfront restaurant. Hotel hosts can arrange tennis, golf, tarpon fishing, canoeing, and other pleasures. $$–$$$.

Plantation Inn & Golf Resort. 9301 West Fort Island Trail; (352) 795-4211 or (800) 632-6262; www.plantationinn.com. This complete, 200-acre resort has something for everyone, including divers and golfers. This is the home of the Florida Women's Open, many state PGA tournaments, and the Original Golf School, one of the nation's most successful teaching programs. The twenty-seven-hole championship golf course, designed by Mark Mahanah, has twenty-one water holes, sloped greens, and plenty of challenges. Swim in the resort's swimming pool or with manatees in the wild. Rent a boat for fishing or sightseeing. Units with kitchen are available. The restaurant has plantation decor and a comprehensive menu of seafood and standards. $$$.

cedar key

From Crystal River, go north on US 19/98 to Otter Creek and take Route 24 southwest to Cedar Key. The ride is part of the fun. You'll see parts of Florida you never knew existed, and the drive out the long causeway to the island is a float through a wonderland of wildlife and waterfowl. Strolling the sleepy streets of the island, it's hard to imagine that Cedar Key was once a thriving seaport and a seething center of wartime activity. So important was salt to the war effort (to preserve meat for the troops), Cedar Key was an early target for Union troops. They attacked from the sea, captured this strategic center, and cut off much of the South's access to supplies brought here by blockade runners.

After the war, lumbering continued to support island residents, who denuded the forests almost down to the last toothpick. Cedar, one of the chief wood products, was harvested for making the pencils you probably used in grammar school. The sea provided fish and tons of oysters. In time, highways and railroads were built elsewhere, deeper harbors were required as ships grew larger, and little Cedar Key languished, battered by the occasional hurricane. Now it has bounced back, a favorite with travelers for its funky, world's-end ambience.

where to go

Cedar Key Scrub State Reserve/Waccasassa State Preserve. Mail address: P.O. Box 187, Cedar Key, FL 32625; (352) 543-5567; www.floridastateparks.org/cedarkeyscrub. The preserve is 6 miles east of Cedar Key on SR 24. The vast Gulf Hammock was once dominated by forested islands threaded by tidal creeks; this 4,000-acre reserve is all that remains. Still, it's a wildlife wonderland bordered by the Waccasassa River, available to visitors on a first-come, first-served basis for hunting, boating, fishing, and hiking. There is a small picnic area off SR 24, 6 miles east of Cedar Key, and service roads can be used as hiking trails. Bring your binoculars, and be prepared to be wowed by sightings of raccoons, black bears, bald eagles, wild turkeys, and gaggles of other bird life. Open 8 a.m. to sundown. Admission is free.

Cedar Key State Museum. Mail address: Box 538, Cedar Key, FL 32625; (352) 543-5350; www.floridastateparks.org/cedarkeymuseum. The museum is found at the northern point of the C-shaped island. Take Gulf Boulevard north, then go east on Hodges Drive to Whitman Drive. See one of the state's great collections of seashells as well as relics from the island's boisterous past. The museum is open 9 a.m. to 5 p.m. daily except Tues and Wed. A small admission fee is charged.

where to eat

The Island Room at Cedar Cove. SR 24 at Second Street; (352) 543-6520; www.island room.com. Located in the Cedar Cove Beach and Yacht Club, this is a good choice for drinks and dinner with a view of the sun sinking into the Gulf. Crab cakes are a specialty of the house. Another is grouper, cooked and sauced in a variety of luscious ways. Or try the chicken Savannah made with roasted pecans. The wine list is impressive and international. Open for dinner daily and Sunday brunch. Reservations are recommended. $$–$$$.

where to stay

The Island Place. First Street at C Street; (352) 543-5307 or (800) 780-6522; www .islandplace-ck.com. This is a rustic condo complex of one- and two-bedroom self-catering apartments within walking distance of the marina and grocery store. Everything you need to do your own cooking is here, or call for delivery from a list of the island's many excellent restaurants. Units have washer, dryer, microwave, cable TV, and a private balcony with a view of the most razzle-dazzle sunsets in Florida. The resort has a swimming pool and hot tub. Hosts can arrange fishing, boating, shelling, or sightseeing. $$–$$$.

regional information

north

day trip 01

Seminole County Convention & Visitors
   Bureau
1230 Douglas Ave. #116
Longwood, FL 32779
(407) 665-2900 or (800) 800-7832
www.visitseminole.com

day trip 02

Cassadaga Spiritualist Camp
Box 319
Cassadaga, FL 32706
(386) 228-2880
www.cassadaga.org

West Volusia Tourism
(800) 749-4350
116 West New York Ave.
Deland, FL 32720
(386) 775-2793 or (800) 749-4350
www.riveroflakesheritagecorridor.com

day trip 03

(Also see West Volusia Tourism.)
Putnam County Chamber of Commerce
1100 Reid St.
Palatka, FL 32177
(386) 328-1503

northeast

day trip 01

South East Volusia Chamber of Commerce
115 Canal St.
New Smyrna Beach, FL 32168
(877) 460-2449
www.sevchamber.com

Southeast Volusia Historical Society
120 Sams Ave.
New Smyrna Beach, FL 32170
www.nsbhistory.org

New Smyrna Beach Visitors Bureau
2238 SR 44
New Smyrna Beach, FL 32168
(800) 541-9621
http://nsbfla.com

day trip 02

Daytona Beach Convention &
Visitors Bureau (walk-ins)
1801 West International Speedway Blvd.
Daytona Beach, FL 32118
(386) 253-8669 or (800) 854-1234
www.daytonabeach.com

Daytona Beach Convention &
Visitors Bureau (mail requests)
126 East Orange Ave.
Daytona Beach, FL 32114
(386) 255-0415

Flagler County Tourist Development
Council
1200 East Moody Blvd., Suite 1
Bunnell, FL 32110
(386) 437-0106
www.flaglercounty.org

day trip 03

St. Johns County Convention & Visitors
Bureau
88 Roberia St., Suite 400
St. Augustine, FL 32084
(904) 829-1711 or (800) OLD-CITY
www.visitoldcity.com

Jacksonville and the Beaches
201 East Adams St.
Jacksonville, FL 32200
(904) 798-9111 or (800) 733-2668
www.visitjacksonville.com

east

day trip 01

Space Coast Office of Tourism
8810 Astronaut Blvd.,
Suite 102
Cape Canaveral, FL 32920
(800) 936-2326 during business hours;
(800) 872-1969 automated line
www.space-coast.com

southeast

day trip 01

Indian River County Chamber of
Commerce
1216 Twenty-first St.
P.O. Box 2947
Vero Beach, FL 32961
(561) 567-3491
www.indianriverchamber.com

day trip 02

(Also see Space Coast Tourism.)
Kissimmee–St. Cloud Convention & Visitors
Bureau
1925 East Irlo Bronson Memorial Hwy.
Kissimmee, FL 34740
(407) 944-2400
www.floridakiss.com

south

day trip 01

(Also see Kissimmee–St. Cloud.)
Lake Wales Area Chamber of Commerce
340 West Central Ave.
Lake Wales, FL 33850
(863) 676-3445
www.lakewaleschamber.com

day trip 02

Avon Park Chamber of Commerce
28 East Main St.
Avon Park, FL 33825
(863) 453-3350
www.apfla.com

Convention & Visitors Bureau of Highlands
   County
309 South Circle St.
Sebring, FL 33870
(863) 385-1316 or (800) 545-6021
www.highlandscvb.com

southwest

day trip 01

Central Florida Convention & Visitors
   Bureau
P.O. Box 61
Cypress Gardens, FL 33884
(863) 298-7565 or (800) 828-7655
www.visitcentralflorida.org

day trip 02

(See Central Florida Convention & Visitors
   Bureau.)

day trip 03

Tampa Bay and Company
401 East Jackson St., #2100
Tampa, FL 33602
(813) 223-2752 or (800) 4-TAMPA
www.visittampabay.com

day trip 04

St. Petersburg/Clearwater Convention &
   Visitors Bureau
14450 Forty-sixth St. North #108
Clearwater, FL 33756
(727) 464-7200 or (877) 352-3224
www.floridasbeach.com

day trip 05

Sarasota Area Visitor Information Center
655 North Tamiami Trail
Sarasota, FL 34236
(941) 957-1877 or (800) 522-9799
www.sarasotafl.org
(The center has a branch office at 5947
   Clark Center Ave. in the Albritton Grove
   Market. The office provides information
   on Sarasota, Longboat Key, Lido
   Key, Siesta Key, Casey Key, Venice,
   Manasota Key, Englewood, and North
   Port.)

Anna Maria Island Chamber of Commerce
5337 Gulf Dr. North
Holmes Beach, FL 34271
(941) 778-1541
www.annamariaislandchamber.org

Bradenton Area Convention & Visitors
   Bureau
(Mail address only; specify Bradenton area
   information.)
12290 Treeline Ave.
Fort Myers, FL 33913
(941) 729-9177 or (800) 4-MANATEE
www.visitbradenton-manatee.com

west

day trip 01

Lake County Convention & Visitors Bureau
315 West Main St.
Tavares, FL 32778
(352) 429-367 or (800) 798-1071
www.lakecountyfl.com

Greater Dade City Chamber of Commerce
14112 Eighth St.
Dade City, FL 33525
(352) 567-3769
www.dadecitychamber.org

day trip 02

Greater Hernando County Chamber of
 Commerce
101 East Fort Dade Ave.
Brooksville, FL 34601
(352) 796-0697
www.hernandochamber.com

day trip 03

Citrus County Tourist Development Council
9225 West Fishbowl Dr.
Homosassa, FL 34448
(352) 628-9305
www.visitcitrus.com

Pasco County Office of Tourism
7530 Little Rd., Suite 340
New Port Richey, FL 34654
(727) 847-8990 or (800) 842-1873
www.visitpasco.net

northwest

day trip 01

Mount Dora Chamber of Commerce
341 Alexander St.
Mount Dora, FL 32757
(352) 383-2165
www.mountdora.com

Lake County Convention & Visitors Bureau
315 West Main St.
Tavares, FL 32778
(352) 429-367 or (800) 798-1071
www.lakecountyfl.com

day trip 02

Ocala/Marion Chamber of Commerce
110 Silver Springs Blvd.
Ocala, FL 34470
(352) 629-8051
www.ocalacc.com

day trip 03

(See Ocala.)

day trip 04

Visitors and Convention Bureau of Alachua
 County
30 East University Ave.
Gainesville, FL 32601
(352) 374-5260 or (866) 778-5002
www.visitgainesville.net
(Visit the Welcome Center at exit 77 on
 I-75.)

day trip 05

Cedar Key Chamber of Commerce
Box 610
Cedar Key, FL 32625
(352) 543-5600
www.cedarkey.org

Citrus County Tourist Development Council
9225 West Fishbowl Dr.
Homosassa, FL 34448
(352) 628-9305
www.visitcitrus.com

general information

Visit Florida
550 Technology Park
Lake Mary, FL 32746
(888) 7-FLA-USA
www.visitflorida.com

Official Florida Vacation Guide
c/o Miles Media
3675 Clark Rd.
Sarasota, FL 34233
(888) 7-FLA-USA
(Contact this organization to request the *Official Florida Vacation Guide.*)

Florida RV Trade Association
10510 Gibsonton Dr.
Riverview, Florida 33578
(813) 741-0488
www.frvta.org
(Contact this group for the *Official RVers Guide,* including campground listings.)

Florida Association of RV Parks and Campgrounds
Camp Florida
1340 Vickers Dr.
Tallahassee, FL 32303
(850) 562-7179
www.campflorida.com
(Write or phone for a list of commercial campgrounds.)

Florida Department of Environmental Protection
Office of Greenways and Trails
3900 Commonwealth Blvd.,
Mail Station 795
Tallahassee, Florida 32399-3000
(850) 245-2052 or (877) 822-5208
www.dep.state.fl.us/gwt
(Write for information on hiking, biking, canoe, and equestrian trails and state and national forests.)

festivals and celebrations

NOTE: Contact numbers can change from year to year. Your best bet is to call tourism information numbers for the cities or counties listed in Regional Information. Dates are always subject to change.

january

Birthplace of Speed Celebration, Ormond Beach. Commemorate the days when gentlemen raced on the beach sands. The two-day event features a gaslight parade, antique car show, swap meet, antique auto races, and much more. www.aaca.org/volusia.

Florida Keys Seafood Festival, Key West. This one-day event features the finest and freshest Florida Keys seafood. (305) 619-0039; http://fkcfa.org/events.aspx

Garage Sale, Sebring. Find bargains galore during an event that calls itself the country's largest garage sale. Sebring does it again every April. (863) 383-8448.

Sarasota Film Festival. The festival screens movies indoors and out as locals and celebrities mingle at parties and special events. (941) 366-6200; www.sarasotafilmfestival.com.

february

Auto and Antique Winterfest, Zephyrhills. This event at Festival Park is highlighted by an antiques-and-car show and auction. (813) 920-7206.

Calusa Wood Carvers Show, New Port Richey. This annual event features master carvers and their works. Vendors from all over the country are here to sell tools and woods. (727) 376-2180.

Mount Dora Art Festival, Mount Dora. One of the leading art events of the region, this festival draws about a quarter of a million visitors on the first full weekend of the month. (352) 383-0880; www.mountdoracenterforthearts.org.

Roaring 20s, Sebring. Dress like a flapper, show up in a tin Lizzie, and enjoy all that jazz. (863) 471-5104.

march

12 Hours of Sebring Grand Prix of Endurance, Sebring. This is one of international auto racing's most sought-after events, attracting big-name drivers, manufacturers, and fans.

Reserve accommodations early because more than 100,000 race fans stream into this small town. (863) 655-1442; www.sebringraceway.com.

Annual Easter Surfing Festival, Cocoa Beach. This becomes the surfing capital of Florida for two weekends, depending on the date of Easter. (321) 799-0493; www.eastersurffest .com.

Antiques Show and Sale, Ormond Beach. The Anderson-Price Memorial Building, built in 1916, is a wonderful setting on the river with exciting antiques to see or buy. (386) 677–7005; www.ormondhistory.org.

Azalea Festival, Palatka. This is central Florida's biggest azalea event, even though the azaleas themselves may be past their prime if it has been a warm winter. A queen is crowned and there are pageants, parades, food and midway attractions; always the second weekend of March. (386) 328-1503; www.flazaleafest.com.

Bach Festival Concerts. Featuring the stellar Bach Festival Chorus and Chamber Orchestra, concerts are staged in several venues this month. Works of other early composers are also featured. (407) 646-2182, www.bachfestival.org.

Chasco Fiesta, New Port Richey. Enjoy one of the state's oldest Native American festivals. (727) 893-8111; www.chascofiesta.com.

Daytona Beach Garden Show, Daytona Beach. The big Ocean Center fills with mountains of blooms plus plants for sale and seminars that sharpen your own gardening skills. (386) 254-4500; www.daytonabeachgardenshow.com.

Grant Seafood Festival, Melbourne. This is one of the state's leading seafood blowouts. Another seafood festival, SeaFeast, takes place at Port Canaveral. (321) 723-8687; www .grantseafoodfestival.com.

Kumquat Festival, Dade City. Experience honest, small-town wackiness with kumquat cooking, concerts, arts, crafts, and food booths. (352) 567-3769 www.kumquatfestival.org.

Art and Heritage Festival, Lake Placid. Remember the good ol' days. Don a bonnet or straw hat and your best gingham, and join the celebrations. (863) 465-4331.

Sarasota Jazz Festival, Sarasota. One of the state's long-established, high-profile jazz events features internationally known musicians. (941) 316-9217; www.jazzclubsarasota .com.

Spring Break, takes over Daytona Beach most of this month with beer, babes, and bawdy behavior. Either come here to join the fun, or run the other way. (386) 255-0981.

april

Blessing of the Fleet, St. Augustine. Blessings take place in many Florida seaports this month, a ceremony that goes back centuries. In St. Augustine, the bishop of the Diocese of St. Augustine performs the rite on Palm Sunday starting at noon with a procession from the Cathedral Basilica to the Cathedral. Pleasure boats and commercial craft participate. (800) OLD-CITY.

Cabbage and Potato Festival, Hastings. This agricultural community 18 miles west of St. Augustine hosts a delightfully cornball, old-Florida event with feasting, street entertainers, arts, games, and contests. Admission is free. It's usually held the last weekend of the month. (904) 692-1420.

Easter Skydiving Boogie, Zephyrhills. Hundreds of skydivers gather for fun and competition. Dates vary with Easter. (800) 404-9399. Another "boogie" is held on Thanksgiving weekend and over Christmas.

Garage Sale, Sebring. Here's a second helping of the country's largest garage sale, also held in Jan. (863) 383-8448.

Indian River Festival, Titusville. This wet and wild funfest features contests, a wacky raft race, food, and music. (321) 615-8111.

La Musica International Chamber Music Festival, Sarasota. This festival attracts top musicians from Europe and throughout North America. (941) 953-3434.

Melbourne Art Festival, Melbourne. More than 275 top artists and exhibitors show their paintings, jewelry, woodworking, sculpture, and textiles. (321) 722-1964.

Rhythm and Ribs Festival, St. Augustine. This yearly festival features championship barbecue, live jazz, and great local wines. It's held at St. Francis Field on Castillo Drive; shuttles run from downtown at San Sebastian Winery. (800) OLD-CITY.

Shark's Tooth Festival, Venice. Comb the beach at the self-proclaimed Shark's Tooth Capital of the World to see how many teeth you can find, then stroll among food and crafts vendors. (941) 412-0402; www.sharkstoothfest.com.

Spring Arts and Crafts Festival, St. Augustine. The festival is held at the Special Events Field on Castillo Drive. Free shuttles run from downtown. Eat, drink, and view the works of more than a hundred artists. (800) OLD-CITY.

Tico Warbird Air Show, Titusville. This show features vintage and modern military aircraft in rousing stunts and flyovers. (321) 268-1941 or (800) USA-1969.

may

Blue Crab Festival, Putnam County. This festival continues over the three-day Memorial Day weekend. (386) 325-4406.

Memorial Weekend Cathedral Festival, St. Augustine. Held Friday through Monday on the grounds of the Mission of Nombre de Dios, the festival features arts, crafts, games, rides, entertainment, food, and fireworks. (904) 824-2806.

Memorial Day weekend also marks the start of **St. Augustine's Summer Concert Series,** sponsored by the Jazz Society. Free concerts are held downtown in the Plaza at 7 p.m. every Thurs through Labor Day.

Mother's Day Native American Powwow, Dade City. Held along the Withlacoochee River, the powwow features Indian dancing, singing, arts, and crafts. (352) 521-3012; www .mothersdaypowwow.embarqspace.com

june

Greek Landing Day Festival, St. Augustine. Celebrate the first colony of Greeks in North America. The festival is held in late June at St. Photius National Greek Orthodox Shrine, 41 St. George St. Admission is free. (904) 829-8205.

Sarasota Music Festival, Sarasota. This two-week chamber music celebration features world-renowned artists. (941) 953-4252.

july

Florida International Festival, Daytona Beach. This festival centers around the London Symphony Orchestra, which calls Daytona Beach their summer home. Classical and popular music are celebrated for two weeks. Buy season tickets well in advance. (866) 978-DBIF; www.fif-lso.org.

Fourth of July is celebrated throughout central Florida, but droughts in recent years have caused a cutback or cancellation of some fireworks. For information on St. Augustine's Bayfront blowout, call (800) OLD-CITY.

august

Playwrights Festival, St. Augustine. The Limelight Theater presents original plays selected in a statewide competition on the first and second weekends. (904) 825-1164.

september

Caladium Festival, Lake Placid. Hundreds of acres of these ornamental plants grow in the area and are celebrated with arts, crafts, music, and fun. (863) 699-1020; www.lpfla.com/events/caladium.htm

Days in Spain/Founders Day, St. Augustine. Spanish dancing, period costumes, music, and entertainers re-create the founding of the nation's oldest city. On the grounds of the Nombre de Dios Mission, a sacred reenactment of the first mass held in the New World is offered. (904) 825-1000.

Fall Fine Arts and Crafts Festival, historic downtown Melbourne. A juried arts-and-crafts show with live entertainment, food and business vendors, and children's activities. Free parking and admission. (321) 724-1741; www.downtownmelbourne.com.

Family Salsa Festival, Melbourne. A city park fills with good music, spicy food, cool drinks, contests, and games. (321) 752-1003; www.fprhcc.org.

Pioneer Florida Day, Dade City. Celebrate at the Pioneer Florida Museum with costumes, reenactments, children's activities, and demonstrations of Cracker crafts. (352) 567-0262; www.pioneerfloridamuseum.org.

october

Biketoberfest, Daytona Beach. The city and county for miles around fill with ear-busting motorcycles and their sometimes bizarrely dressed riders. Drive carefully; these are fast machines that aren't always easy to see. (386) 255-0415 or (866) 296-8970; www.bike toberfest.org.

The Colony's **Annual Stone Crab, Seafood, and Wine Festival** brings in celebrity chefs who celebrate the yearly stone crab season in this resort's gourmet restaurants and around the grounds. Reserve early and stay the weekend. (800) 426-5669.

Cracker Day, St. Augustine. Enjoy bluegrass, banjos, and barbecue in the St. Johns County Fairgrounds off SR 207 near St. Augustine. (800) OLD-CITY.

Mount Dora Bike Festival, Mount Dora. This festival is three days of rides, contests, and picnicking for riders of all levels—including families—on picturesque streets and rural roads that *Bicycling* magazine named one of the planet's top fifty bicycling destinations. (352) 383-2165.

Native Rhythms Festival, Melbourne. Celebrates Florida's rich and varied tribal history from pre-Columbians through the Seminole era using music, especially flute music. Visiting tribes add color with dancing, feasting, and native dress. (321) 639-3561; http://native rhythmsfestival.com.

Polish American Festival, Titusville. Serve up Polish dancing, crafts, and great food. (321) 633-3099.

Rattlesnake Festival, San Antonio. See professionals handle rattlesnakes at this yearly gathering. The party includes foods, crafts, music, and fun. (352) 588-4444; www.rattle snakefestival.com.

St. Armand's Circle Art Festival. More than 200 national and international artists show their works in this chichi shopping center. (941) 388-1554.

november

Art Festival, Sebring. It's one of the best regional art festivals in the South with paintings, photographs, gifts, food, and festivities for all ages. (863) 385-8448.

Bug Jam, Dade City. The jam brings together hundreds of Volkswagens for viewing, parts swapping, and camaraderie. (352) 567-6678; www.pascobugjam.com.

Great Chowder Debate, St. Augustine. Every year at Conch House Marina, 57 Comares Ave., St. Augustine, the "debate" serves up barrels of the best seafood chowder ever created. (904) 829-8646.

Greek Festival, Daytona. Held in the spectacular gold-domed St. Demetrios Greek Orthodox Church, the festival features authentic food, music, dance, and crafts. (386) 252-6012.

Nights of Lights, St. Augustine. More than a million tiny, twinkling lights burn along the bay and downtown. It starts mid-Nov and continues through Jan, with various ceremonies and programs throughout. (800) OLD-CITY.

Thanksgiving Bluegrass Festival is held at the Sentoma Youth Ranch between Brooksville and Dade City. Money is raised for the ranch, where youths are housed. Make reservations for camping. (352) 754-3082.

Space Coast Art Festival, Cocoa Beach. This is one of the oldest, largest art shows in Florida. See extensive displays of paintings, photography, glass, sculpture, and weaving. (321) 784-3322; www.spacecoastartfestival.com.

Turkey Run Car Show and Swap Meet, Daytona International Speedway. This is one of the year's biggest events for car fanciers. (800) PIT-SHOP

december

Christmas Boat Parades feature boats sparkling with lights that reflect in the water. They're held in most waterfront communities, including Anna Maria, Cocoa, DeLand, Edgewater, and Sarasota Bay.

Grand Illumination, St. Augustine. Bring a candle and join the parade to the plaza to hear the governor's proclamation at Government House, 48 King St. Soldiers fire muskets, and the Christmas season is serenaded with ancient carols. (904) 460-9368. **British Night Watch Weekend** is part of the centuries-old celebration, a two-day event with a cast of British soldiers and citizens reenacting ceremonies that took place during the British occupation. Later in the month, usually about the second weekend, boat parades begin. St. Augustine's **Regatta of Lights** floats along the Bay of Lions and the Castillo de San Marcos. (904) 824-9725.

ongoing events

The second Saturday of every month is **East Coast Cruiser Night** on Canal Street in New Smyrna Beach, 6 to 9 p.m. Antique cars, street rods, and other interesting iron make the scene, while people party and listen to live music.

The last Thursday of every month is **Gallery Stroll** in downtown DeLand. Visit a half dozen art galleries, linger over a glass of wine in one of the pubs, and have dinner in one of the restaurants.

Every Saturday morning on Lemon Avenue, Sarasota hosts a **Farmers' Market** downtown.

Living history events are portrayed on Sunday afternoon January through mid-April at **Historic Spanish Point,** Osprey. (941) 966-4215.

Circus Sarasota performs in season at the Sarasota Fairgrounds. (941) 355-9335.

On the first Friday of the month, 6 to 9 p.m., join a **Friday Walk** of Palm Avenue, Sarasota, to visit shops, galleries, and restaurants. Special events include live music, gallery openings, and special menus. (941) 365-7414. On the fourth Friday, the same sort of event takes place at **St. Armand's Circle.** (941) 388-1554.

index

A

A1A Ale Works, 54
Aardvark's Florida Kayak Company, 189
Accents by Grace and Friends, 155
Ace of Hearts Ranch, 67
Adventure Island, 114
African American Museum of the Arts, 14
airboat rides, St. Johns River, 67
Akina Sushi, 144
Alafia River State Recreation Area, 114
Ale House & Raw Bar, 180
Alexander Springs Recreation Area, 173
Amapola Guest House, 150
America's Best Value Inn, 182
Amtrak, xii
Anastasia Inn, 58
Anastasia State Park Canoe and Kayak Concession, 51
Anclote Key State Preserve, 121
Angell & Phelps, 42
Angel's Diner, 25
Angevine's, 16
Anna Maria Island Chamber of Commerce, 195
Anna Maria Island Historic Museum, 136
Ann Steven's House, 12
Annual Easter Surfing Festival, 199

Annual Stone Crab, Seafood, and Wine Festival, 202
Antiques Show and Sale, 199
Appleton Museum of Art, 165
Archie Carr National Wildlife Refuge, 84
area codes, xii
Around the Bend Nature Tours, 136
Art and Heritage Festival, 199
Art Festival, 203
Arthur's, 167
Artists Guild Gallery, 80
Arts on Douglas, 35
Ashley Street Grille, 117
Athens Theatre, 14
Atlantic Plaza Condo Hotel, 36
Aunt Catfish's on the River, 32
Auto and Antique Winterfest, 198
Avilés Restaurant, 55
Avon Park Chamber of Commerce, 194
Azalea Festival, 199
Azalea House, 26

B

Bach Festival Concerts, 199
Back Home Antiques, 17
Back Porch Garden and Tea Bar, The, 190
Back Porch Tea Room, The, 105

BageLicious Bakery & Cafe, 167
Banyan's Restaurant, 180
Barberville, 22
Barnacle Bill's, 55, 132
Barnacle's Restaurant & Lounge, 30
Barn Antique, The, 105
baseball, xii
Beach Bistro, 137
Beacher's Lodge, 58
beaches, xii
Beach House, The, 137
Beauclaire Restaurant, 161
Bella Luna Cafe, 167
Belly Busters, 17
Bern's, 117
Best Western Crystal River Resort, 191
Best Western Deltona Inn, 14
Best Western Gateway Grand, 182
Best Western Inn of Palatka, 26
Best Western Mayan Inn Beachfront, 43
Best Western Space Shuttle Inn, 72
bicycling, xii
bicycling, Flagler and St. Johns Counties, 61
Biggar Antiques, 105
Big Scrub, 173
Biketoberfest, 202
bird-watching, xiii
Birthplace of Speed Celebration, 198
BJ's Brewhouse, 180
Black Hammock, 2, 4
Black 'n Brew, 106

Blackwater Inn, 167
Blessing of the Fleet, 200
Blue Crab Festival, Putnam County, 201
Blue–Dining with a View, 45
Blue Spring State Park, 13
Boathouse restaurant, 134
Bok Tower Gardens, 90
Bonefish Willy's Riverfront Grille, 85
Boondocks at Adventure Yacht Harbor, 42
Bradenton, 135
Bradenton Area Convention & Visitors Bureau, 195
Brevard Art Museum, 84
Brevard Zoo, 84
BridgeWalk, 138
British Night Watch Weekend, 204
Bronson-Mulholland House, 25
Brooke Pottery, 105
Brooksville, 148
Buccaneer Bay Water Park, 150
Buena Vista Inn, 36
Bug Jam, 203
Bulow Plantation Ruins State Historic Site, 44
Busch Gardens Tampa Bay, 114
Bushnell, 145

C

Cabana Cove Caribbean Grille, 180
Cabbage and Potato Festival, 200
Cabot Lodge, 182
Cà d'Zan, Ringling mansion, 131
Caffe Paradiso, 117
Caladesi Island State Park and Honeymoon Island State Recreation Area, 123

Caladium Festival, 202
Calico Jack's, 180
Calusa Wood Carvers Show, 198
camping, xiii
Camp Mack's River Resort, 91
Canaveral National Seashore, 34, 67, 70
Canoe Escape Inc., 114, 123
Cantina Toscana, 137
Capdevila's at La Teresita, 118
Cape Canaveral, 67
Captain Memo's Pirate Cruise, 123
Casa Coquina Bed and Breakfast, 73
Casa Monica Hotel, 59
Casements, The, 30
Cassadaga, 9
Cassadaga Hotel, 11, 12
Cassadaga Spiritualist Camp, 9, 193
Cassadaga Spiritualist Camp Bookstore, 12
Castillo de San Marcos National Monument, 50
Cedar Key, 191
Cedar Key Chamber of Commerce, 196
Cedar Key Scrub State Reserve/Waccasassa State Preserve, 192
Cedar Key State Museum, 192
Centennial House, 59
Central Florida Convention & Visitors Bureau, 195
Central Florida Kayak Tours, 160
Central Florida Zoo, 5
CFT Sommer Sports, 142
Chalet Suzanne Restaurant and Inn, 91
Chamber of Commerce, 34, 96, 160

Channelside Bay Plaza, 115
Charlie's Fish House Restaurant, 190
Chart House, 85
Chasco Fiesta, 199
Chase Suite Hotel, 119
Chateau Élan, 98
Chef's Table, 144
Chicanes, 97
Chicken Pantry, 45
Christmas, 64
Christmas Boat Parades, 203
Cinnamon Sticks Restaurant and Bakery, 155
Circus Sarasota, 204
Citrus County Heritage Tour, 154
Citrus County Tourist Development Council, 196
Citrus Hills Lodge, 156
Citrus Tower, 142
Clarion Hotel, 73
Classic Impressions, 25
Clearwater, 121
Clearwater Lake, 173
Clearwater Marine Aquarium, 123
Clermont, 142
Coastal Heritage Museum, 189
Cocoa Village, 67
Coconut's Comedy Club, 180
Colby Memorial Temple, 11
Colony Beach & Tennis Resort, 133
Columbia, 118
Columbia Restaurant, 55, 132
Comfort Inn, 19, 59
Comfort Suites at World Golf Village, 59
Compass Rose, 104
Conch House, 55
Coney Island Drive Inn, 150

Connors Gifts, 155
Continental Cafe, 132
Convention & Visitors
    Bureau of Highlands
    County, 195
Coquina on the
    Beach, 133
Coquina Wharf Bed and
    Breakfast, 37
Coral Beach Motel, 31
Corky Bell's Seafood, 70
Corky Bell's Seafood of
    Palatka, 26
Coronado del Ma, 37
Cortessés Bistro, 55
Country at Home, 155
Country Cottage
    Crafts, 160
Country Hearth Inn, 46
Cove, The, 71
Cow Camp, 90
Cracker Barrel, 46
Cracker Creek
    Canoeing, 32
Cracker Day, 202
Cracker's Bar & Grill, 190
Cravings on the Water, 191
Crazy Buffet, 118
Crescent City, 22
Crispers, 106
Crowne Plaza Melbourne
    Oceanfront Resort and
    Spa, 85
Cruise out of the Port of
    Tampa, 115
cruising, xiii
Crumps, 189
Crystal River, 189
Crystal River National
    Wildlife Refuge, 189
Crystal River State
    Archaeological Site,
    190
Curtis Hixon Waterfront
    Park, 116
Cypress Gardens, 108
Cypress Inn, 110
Cypress Restaurant, 84

D
Dade Battlefield State
    Historic Site, 146
Dade City, 146
Dairy Queen, 56
David's Barbecue, 180
Day Away Kayak Tours,
    A, 68
Days Inn Fairgrounds, 119
Day's Inn Historic
    Downtown, 59
Days Inn Silver
    Springs, 170
Days in Spain/Founders
    Day, 202
Daytona Beach, 38
Daytona Beach Convention
    & Visitors Bureau,
    193, 194
Daytona Beach Drive-in
    Christian Church, 40
Daytona Beach Garden
    Show, 199
Daytona Flea and Farmers'
    Market, 42
Daytona USA, 40
DeBary, 8
DeBary Hall Mansion, 8
Deep Creek Stables, 20
Deep South Family Bar-B-
    Que, 150
DeLand, 14
DeLand Artisan, 17, 19
DeLand Country Inn, 19
DeLand Historic Mural
    Walk, 15
DeLand House
    Museum, 15
DeLand Museum of Art,
    The, 15
DeLand Naval Air Station
    Museum, 15
DeLeon Springs, 19
DeLeon Springs State
    Park, 20
Denny's Restaurant, 59
Devil's Millhopper State
    Geological Site, 178
Dinosaur World, 115

Discovery Gardens, 163
Disney's Vero Beach
    Resort, 81
Disney Wilderness
    Preserve, 88
Dixie Crossroads, 70, 71
Doll & Hobby Shop, 17
Don CeSar Beach Resort &
    Spa, 127
Don Garlits Museum of
    Drag Racing, 167
Don Pablo's Mexican
    Kitchen, 7
Double Tree Beach
    Resort, 128
Doubletree Oceanfront
    Hotel, 73
Dove, The, 71
Dow Museum of Historic
    Houses, 50
Down the Hatch, 33
Driftwood Beach Motel, 31
Driftwood Resort, 81
Durango Oak Fire
    Steakhouse, 71

E
East Coast Cruiser
    Night, 204
Easter Skydiving
    Boogie, 200
EconoLodge, 164, 182
El Leoncito, 70, 71
El Paso Tienda, 95
El Potro Mexican
    Restaurant, 4
Elsie Bell's Antique and Art
    Mall, 25
Environmental Learning
    Center, 79
Euphemia Haye
    Restaurant, 137
Everything Under the
    Sun, 137

F
Fall Fine Arts and Crafts
    Festival, 202
Family Salsa Festival, 202

Fantasy of Flight, 102
Farah's, 180
Farmers' Market, 204
Faver-Dykes State Park, 50
Felasco Hammock State
    Preserve, 178
Ferris Groves, 155
ferry ride, Crescent City, 24
Fiddlers Green Ranch, 162
Fifth Avenue Café, 161
Fisherman's
    Restaurant, 155
Fisher's Seafood Bar and
    Grill, 72
fishing and hunting, xiv
Flagler Avenue, New
    Smyrna, 35
Flagler Beach, 44
Flagler County Tourist
    Development
    Council, 194
Fleaworld, 6, 7
Florida Air Museum, The,
    at Sun-n-Fun, 104
Florida Aquarium, 115
Florida Association
    of RV Parks and
    Campgrounds, 197
Florida Department
    of Environmental
    Protection, 197
Florida International
    Festival, 201
Florida Keys Seafood
    Festival, 198
Florida Museum of Natural
    History, 178
Florida National Scenic
    Trail, xiv
Florida RV Trade
    Association, 197
Florida Southern
    College, 104
Forever Florida and the
    Crescent J Ranch, 82
Fort Christmas Historical
    Park, 66
Fort Cooper State
    Park, 154

Fort Mose, 50
Fountain of Youth, 51
Fourth of July, 201
Francesca's Trattoria, 181
Frappes North, 30
Frenchy's Rockaway
    Grill, 125
Friday Walk, 204

G
Gainesville, 177
Gallery on First, 6
Gallery Stroll, 204
Gamble Place, 32, 41
Gamble Plantation State
    Historic Site, 136
Gamble Rogers Memorial
    State Recreation
    Area, 45
Garage Sale, 198, 200
Gator Ventures, 2
Gemini Springs Park, 8
Ghostly Experience, A,
    walking tour, 51
Gillespie Museum of
    Minerals, 16
Ginny's and Jane E's at the
    Old IGA, 137
Ginny's Antiques & Art, 137
Giovanni's Italian
    Restaurant &
    Pizzeria, 4
Glazer Children's
    Museum, 116
Goblin Market, 161
Golden Apple Dinner
    Theater, 129
golf, xv
Government House
    Museum, 51
Grand Illumination, 204
Grand Villas at World Golf
    Village, 59
Grant Seafood
    Festival, 199
Great Chowder
    Debate, 203

Greater Dade City
    Chamber of
    Commerce, 196
Greater Hernando
    County Chamber of
    Commerce, 196
Greek Festival,
    Daytona, 203
Greek Landing Day
    Festival, 201
Green Gables Inn, 91
Gregory's Steak & Seafood
    Grille, 72
Greyhound bus, xv
Guana River State Park, 61
Gulf Coast Museum of
    Art, 123
Gulfside Resort, 127
Gypsy Bar & Grill, The, 56
Gypsy Cab Company, 56

H
Halifax Historical
    Museum, 40
Hampton Inn, 60
Harbor Branch
    Oceanographic
    Institute's Ocean
    Discovery Center, 80
Harrington House Bed &
    Breakfast, 138
Harry's Seafood, Bar, and
    Grille, 56, 106, 168
Harvest Thyme Cafe, 181
Hawthorne, 183
Hawthorne Museum and
    Cultural Center, 184
Heavenly Sandwiches &
    Smoothies, 35
Helmsley Sandcastle
    Hotel, 133
Henscratch Farms Vineyard
    and Winery, 99
Herlong Mansion, 177
Hernando Heritage
    Museum, 148
Heron Cay Lakeview Bed
    and Breakfast, 162
Heron's Garden, 100

High Jackers, 46
Highlands Hammock State
    Park, 97
Hilton Daytona Beach
    Oceanfront Resort, 43
Hilton Daytona Beach
    Resort, 43
Hilton Longboat Key
    Beachfront
    Resort, 134
Hilton Melbourne
    Airport, 85
Hilton University of Florida
    Conference
    Center, 182
Historical Museum, 99
Historic Conner Library
    Museum, 35
Historic Spanish Point, 204
Holiday House, 18
Holiday Inn Lido
    Beach, 134
Holiday Inn, St. Augustine
    Beach, 60
Holiday Inn University
    Center, 182
Holiday Inn,
    Vero Beach, 81
Holiday Inn
    Winter Haven, 110
Hollerbach's Willow Tree
    Cafe, 8
Homosassa, 185
Homosassa Riverside
    Resort, 188
Homosassa
    Springs, 185, 188
Homosassa Springs State
    Wildlife Park, 185
Hontoon Island State
    Park, 16
Hotel Jacaranda, 96
Hotel Valencia, 100
Howard Johnson Express
    Inn, 145
Hungry Harry's, 118
Hurricane Seafood, 125
hurricane season, xv

Hyatt Regency
    Westshore, 119
Hyatt Sarasota, 134

I
Indian River Citrus
    Museum, 80
Indian River County
    Chamber of
    Commerce, 194
Indian River Festival, 200
Inlet Harbor Marina &
    Restaurant, 33
Inn on the Lakes, 98
Inn Place, The, 111
International Market
    World, 105
International Plaza, 116
Inverness, 152
Island Place, The, 192
Island Room at Cedar
    Cove, The, 192

J
Jackie's Mango's on the
    Beach, 42
Jacksonville and the
    Beaches, 194
Jax Place, 13
J.B.'s Fish Camp and
    Restaurant, 35
Jerusalem Kosher
    Restaurant, 31
John and Mable Ringling
    Museum of Art, 131
Johnny Leverock's Seafood
    House, 125
Johnson Field, 173
John's Pass Village and
    Boardwalk, 115
Jungle Adventures, 66
Juniper Springs and Fern
    Hammock Springs,
    173
Just Olde Stuff, 17

K
Kafe Kokopelli, 147
Karling's Inn, 20

kayaking, St. Augustine, 51
Kenilworth Lodge, 98
Kennedy Space Center
    Visitor Complex, 68
Key West Inn, The, and
    Capt. Hiram's Resort,
    79
Kings Head British Pub,
    The, 56
Kissimmee–St. Cloud
    Convention & Visitors
    Bureau, 194
Kumquat Festival, 199

L
La Crepe en Haut, 31
Lake Brentwood Motel, 96
Lake County Convention &
    Visitors Bureau, 195,
    196
Lake Dorr, 173
Lake Eaton Sinkhole
    Trails, 173
Lake Griffin State
    Recreation Area, 163
Lake Harris Lodge, 163
Lake Jackson, 97
Lake Kissimmee State
    Park, 90
Lakeland, 104
Lakeland Terrace
    Hotel, 107
Lake Louisa State
    Park, 144
Lake Morton Bed &
    Breakfast, 107
Lake Placid, 99
Lakeridge Winery, 144
Lakeside Inn, 162
Lakeside Landings Bed &
    Breakfast, 162
Lake Verona Lodge Bed
    and Breakfast, 96
Lake Wales Area Chamber
    of Commerce, 194
Lake Wales Ridge, 95
Lakewood Retreat, 150
Lake Woodruff National
    Wildlife Refuge, 20

La Luna Italian
Restaurant, 156
La Musica International
Chamber Music
Festival, 200
La Pentola, 56
La Strada, 57
Lavender & Lace Tearoom
& Gift Shop, 106
Leesburg, 163
Le Pavillon, 57
Lightner Museum, 51
Lloyds Lakeland
Antiques, 105
Lost in Time Cafe, 12
Lower Wekiva River State
Preserve, 5
LPGA International, 40
Lunch on Limoges, 147

M
MacRae's of
Homosassa, 189
Magnolia Gift Shop and
Tea Room, 105
Magnolia Inn Bed and
Breakfast, 162
Magnolia Plantation Bed &
Breakfast, 183
Main Street America, An
Eatery, 100
Main Street Pier, 40
Manatee Connection,
The, 187
Marie Selby Botanical
Gardens, 131
Marion County Museum of
History, 167
Marjorie Kinnan Rawlings
Historic State Park,
184
Marko's Chick-fil-A
Heritage Inn, 33
Marriott Suites Clearwater
Beach at Sand Key,
128
Mary A. Coogler
Cottage, 150

Matheson Historical
Center, 178
Matter of Taste, A, 147
McKee Botanical
Garden, 80
Melbourne, 67, 84
Melbourne Art Festival, 200
Mel Fisher's Treasure
Museum, 76
Melting Pot, The, 181
Memorial Presbyterian
Church, 51
Memorial Weekend
Cathedral Festival, 201
Merritt Island National
Wildlife Refuge, 68, 70
Micanopy, 175
Micanopy Historic Society
Museum, 177
Mile-Long Mall, The, 93
Mill at Lake Hamilton, The,
90, 110
Mill Creek Farm, 178
Mill Dam Lake, 174
Mise en Place, 118
Mission Inn Golf & Tennis
Resort, 145
Mission Park Florida
Vacation Homes, 145
Morning Glori Antique
Mall, 164
Morningside Nature
Center, 179
MOSI (Museum of Science
and Industry), 116
Mote Aquarium, 131
motels, xiii
Mother's Day Native
American Powwow,
201
Mount Dora, 158
Mount Dora Art
Festival, 198
Mount Dora Bike
Festival, 202
Mount Dora Chamber of
Commerce, 196
Mount Dora Historic Inn
Bed & Breakfast, 162

Mr. Bones BBQ, 138
Mulberry Phosphate
Museum, 104
murals, Lake Placid, 99
Murray Brothers' Caddy
Shack, 53
Muse Book Shop, The, 17
Museum of Arts and
Sciences, 41
Museum of Fine Arts, 124
Museum of Science and
Industry (MOSI), 116
Museum of Seminole
County, 5
Mykonos II, 150

N
Native Rhythms
Festival, 202
New Smyrna Beach, 34
New Smyrna Beach
Visitors Bureau, 193
Nights of Lights, 203
Night Swan Intracoastal
Bed & Breakfast, 37
95 Cordova, 57
No Frills Grill, 100
Norwood's Restaurant &
Wine Shop, 36

O
Ocala, 165
Ocala/Marion Chamber of
Commerce, 196
Ocala National Forest, 171
Ocala Silver Springs
Hilton, 168
Ocean Deck, 42
Ocean Waters Spa, 41
O. C. White's, 57
Official Florida Vacation
Guide, 197
Old Bicycle Inn, The, 145
Old City Farmers'
Market, 54
Old Courthouse Heritage
Museum, 154
Old House Café, The, 18
Old Hyde Park Village, 117

Old Spanish Sugar Mill
   Restaurant, 21
Olive Branch, The, 161
Olympic Restaurant, 95
Orange City, 13
Orchid Beach Trading
   Company, 85
Orlando Wetlands Park, 66
Ormond Beach, 28
Ormond Memorial Art
   Museum and Garden,
   30
Oudoms Thai
   Restaurant, 18
Outback Steak House, 144
Outdoor Adventures, 51
Outlets at Vero Beach,
   The, 81
Oviedo, 2

P
Palatka, 24
Palm Coast, 44
Palm Island Park, 160
Pappy's Patch U-Pick
   Strawberries, 4
parks, Cassadaga, 11
parks, state, xvi
Parrots of the Caribbean
   Trolley Boat Tours, 115
Pasco County Office of
   Tourism, 196
Pasco Motel, 147
Patrick's Bayside Grill, 125
Paynes Prairie State
   Preserve, 177
Pelican Island National
   Wildlife Refuge, 76
Penny Farthing Inn, 60
Peppino's Ristorante, 4
Perfect Spot Restaurant
   and Bar, The, 18
pets, xv
Pig & Whistle, 72
Pioneer Center for the
   Creative Arts, 24
Pioneer Florida Day, 202
Pioneer Florida
   Museum, 146

Placid Tower, 100
Plantation Inn & Golf
   Resort, 191
Playalinda Beach,
   Canaveral National
   Seashore, 70
Playwrights Festival, 201
Polish American
   Festival, 203
Polk Museum of Art, 105
Ponce de Leon Inlet
   Lighthouse, 33
Ponce Inlet, 33
Ponte Vedra Beach, 61
Ponte Vedra Inn & Club, 61
Port Canaveral, cruises, xiii
Port Manatee, cruises, xiii
Port Orange, 32
Prime Outlets St., 54
Prince of Wales Motel,
   A, 92
Princess Place
   Preserve, 45
Publix Supermarket, 181
Punjab, 72
Purple Rose, 12
Putnam County Chamber
   of Commerce, 193

Q
Quality Inn, 98
Quality Inn Riverfront, 26
Quality Inn Weeki
   Wachee, 151

R
Radisson Hotel at the
   Port, 73
Raintree, 57
Rattlesnake Festival, 203
Ravine State Gardens, 25
Red Roof Inn, 183
Regatta of Lights, 204
Reitz Union Hotel, 183
Renaissance Vinoy Resort
   and Golf Club, 128
Renninger's Antique
   Center, 161

Reptile Discovery
   Center, 16
Residence Inn by
   Marriott, 183
resident discounts, xiv
Resort at Longboat Key
   Club, The, 134
Rhythm and Ribs
   Festival, 200
Riley's Pub, 59
Ritz-Carlton Sarasota, 134
Riverfront Marketplace, 42
River Queen cruises, 78
River Safaris and Gulf
   Charters, 187
Rivership *Romance,* 5
Riverside Crab House, 187
Riverside Theatre, 80
Riverview Hotel, 37
Riverview Restaurant, 36
Roaring 20s, 198
Roberto's Little Havana, 72
Rogers' Christmas House
   and Village, 148
Rotten Ralph's, 138
Royal Oak Resort & Golf
   Club, 73
Rum Runners, 72
Rusty's Seafood and
   Oyster Bar, 72
Rutabagas Etc., 156
Ruth's Chris Steak
   House, 132

S
Safety Harbor Resort and
   Spa, 119
sales tax, xv
Salt Rock Grill, 127
Salt Springs Recreation
   Area, 174
Salvador Dalí Museum,
   124, 126
Sam Snead's Tavern, 53
Samuel P. Harn Museum of
   Art, 179
Sand Pebble
   Apartments, 139
Sandpiper Inn, 135

Sanford, 4
Sanford Historic District
    Shopping Area,
    Downtown Sanford, 7
Sanford Museum, 6
San Sebastian Winery, 53
Santa Fe Community
    College Teaching
    Zoo, 179
Sarasota, 129
Sarasota Area Visitor
    Information
    Center, 195
Sarasota Film Festival, 198
Sarasota Jazz Festival, 199
Sarasota Jungle
    Gardens, 131
Sarasota Music
    Festival, 201
Sawgrass Marriott
    Resort, 62
Scottish Inns, 111
Scuttles New England
    Seafood, 91
SeaFeast, 199
Seagrass Pub & Grill, 187
Seagrass River Resort, 189
Sea Hagg, The, 137
Seaside Music Theater, 41
Sebastian Inlet, 76, 78
Sebastian Inlet State
    Park, 78
Sebring Lakeside Golf
    Resort Inn, 99
Second Hand Rose, 106
Seminole County
    Convention & Visitors
    Bureau, 193
Seminole Towne Center, 7
Sergio's, 8
Seven Sisters Inn, 168
Seven Sisters Inn Bed and
    Breakfast, 170
Shady Oak, 177
Shamrock, Thistle &
    Crown, 168
Shark's Tooth Festival, 200
Sheraton Tampa
    Riverwalk, 120

Shoppes of Heritage
    Village, The, 190
Shutters, 81
SideBern's, 119
Silver River State Park, 167
Silver Sands Gulf Beach
    Resort, 135
Silver Springs, 169
Silver Surf Gulf Beach
    Resort, 139
Skip Barber Racing
    School, 97
Skydive DeLand, 16
Skydive Sebastian, 79
smoking, xvi
Smyrna Dunes Park, 35
Sonya's Restaurant, 81
South Beach Grill, 58
South East Volusia
    Chamber of
    Commerce, 193
Southeast Volusia Historical
    Society, 193
Southern Cassadaga
    Spiritualist Camp
    Meeting, 9
Space Coast Art
    Festival, 203
Space Coast Office of
    Tourism, 194
Spanish Quarter
    Museum, 53
Sprague House Inn &
    Restaurant, 24
Spring Arts and Crafts
    Festival, 200
Spring Break, 199
Stable Gifts, The, 105
St. Armand's Circle, 204
St. Armand's Circle Art
    Festival, 203
St. Armands Key, 132
StarShip Dining Yacht, 119
state parks, xvi
St. Augustine, 47
St. Augustine Alligator
    Farm and Zoological
    Park, 52

St. Augustine Lighthouse &
    Museum, 52
St. Augustine Sightseeing
    Trains, 52
St. Augustine's Summer
    Concert Series, 201
St. Augustine Trolley
    Tours, 52
Stavros Pizza, 14
St. Charles Inn Bed and
    Breakfast, 147
St. Cloud, 82
St. Francis Inn, 60
St. Johns County
    Convention & Visitors
    Bureau, 194
St. Johns River, 2
St. Johns River Cruises &
    Tours, 13
Stonewood Tavern &
    Grill, 31
St. Petersburg, 121
St. Petersburg/Clearwater
    Convention & Visitors
    Bureau, 195
Stromboli's, 144
Sugar and Spice Family
    Restaurant, 133
Sugar Mill Gardens, 32
Summer Bay Resort, 145
Sun House Restaurant and
    Bar, The, 138
Sunken Gardens, 124
Sun 'n Fun, 104
Sunrise Fish Camp, 18
Sun Viking Lodge, 43
Super 8 Motel, 183
Super Flea and Farmers'
    Market, 85
Surf Restaurant, The, 72
Sweetwater Branch
    Inn, 183
swimming, safety, xvi

T

Tampa, 112
Tampa Bay and
    Company, 195

Tampa Bay Port Authority, 115
Tampa, cruises, xiii
Tampa Museum of Art, 116
Tavares, 163
Tavares Heritage Ecotours, 163
Tea Room, The, Sebring Lakeside Golf Resort Inn, 98
Teauila's Hawaii Dinner Show, 43
Ted Williams Museum and Hitters Hall of Fame, 124
Terrace Grille, 107
Thanksgiving Bluegrass Festival, 203
This Olde House, 106
Tico Warbird Air Show, 200
Tijuana Willie's, 156
Tiny Cruise Line, A, 41
Tomoka State Park, 30
Topaz Motel & Hotel, 46
Tosohatchee Wildlife Management Area, 66
Towles Court, 132
Tradewinds Beach Resorts & Conference Centers, 128
Tradewinds Resort, 139
Tropical Manor Beach Motel, 44
Turkey Run Car Show and Swap Meet, 203
Turtle Beach Resort, 135
12 Hours of Sebring Grand Prix of Endurance, 198

U
University Galleries, The, at the University of Florida, 179
Uppity Woman, 17
U.S. Astronaut Hall of Fame, 69
U.S. Postal Museum, 13

V
Valencia Suites, 100
Van der Valk Inverness, 156
Van der Valk Lakeside, 156
Vero Beach, 79
Vero Beach Inn Resort on the Beach, 81
Verrazano Pizza & Sub, 58
Victorian Lace Bed and Breakfast, 19
Victory III, 53
Visit Florida, 197
Visitors and Convention Bureau of Alachua County, 196

W
Waldo's Open Air Deck, 81
walking tour, Cassadaga, 11
walking tour, Sanford, 6
Warbird Air Museum, 69
Washington Oaks State Gardens, 45
Weedon Island Preserve Cultural and Natural History Center, 125
Weeki Wachee, 150
Weeki Wachee Springs State Park/Buccaneer Bay Water Park, 150

Wekiwa Springs State Park, 6
West Volusia Tourism, 193
wheelchair access, xvi
Whetstone Chocolate Factory, 54
White Orchid Bed & Breakfast, 46
Wild Waters Water Park, 169
Windemere Inn by the Sea, 86
wineries, xvi
Winter Haven, 108
Withlacoochee State Trail, 154
Wolfe Contemporary Gallery, 17
World Golf Village, 53, 54
World Golf Village Renaissance Resort, 60
World's Most Famous Beach, 41
Wright, Frank Lloyd, 104

Y
Yalaha Country Bakery, 164
Yamato Japanese Restaurant, 181
Ybor City State Museum, 116
Yoder's Amish Restaurant, 133
Yulee Sugar Mill Ruins State Historic Site, 187

Z
Zaharia's Restaurant & Lounge, 58

about the author

In addition to guiding fly and light-tackle anglers around the nether reaches of Florida's Indian River Lagoon by skiff, canoe, and kayak, **John Kumiski** writes books and freelance magazine articles and indulges in photography. One of his two most recent books centers on his beloved Space Coast area and is entitled, appropriately enough, *Fishing Florida's Space Coast*. The other is a revision of the very popular *Flyrodding Florida Salt*. John lives in Chuluota, Florida, and can be reached via his Web site, www.spottedtail.com.